THE ART OF MANAGING FINANCE
Third Edition

David Davies

McGraw-Hill

A Division of The McGraw·Hill Companies

THE McGRAW-HILL COMPANIES

London · New York · St Louis · San Francisco · Auckland · Bogotá · Caracas
Lisbon · Madrid · Mexico · Milan · Montreal · New Delhi · Panama · Paris
San Juan · São Paulo · Singapore · Sydney · Tokyo · Toronto

Published by
McGraw-Hill Publishing Company
Shoppenhangers Road, Maidenhead, Berkshire, SL6 2QL, England
Telephone 01628 502500
Facsimile 01628 770224

Library of Congress Cataloging-in-Publication Data

Davies, David B. (David Basil)
    The art of managing finance / David B. Davies. — 3rd ed.
      p. cm.
    Includes bibliographical references and index.
    ISBN 0-07-709178-7 (paperback)
    1. Business enterprises—Finance.   2. Corporations—Finance.
  I. Title.
  HG4028.D378   1997
  658. 15—dc21
                                                  97-5060
                                                  CIP

British Library in Publication Data

The CIP data has been applied for and may be obtained from the British Library, London.

McGraw-Hill

A Division of The McGraw·Hill Companies

Typeset by Mackreth Media Services, Hemel Hempstead
Printed and bound in Great Britain by the University Press, Cambridge
Printed on permanent paper in compliance with ISO Standard 9706

To Ann
with thanks for her help and support

CONTENTS

ONE

SCOPE OF FINANCIAL MANAGEMENT

OBJECTIVE

To provide an understanding of the financial requirements of a manufacturing organization and the sources from which they might be obtained.

At the end of this chapter you will be able to explain:

1. The scope of financial management
2. Equity capital
3. Loan capital
4. Stock
5. Work in progress
6. Working capital
7. Debtors

Any business must have money if it is to survive. Surprisingly the great majority of businesses are profitable when they fail. In the United Kingdom 75–80 per cent cease to trade because they lack money and not because they are unprofitable. This book sets out to explain the difference between liquidity, the ability of an organization to pay its way, and profitability, the return on investment. The balance sheet, income statement and cash budget as the main financial statements are fully explained; once these are understood the ways in which the finances employed in an organization may be managed are discussed. Contrary to general belief, financial management is an art and not an exact science, which explains why many people are good at it but some are bad at it. The available techniques can be learnt but their application depends on the time, place and situation in which they are to be applied and on the person applying them.

Accounting has developed from its original role of stewardship, when it was used to reassure merchants that their goods were not being stolen, to its present purpose of not only maintaining stewardship of the property of an organization but also as an aid to management in planning, decision making and control. Accounting has come a long way

1

but it still does not replace the managers who make decisions based on the information that is available.

Prior to the twentieth century, financial accounting, with its emphasis on past events, enabled a report to be prepared on the profit that had been made, or the loss incurred by an organization in a financial period, generally a year. This, together with its ability to account for the resources of an organization, provided owners/managers with the information that they felt was needed. The twentieth century, particularly since the end of the Second World War, has been a period of accelerating growth and change. Financial accounts, which provide largely historical information, are still essential but no longer sufficient to meet the needs of owners/managers. To enable business to survive, plans have to be prepared to cope with changing needs and the plans themselves must be capable of modification. This led to the development of management accounting, which enables owners/managers to plan the course of their organizations and control their operations more effectively.

This book covers financial accounting, which is largely for external users, although much information is also provided internally through the key ratios that are discussed later. It also describes management accounting with its emphasis on providing the right information at the right time for the right people. It is not good to wait until the end of the financial year to discover that your plan started to go wrong 11 months ago. To be useful, information must be obtained quickly and accurately and be transmitted to the person most directly concerned. In order for this to be done, information must be provided regularly and quickly. Financial analysis should be carried out at least monthly and if possible weekly. Modern management information systems enable this to be done and data can be transmitted electronically and instantaneously to the relevant manager. If plans are to work, and control is to be maintained, management must be able to respond to changing conditions as they arise.

1.1 FLOW OF FUNDS

The diagram (Figure 1.1), which resembles a water system, represents a business and the money circulating in it. To start any business funds must first of all be obtained. The money may come from the owner's savings, in which case it is equity capital. It may be borrowed for periods of five years or more (long-term loan), or for between one and four years (short-term loan). Having obtained the money that is needed to start a business it has to be managed. The type of business will have been decided before the finance is obtained, so the next major decision may be what premises are to be used and, if it is a manufacturing concern, what plant and machinery are needed. These items are known as fixed assets and require a heavy outlay of money. The next decision is which supplier to use to provide the items that are needed to manufacture the product, and what credit can be obtained. These items, once obtained, become the stock of raw materials. Decisions will have to be made on the number of people that are to be employed, the number of telephones to be installed, and a multiplicity of other matters, all of which require financing.

Once these decisions have been made it will be necessary to implement them and start the manufacturing process as soon as possible. Until the business has a product for which there is a demand and has succeeded in selling that product, there will be a continuous drain from the pool of money and if the business finances are not properly managed it may well disappear altogether. The 'pumps' in the chart represent the points at which good management can speed up the whole process. The successful integration of people and

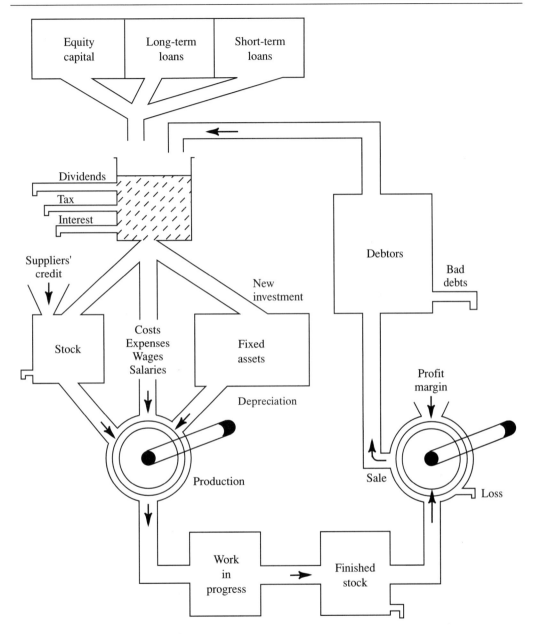

Figure 1.1   Chart of business funds flow

materials requires good management and the more effectively this is done the better for the business.

There is a leak of resources through the tap at the pool of stock. This is a controllable leak and its size depends upon the success or otherwise with which the raw materials are managed. If store facilities are poor and the storeperson is not very interested in the job the leak will be large due to breakages, obsolete items, rust and pilfering. The loss will be minimized by a good system of stores control backed by well-trained staff.

During and immediately following the production process, there are two other 'pools' in which the resources employed in a business become trapped. These are work in progress (WIP) and finished stock. In even the most successfully managed businesses there will be at the end of each accounting period some items that are between the raw material and finished goods stage. Management would like all items to be produced as quickly as possible but as things take time to be made, work in progress can never be eliminated. It should not, however, be allowed to build up to an unnecessarily high level. There are problems too in deciding how work in progress should be valued and the system necessary to keep track of it has to be detailed. Finished stock should be sold and delivered as quickly as possible, although in some cases where the demand for the goods is seasonal it may be necessary to have facilities to hold quite a lot of finished stock. Toy manufacture, where the bulk of the sales take place at Christmas, is one example of this. The loss of resources at the finished stock stage can be serious unless a good system of stores control is employed. The loss can be due to pilfering, obsolescence, breakages and general deterioration. Stock levels in this country used to be much higher in the manufacturing sector than in America, Germany and Japan, but the destocking brought about by the last recession has lowered them quite dramatically. Indeed the *just in time* method of stock control attempts to eliminate the need to hold raw material stocks at all.

The next point at which good management can greatly improve the resources available to the business, is by selling and distributing the finished goods as quickly as possible and obtaining the money from the firm's customers in the shortest possible time. There may be a loss at the time of sale, which good procedures can largely eliminate, caused by damage, pilferage and below-standard items that are returned, as well as items incorrectly delivered. It is here that the greatest potential loss occurs, that of *bad debts* (people who take delivery of goods but do not pay for them). Most business is conducted on credit and with the difficulty in obtaining sales, credit has become easier to obtain. It is one element in the *marketing mix* and its terms depend on many factors, including custom and practice of the trade and the pressures on the company to make a sale. Nearly all businesses suffer from bad debts, and, in order to keep them to a minimum, an efficient system of *credit control* is essential. The practice of *factoring* your debts, which entails employing a third person who obtains your money for you for a fee, is widespread in America and growing in this country. It has the advantage of giving the business money to use more quickly than would otherwise be the case. The criticism most usually levied against it is that it destroys the special relationship between the organization and its customers.

The money having been collected from the customers is now replacing some of that used in starting the business, but the 'taps' of dividends, tax and interest have to be considered. Shareholders' dividends can be paid only out of profits so if no profits have been made no dividends will be expected. If profits have been made, dividends may be paid at the discretion of the owners but it is not a requirement. If a business is continually making a profit but refuses to pay dividends without good reason, it will find it difficult to obtain money from the public when it next needs it. Interest has to be paid whether the business is profitable or not, which means that businesses have to ensure that they do not borrow so much that they cannot afford the interest charges. Examples of this include the Channel Tunnel company which has had to restructure its debt in order to survive. The amount of interest to be paid depends on the size and terms of borrowing which good management can ensure remain within the capability of the business. Tax is chargeable on profit but is at a minimum in the early years of manufacturing businesses because of capital allowances, as well as when any large capital investment programme has been undertaken.

The amount of money that a business has to enable it to operate until more money has been received is called its working capital, the difference between the capital it will have available within the next four or five months and what it will have to pay within the same period. It may need enough working capital to keep it going for five months before it receives any further resources.

This may be broken down as:

Obtaining raw materials	4 weeks	
Manufacturing process	4 weeks	
Held in stock	4 weeks	These periods are for example only and
Collect money from customer	8 weeks	will vary from industry to industry
Total	20 weeks	

All this time the costs, expenses, wages and salaries have to be met. It is for this reason that it is important to ensure that the working capital and other financial resources of the business are properly managed. The following chapters demonstrate how this may be achieved.

SELF-TEST QUESTIONS

1. Why is liquidity important?
2. What is profitability?
3. What is the purpose of working capital?

TWO

BALANCE SHEET

OBJECTIVE

To provide an understanding of the balance sheet and to enable you to prepare a balance sheet using diverse information.

At the end of this chapter you will be able to explain:

1. The purpose of the balance sheet
2. The limitations of the balance sheet
3. The difference between the vertical and narrative form of balance sheet
4. Reserves
5. Net capital employed

The *balance sheet* is a map, or photograph, of a business's financial position on a specific date. It refers *only* to that date and covers no period of time. It shows where the business has obtained its resources, and the purpose to which they have been put at that date. The balance sheet must always balance because no business can ever use more or fewer resources than it has obtained.

The business and its owner are separate entities, and because of this the balance sheet tells us something about the business but *nothing at all* about the owner.

2.1 CAPITAL

The capital of a business is the sum of the *resources* for which the business has to account to the owner, i.e. if a man started a business with life savings of £5,000 which he paid into the business bank account and his own car valued at £3,000 to be used solely in the business, the balance sheet on the first day of business would be:

Uses	£	*Sources*	£
Motor vehicle	3,000	Capital	8,000
Bank	5,000		
	8,000		8,000

The resources have been obtained from the owner. The uses to which they have been put are a motor vehicle and business bank account. Another way of describing the resources of the business is as liabilities. The capital of the business is a liability of it to the owner, i.e. in certain circumstances, like business failure, it is due to be paid by the business to the owner. The 'uses' to which the resources have been put could also be described as assets, i.e. the motor vehicle and the bank balance belong to the business, and are assets used in the operation of the business.

The business would not survive if it remained in its present form. In order to function it needs premises and some commodity with which to deal or service to offer. This commodity in which a business deals is called stock. The business buys premises for £14,000 and stock for £1,000, both of which it pays for in cash. It borrows £10,000 from the bank. The balance sheet would now look like this:

Uses (assets)	£	Sources (liabilities)	£
Fixed assets:		Capital	8,000
Premises	14,000	Loan	10,000
Motor vehicle	3,000		
	17,000		
Current assets:			
Stock	1,000		
	18,000		18,000

The capital remains unaltered but the uses to which it has been put have changed.

2.2 FIXED ASSETS

Fixed assets are those that are retained in the business for several accounting years and are used within the business over their useful life to enable it to operate. In the example, premises and motor vehicles are fixed assets because the business is retaining and using them. However, if the business traded in motor vehicles or premises only those retained by the business for its own use would be fixed assets, the remainder would be 'stock'.

2.3 CURRENT ASSETS

Current assets are those that are usually consumed by the business in the course of one accounting year. The stock of the business would normally be sold and replaced at least once in an accounting year, and therefore it is a current asset.

The business has been established but needs to start trading. The owner sells stock that cost £500 on credit for £900. The effect on the balance sheet is:

Uses (assets)	£	£	Sources (liabilities)	£	£
Fixed assets:			Capital	8,000	
Premises	14,000		Reserves:		
Motor vehicle	3,000	17,000	Retained profit	400	
Current assets:			Owner's equity		8,400
Stock	500		Loan		10,000
Debtor	900	1,400			
		18,400			18,400

2.4 PROFIT

The profit of £400 is shown as a source of funds and is added to the reserves which are profits that are kept in the business. It is due to the owner by the business. The profit is the excess of the selling price over the cost price of the stock (£900 − £500). *Note that although the business has made a profit of £400 is has no cash. Profit does not equal cash. Neither do reserves!*

2.5 DEBTOR

A debtor is any institution or person owing money to the business for goods or services received from the business. It is therefore both an asset of the business, because it can be called upon to pay what it owes, and a use of funds because the debtor has received benefits for which no payment has yet been made.

In order to expand further his business operations the owner feels it necessary to extend the credit facilities that he is able to offer his customers, and improve his premises internally with some filing cabinets and general office equipment. To do this he obtains a further loan of £6,000 which will be repayable in five years' time. The money is used to buy furniture and equipment for £4,000 and stock for £1,000. The balance sheet redrawn will be:

Uses (assets)	£	£	Sources (liabilities)	£	£
Fixed assets:			Capital	8,000	
Premises	14,000		Reserves:		
Furniture and			Retained profit	400	
equipment	4,000				
Motor vehicle	3,000	21,000	Owner's equity		8,400
			Loan		16,000
Current assets:					
Stock	1,500				
Debtor	900				
Cash	1,000	3,400			
		24,400			24,400

Furniture and equipment is a fixed asset because it will be retained in the running of the business for several years.

Cash is a current asset because it will be very quickly used in the normal course of business events.

Loan is a long-term liability and so comes between capital and reserves, which are permanent, and current liabilities, which are sources that are repaid in the course of one financial period.

The business is ready to operate at full throttle so it obtains £4,000 worth of stock on credit, and sells stock that costs £2,000 for £5,500; of this £2,500 represents cash sales and £3,000 credit sales. The balance sheet shows:

Uses (assets)	£	£	Sources (liabilities)	£	£
Fixed assets:			Capital	8,000	
Premises	14,000		Reserves:		
Furniture and			Retained profit	3,900	
equipment	4,000				
Motor vehicle	3,000	21,000	Owner's equity		11,900
			Loan		16,000
Current assets:			Current liabilities:		
Stock	3,500		Creditors		4,000
Debtor	3,900				
Cash	3,500	10,900			
		31,900			31,900

Creditors are people to whom the business owes money for goods or services received.

The *profit* figure of £3,900 is made up of the £400 previous profit, plus the profit on this sale of £3,500 (£5,500 − £2,000).

The *stock* figure of £3,500 is made up of the £1,500 previous stock plus the stock purchased of £4,000, minus the stock sold which cost the business £2,000 to buy (£1,500 + £4,000 − £2,000 = £3,500).

The *debtor* figure of £3,900 is made up of the £900 previous debtors plus the £3,000 owing for stock sold.

The *cash* figure of £3,500 is made up of the £1,000 previous cash balance plus the £2,500 received from cash sales.

The businessman needs extra resources to take full advantage of an expanding market. He is also a little nervous of the liabilities and so he decides to convert his business to a *private limited company*, with an authorized and issued capital of £30,000 in £1 ordinary shares. He issues shares at par (that is a £1 share for £1) as follows:

£11,900 for the owner's interest in his own name to the owner (himself)
£3,100 for the goodwill in his own name to the owner
£5,000 for cash in his own name to the owner
£10,000 Every Finance Company Ltd for cash

The costs of company formation were paid by the owner and confirmed by the company after incorporation. The costs were:

	£
Capital duty 50p per cent of £30,000	150
Conveyance duty	100
Legal, printing and postage costs	80
	330

Before the new balance sheet can be drawn up the new cash balance must be calculated:

	£	£
Receipts:		
Opening cash	3,500	
Cash for his own shares	5,000	
Cash from finance company	10,000	18,500
Payments:		
Formation expenses shown above		330
Cash balance in hand		18,170

Business Ltd
Balance sheet as at Day 0

	£	£		£
Goodwill		3,100	Authorized capital:	
Fixed assets:			30,000 £1 ordinary shares	30,000
Premises	14,000		Issued capital:	
Furniture and			30,000 ordinary shares	30,000
equipment	4,000		Loan	16,000
Motor vehicle	3,000	21,000		
Current assets:			Current liabilities:	
Stock	3,500		Creditors	4,000
Debtors	3,900			
Cash	18,170			
Preliminary expenses	330	25,900		
		50,000		50,000

Ordinary shares are shares that carry voting rights and the person or group with over 50 per cent controls the business. In this case the owner has retained control with 20,000 out of the 30,000 shares issued.

Authorized capital is the amount authorized to be issued in the Memorandum of Association.[1]

Goodwill represents the value that a prospective purchaser would be prepared to pay for the business over its book value, because its contacts enable it to make more profit than an entirely new business in the same field could make. It appears in the balance sheet only when more has been received for a business than the book value of the assets acquired.

Preliminary expenses are carried in the balance sheet until the owner of the business decides to write them off against profits. They are shown as an asset because the business gets the benefit of them over its whole life. They are the formation expenses shown above.

The business buys £30,000 of stock. It pays £15,000 cash and gets the other half on credit. It sells £20,000 of it for £40,000, half cash and half on credit. The balance sheet now shows:

Business Ltd
Balance sheet as at Day 1

	£	£		£	£
Goodwill		3,100	Authorized capital:		
Fixed assets:			30,000 £1		
Premises	14,000		ordinary shares		30,000
Furniture and			Issued capital:		——
equipment	4,000		30,000 £1		
Motor vehicle	3,000	21,000	ordinary shares	30,000	
	——		Reserves:		
Current assets:			Retained profits	20,000	
Stock	13,500			——	
Debtors	23,900		Equity interest		50,000
Cash	23,170		Loan		16,000
			Current liabilities:		
Preliminary expenses	330	60,900	Creditors		19,000
	——	——			——
		85,000			85,000

Reserves in this case consist solely of retained profits, that is, profits that have been retained in the business in order to strengthen it rather than distributed to the shareholders as dividends. *Reserves do not represent cash.* In studying company balance sheets you will see that it is possible to have very large reserves but very little money. This is because reserves are simply another source of the resources that are being used on the assets side of the balance sheet to buy premises, equipment, stocks or some other assets which may well include, but will not solely be, cash.

The business buys a further £20,000 of stock for cash and sells stock that cost £30,000 on credit for £60,000. A general reserve of £20,000 is created by the business and the preliminary expenses are written off. The balance sheet becomes:

Business Ltd
Balance sheet as at Day 2

	£	£		£	£
Goodwill		3,100	Authorized capital:		
Fixed assets:			30,000 £1 ordinary shares		30,000
Premises	14,000				
Furniture and			Issued capital:		
equipment	4,000		30,000 £1 ordinary shares		30,000
Motor vehicle	3,000	21,000	Reserves:		
			Retained profits	29,670	
Current assets:			General reserve	20,000	49,670
Stock	3,500				
Debtors	83,900		Equity interest		79,670
Cash	3,170	90,570	Loan		16,000
			Current liabilities:		
			Creditors		19,000
		114,670			114,670

The *stock* figure is arrived at in the following way:

	£
Opening stock (previous balance sheet)	13,500
Purchases	20,000
	33,500
Less Sales at cost	30,000
	3,500

The *cash* figure is calculated as follows:

	£
Opening cash (previous balance sheet)	23,170
Less Cash purchases	20,000
	3,170

   The *debtors'* figure consists of previous debtors' £23,900 plus this period's credit sales of £60,000.

The *retained profits* consist of:

	£
Opening balance (previous balance sheet)	20,000
Add This period's profit	30,000
	50,000

Deduct:		
Transfer to general reserve	20,000	
Preliminary expenses written off	330	20,330
		29,670

Notice that the reserves are undistributed *profit* and usually *not cash*. The balance sheet now has reserves of £49,670 but cash of only £3,170. The preliminary expenses have been written off against profits with no effect on cash.

All the balance sheets shown so far have been in the traditional two-sided form. Most published balance sheets are in the narrative or vertical form as this format is said to be easier to understand. The balance sheet of Business Ltd on Day 2 can be redrawn in the vertical form as follows:

Business Ltd
Balance sheet as at Day 2

	£	£
Goodwill		3,100
Fixed assets:		
Premises	14,000	
Furniture and		
equipment	4,000	
Motor vehicle	3,000	21,000
Current assets:		
Stock	3,500	
Debtors	83,900	
Cash	3,170	
	90,570	
Less Current liabilities:		
Creditors	19,000	
WORKING CAPITAL		71,570
NET CAPITAL EMPLOYED		
(total assets *less* current liabilities)		95,670
Less Long-term loan		16,000
Net assets		79,670
Financed by:		
Authorized capital:		
30,000 £1 ordinary shares		30,000
Issued capital:		
30,000 £1 ordinary shares		30,000
Reserves:		
Retained profit	29,670	
General reserve	20,000	49,670
Equity interest		79,670

The vertical form of a balance sheet readily gives more information, without the need for calculation, than the two-sided form.

Working capital and *net capital employed* are both visible at a glance in the vertical form, but must be calculated in the two-sided balance sheet. *Equity interest* is that part of the business belonging to the owners.

The importance of having sufficient working capital to enable your business to operate while it awaits receipts from its activities cannot be overemphasized, although it should be remembered that to have too much is as bad as having too little. The objective is to decide what a sensible level is for the particular business and endeavour to maintain it at that level.

SELF-TEST QUESTIONS

1. What is another name for 'uses' in the balance sheet?
2. What is another name for 'liabilities' in the balance sheet?
3. Which form of balance sheet provides the most useful information?
4. What is the owner's equity?
5. What is a current asset?

QUESTIONS

2.1.1 Evans has decided to start his own business. After careful thought he decided to open a shop selling video cassettes. He has £20,000 which he obtained by increasing the mortgage on his house. The £20,000 is paid into the business bank account. Draw up the business balance sheet as at 30 September, the day on which he paid the money into the business bank account.

2.1.2 On 4 October he rents shop premises at a monthly rental of £500 payable in arrears. He also buys cassettes for £4,000 with which he intends to stock the shop. He pays for the cassettes. His mother will work part-time in the shop and is to receive wages of £50 per week. Draw up his business balance sheet as at 4 October.

2.1.3 He buys a further £10,000 worth of cassettes and cassette players on 7 October for which he will pay at the end of the month. On the same date he sells cassettes that cost him £300 for £400 cash. Draw up his balance sheet as at 7 October.

2.1.4 On 8 October he sells cassettes that cost him £500 for £666. Cash to be received in 30 days. Draw up his business balance sheet at that date.

2.1.5 He pays his mother her wages of £50 on 11 October. Draw up his business balance sheet at that date.

2.1.6 Business is going well, and so on 14 October he decides to buy the lease of his premises for £25,000. To enable him to do so he has a bank loan of £15,000 and pays cash. Draw up his balance sheet at that date.

2.2 Draw up the balance sheet for Universal Activities using the following information.

	£		£
Capital	200,000	Creditors	40,000
Bank	40,000	Land and buildings	160,000
Debtors	90,000	Plant and machinery	50,000
Loan	70,000	Motor vehicles	10,000
Stock	20,000	Reserves	60,000

Employ the two-sided form of balance sheet.

2.3 Employ the vertical form to draw up a balance sheet using the information provided below.

	£		£
Accruals	10,000	Loan	50,000
Furniture and fittings	80,000	Stock	60,000
Debtors	40,000	Share capital	290,000
Creditors	90,000	Goodwill	20,000
Reserves	70,000	Land and buildings	190,000
Plant and machinery	110,000	Bank	10,000

2.4 Redraw the following balance sheet in the correct form so that it balances. There is no need to alter any of the numbers other than by repositioning items.

	£	£		£	£
Fixed assets:			Capital		90,000
Land and buildings	80,000		Plant and machinery		60,000
Reserves	20,000		Fixture and fittings		20,000
Motor vehicles	30,000		Loan		70,000
		130,000			240,000
Current assets:					
Stock	40,000		Current liabilities:		
Creditors	90,000		Debtors		80,000
Bank	10,000	140,000	Accruals		50,000
		270,000			370,000

NOTES

1. The Memorandum of Association gives the name of the company, where the registered office is to be situated and the objectives of the company.

THREE

INCOME STATEMENT

OBJECTIVE

To provide an understanding of the income statement and to enable you to prepare an income statement showing both the gross profit and the net profit.

At the end of the chapter you will be able to explain:

1. The purpose of the income statement
2. Gross profit
3. Net profit
4. Depreciation
5. Capital expenditure
6. Revenue expenditure
7. Turnover

An *income statement* is used to determine the profit a business has made or the loss it has incurred over a trading period. Trading, profit and loss accounts, revenue account, and receipts and payments account are other names used for the income statement. Usually a trading period is taken as one year, but these accounts will be more useful if they are prepared more frequently, i.e. half-yearly, quarterly, or monthly.

The income statement collects together revenue items of income and expense, that is, items that are largely discharged in the financial period and are not held in their present form by the company, nor involve the company in any lasting commitment. In collecting the items for inclusion in the income statement certain accounting principles are followed to ensure comparison is possible between different accounting periods. The main principles are shown below.

3.1 DISTINCTION BETWEEN CAPITAL AND REVENUE EXPENDITURE

Revenue expenditure has an immediate and single impact on profit; examples are wages, rent and rates, heat and light, and postage. *Capital expenditure* has a lasting impact on the business as it normally results in the acquisition of an asset that will be employed within the business for the purpose of earning resources over several years. Because of this it would not be fair to charge the whole cost of the new capital asset to one accounting period, and so an attempt is made to spread the cost over the accounting periods that will benefit from its use. This annual charge for the use of an asset is called *depreciation*, and that is the only way that capital expenditure affects profit. Examples of capital expenditure are purchases of plant and machinery, fixtures and fittings, land and buildings, and vehicles.

3.2 PRINCIPLE OF CONSERVATISM

It is considered to be good business practice to provide for all anticipated losses, but ignore any anticipated gains until they are actually realized. This is exactly the principle applied by accountants when they prepare the annual accounts. An example of this is the valuation of stock which is always the lower of cost or current market price. Any rise in price since purchase is ignored until the stock is sold, when the selling price contributes to income.

3.3 PRINCIPLE OF CONSISTENCY

In order to facilitate comparison between one accounting period and another the accounts must be prepared on a consistent basis. Once the method of depreciating a fixed asset has been decided upon, it must be adhered to over the whole life of that asset.

3.4 GOING CONCERN CONCEPT

Balance sheets are prepared on the assumption that the business is going to continue, and the assets are valued on the basis of cost, not what they could be sold for if the business were to fail.

An example of an income statement is:

Business Ltd
Income statement
(trading and profit and loss account)
for the year ending 30 November 19—

	£	£
Sales (turnover)		80,000
Cost of sales (cost of goods sold):		
Opening stock	5,000	
Add Purchases	100,000	
	105,000	
Deduct Closing stock	45,000	
Cost of sales		60,000
Gross profit		20,000
Administrative and selling expenses:		
Wages	8,000	
Advertising	1,000	
Business rate	2,000	
Light and heat	500	
General expenses	500	
Depreciation	1,700	
Bank charges	200	13,900
Net profit		6,100

Corporation tax } These entries depend on the rate of corporation tax and necessary
Net profit after tax } adjustments.
Sales £80,000   This is the *total* sales figure for the financial year whether the money has been received or not. The figure can be obtained by adding all your sales invoices for the financial year. Sales is also turnover. The total earnings of the financial year.
Opening stock £5,000   This will have been obtained from a physical count of your stock at the end of the previous financial year and the value put on the stock held.
Purchases £100,000   This is the total of goods purchased during the year, whether or not you have paid for them. This figure can be obtained by totalling all your purchase invoices for the financial year.
Closing stock £45,000   This will be obtained from a physical count of your stock at the end of the financial year with which you are dealing, and a value being put on the stock held.
Gross profit   This represents the difference between the cost price of the goods that you have sold and their selling price (£80,000 − £60,000).
Wages £8,000   This represents total wages for the year and can be obtained from the weekly pay schedules.
Advertising £1,000   This is obtained from bills received or contracts entered into.
Business rate £2,000   This is obtained from the rate accounts received from the local

authority. It is important to remember that only the part of the rates that relate to *this* financial year go in the Income Statement. The balance overpaid or underpaid will appear in the balance sheet.

Light and heat £500   This can be obtained from the electricity bills relating to the financial year. Any that relate to any other financial year are excluded from the income statement.

General expenses £500   These are obtained from bills paid for stationery and from the postage book for stamps used on postage.

Depreciation £1,700   This will be obtained as a result of a managerial (or owner's) decision at the time the asset is acquired. Depreciation is a rent or charge for the use of a fixed asset. If a machine costing £10,000 has an anticipated scrap value of £2,000 and is expected to last eight years, then the depreciation charged in each year would be £1,000, calculated by using the following formula (which is one of several available):

$$\frac{\text{Cost} - \text{Scrap (or resale value)}}{\text{Number of years useful life}} = \frac{£10,000 - £2,000}{8} = £1,000 \text{ p.a.}$$

Of the three facts used in the calculation only one is known, that is the cost. The other two—life and scrap value—are estimates; as a result depreciation is rarely, if ever, completely accurate. But it is an attempt to spread capital outlay over all the accounting periods that benefit from it. The depreciation of £1,700 was arrived at by:

	£
1. Depreciating the premises in Business Ltd balance sheet by 5 per cent, i.e. $5/100 \times 14,000$	700
2. Depreciating the furniture and equipment by 10 per cent, i.e. $10/100 \times 4,000$	400
3. Depreciating the vehicle by 20 per cent, i.e. $20/100 \times 3,000$	600
	1,700

Bank charges £200   These would be obtained from the bank statement.

3.5 INCOME STATEMENT FOR A MANUFACTURING CONCERN

If the business is in manufacturing (as opposed to the retail or service sectors) it will be necessary to prepare a manufacturing account or statement in which all costs of manufacture are collected. The manufacturing statement is part of the income statement and comes at the start of it. When the manufacturing statement is included, the income statement summarizes costs and profits at different levels:

1. Cost of goods made
2. Gross profit
3. Net profit

This is illustrated below:

Manufacturing Business Ltd
Income statement
(manufacturing, trading and profit and loss account)
for the year ending 30 November 19—

	£	£
Cost of material used:		
Opening stock of raw materials	20,000	
Add Purchases of raw materials	70,000	
	90,000	
Deduct Closing stock of raw materials	40,000	
Raw materials used		50,000
Manufacturing labour		120,000
PRIME OR DIRECT COST OF GOODS MADE		170,000
Indirect manufacturing costs:		
Labour (supervisors and cleaning staff)	65,000	
Heat and light of factory or workshop	2,000	
Rent and rates of factory or workshop	30,000	
Depreciation of factory/workshop equipment		
and machinery	8,000	
General manufacturing expenses	3,000	108,000
		278,000
Add Opening work in progress (WIP)		3,000
		281,000
Deduct Closing work in progress (WIP)		1,000
FACTORY COST OF GOODS MADE		280,000

	£	£
Sales (turnover)		490,000
Cost of sales (cost of goods sold):		
Opening stock of finished goods	5,000	
Add Factory costs of goods made	280,000	
	285,000	
Deduct Closing stock of finished goods	45,000	
Cost of sales		240,000
Gross profit		250,000
Administrative and selling expenses:		
Wages	68,000	
Advertising	1,000	
Business rates	12,000	
Light and heat	500	
General expenses	500	
Depreciation	1,200	
Bank charges	200	83,400
NET PROFIT BEFORE TAX		166,600

Corporation tax } These entries depend on the rate of corporation tax and the
Net profit after tax } necessary adjustments.

We have three different types of stock which enter the profit calculation at different times:

1. *Raw material stock*   This is calculated by counting the stock of unworked materials that have been bought in and valuing it.
2. *Work in progress (WIP)*   This is calculated by counting the stock of items started but not yet completed. It is extremely difficult to arrive at an accurate figure for this item as it must include a value for both the labour and the materials so far used in the manufacture of the partly finished items as well as other costs.
3. *Finished goods stock*   This is calculated by counting the finished goods and valuing them. It is the stock of goods that is ready for sale.

Raw material purchased   This item is calculated by totalling the purchase invoices or orders.
Manufacturing labour   This is calculated by totalling the hours on the time sheets or cards and multiplying them by the appropriate hourly rate. It will equal the payment of wages.
Prime or direct cost of goods made   This consists of cost items that alter with the volume of output. They are the ones that management can most easily control and should be closely watched.
Indirect labour   This is difficult to calculate accurately unless the staff spend their whole time in the workshop, in which case their whole wage will be charged to the manufacturing section. In other cases some sort of apportionment will have to be made, usually on a time basis.
Indirect manufacturing costs   This consists of cost items that do not alter with the volume of output, but are fixed in the short term as a matter of business policy. Little can be done

about rent, rates or depreciation in the short term, and so not much time should be spent on controlling them. In long-term planning, however, they can have a significant impact and management must be aware of the need to control them.

Heat and light   This item is difficult to calculate unless the workshop is separately metered, in which case the total of the bills will give the figure required. In other cases the cost would be apportioned according to floor area.

Rent and rates   Rent and rates are difficult to calculate unless the workshop is separately assessed. In other cases the charge relating to the workshop should be calculated on the basis of floor area.

Depreciation of machinery and factory or workshop equipment   This will be calculated on the basis of:

$$\frac{(\text{Cost} - \text{Residual value})}{\text{Estimated life}}$$

General manufacturing expenses   This item is calculated by totalling the miscellaneous invoices for such items as telephones, postage and cleaning materials.

Factory cost of goods made   This is used instead of *purchases* in the gross profit or 'trading' section of the income statement.

The income statement will reveal how much profit or loss an undertaking has made in an accounting period but it will not show the change in the cash balance. *Profit is not equal to increase in cash* and this may be illustrated as follows. Suppose a business has revenues of £50,000 and expenses of £40,000 then the profit will be:

	£
Revenue	50,000
Expenses	40,000
Profit	10,000

Now if the revenue is made up of cash sales £20,000, credit sales £30,000 and the expenses consist of cash purchases £25,000, credit purchases £15,000, then the effect on the cash balance will be:

	£
Receipts	20,000
Payments	25,000
Cash outflow	5,000

A profit of £10,000 has resulted in a deterioration in the cash position of £5,000.

This illustrates how it is that so many profitable organizations fail. They may have poor credit control and eventually run out of money or they may be 'overtrading'—that is growing too rapidly for the resources of the organization to be able to meet the demands put on them. Chapter 9 suggests a way in which the business can monitor its cash position.

SELF-TEST QUESTIONS

1. Why do businesses require profit?
2. How is the liquidity of an organization calculated?
3. What is the formula for calculating gross profit?
4. Why is it important to separate personal expenses and business expenses?
5. What are the accounting conventions/principles?

QUESTIONS

Tom Smith—Barrow boy

3.1.1 Smith has £3,000 available for starting a business. He decides to become a barrow boy and buys a barrow costing £832, estimated two-year life, and scales costing £208, estimated four-year life.

During the first four weeks he buys second-grade fruit for cash costing £1,500 out of his original fund. After the four weeks he has £4,000 left of his takings after paying out:

	£	
Rent of yard	90	(£30 per week)
Weekend help	60	
Obstruction fines	80	

At the end of the four weeks he owes £30 rent and has fruit unsold which cost £100. He considers half to be still saleable.

In order to determine how much he can spend on personal living costs, he asks you to calculate his first four weeks' profit from his business.

3.1.2 Smith starts his second four weeks' operation with:

	£
One week's rent owing	30
Stock of saleable fruit in hand	50
Cash in hand	4,460
One barrow and one pair of scales	

During the second four weeks he buys fruit for cash to the value of £2,000.

He gives his wife £1,200 housekeeping money in accordance with his accountant friend's advice.

He takes out a loss of profits insurance policy in case of personal illness at the beginning of the period, payable in advance at an annual premium of £208.

Other payments are:

	£	
Rent	90	(3 weeks)
Fines	150	
Weekend help	60	
Cash takings for month	4,800	

Closing stock of fruit valued at cost price is £120, half of which is in good condition and half of which he thinks will only fetch £40 (two-thirds of cost).

What is his profit for the second period, his cash balance and financial position at the end of the second period? His wife says she requires more housekeeping money. Can he afford to give it to her?

3.1.3 Smith starts his third four weeks' operation with:

	£
Two weeks' rent owing	60
Stock of saleable fruit	100
Cash in hand	5,552
Insurance paid in advance	192
One barrow and one pair of scales	

During the four-week period he buys fruit for cash to the value of £2,500.

He decides he can afford to give his wife more housekeeping, and so gives her £1,450, keeping the balance of the money in the business.

Other payments are:

	£	
Rent	150	(5 weeks)
Fines (nil but one prosecution is pending, the current obstruction fines being imposed are £25)	NIL	
Weekend help	60	
Cash takings for the month	4,100	

Sale of the barrow realized £500 on the last day of the period. He purchased a motor van for delivery purposes, also on the last day, for £3,003. Stock of fruit at the end of the period £200 valued at cost.

What is Smith's profit for the period? Was there a profit or loss on the sale of the barrow? What is his financial position at the end of the period?

3.1.4 Smith starts his fourth four weeks' operation with:

	£
One week's rent owing	30
Stock of saleable fruit which cost	200
Cash in hand	2,989
Insurance paid in advance	176
Provision for pending fine	25
One motor van and one pair of scales	

His wife feels that £1,450 housekeeping money is not sufficient because of some necessary repairs and despite his protestations of the need to plough more money back into the business, Smith has to give her £4,000.

At the magistrate's court he is fined £20 in respect of the outstanding case of obstruction.

During the first week he commences a delivery round on a new estate and enlarges his range of goods to include fresh vegetables. He expects his van to remain in use for two years and it will then have a scrap value of £793.

He arranges a credit account for the purchase of supplies.

His transactions for the period are:

	£
Total cash purchases	1,500
Total purchases on credit	2,500
Cash takings	4,500

Sales to friends living on the estate, who are financially embarrassed and unable to pay him until next month, £100.

Stock of fruit and vegetables at end of period at market value £1,500.

Payments made during period:

	£
Vehicle running expenses	200
Vehicle licence—annual	260
Rent paid	120
Weekend help	60
Payments made to creditors for supplies	2,000

What is his profit for the period? What is the financial position at the end of the period? Does this represent accurately the worth of his business?

3.2

Brown's income statement for the year ending
31 August 1997

	£	£
Sales		120,000
Cost of goods sold:		
Opening stock	15,000	
Add Stock purchased	100,000	
	———	
Stock available to sell	115,000	
Less Closing stock	60,000	
	———	
Cost of goods sold		55,000
		———
Gross profit		65,000
Expenses:		
Wages	25,000	
Heat & light	1,000	
Rent	4,000	
Business rate	6,000	
Postage, etc	1,500	
Depreciation	3,500	
	———	
		41,000
		———
NET PROFIT		24,000
		═══

Brown's balance sheet
as at 31 August 1997

	Cost	Depreciation	Net book value		£	£
				Capital		80,000
Fixed assets	£	£	£	Reserves		
Land & building	280,000	100,000	180,000	Retained profit		52,000
Plant & machinery	76,000	61,000	15,000	Loan		60,000
Vehicles	20,000	16,000	4,000			
	376,000	177,000	199,000	Current liabilities		
				Creditors	30,000	
				Accruals	10,000	
Current assets						
Stock		18,000				40,000
Debtors		14,000				
Bank		1,000	33,000			
			232,000			232,000

1. Redraw the balance sheet in the vertical or narrative form.
2. Has the business been operating for one year or more than one year?
3. Do you think Brown will be able to pay his way?

FOUR

INTERPRETATION

OBJECTIVE

To provide an understanding of financial information and its application in assessing the performance of an organization.

  At the end of this chapter you will be able to explain:

1. The purpose of ratios
2. the importance of trends
3. Long-term and short-term solvency measures
4. The importance of average figures for the sector
5. The limitations of ratios in assessing performance

  The final accounts of companies contain many indications of their financial health. This information is of value to shareholders and creditors as well as to the management of the company. The data contained in the accounts may be interpreted by means of ratio analysis, which defines meaningful relationships between business results. Examples are profit on sales and return on capital employed. There are four broad categories of ratios that are useful in assessing a company's performance and financial position. These are:

1. Profitability ratios
2. Short-term liquidity ratios
3. Long-term solvency ratios
4. Efficiency ratios

It is important to realize that with financial ratios the figures alone have very little meaning. They have to be compared with something, i.e.

1. The figures for the previous three years, say, so that a trend may be seen
2. Figures for similar firms in the same industry
3. Where possible, the industry average
4. The business plan

It should always be borne in mind that while ratios are extremely helpful they do not provide answers. They merely suggest lines of enquiry that should be pursued by the competent manager.

These ratios are further explored using the example of a manufacturing concern shown below.

Manufacturing Business Ltd
Income statement
(manufacturing, trading and profit and loss account)
for the year ending 30 November 19—

	£	£
Cost of material used:		
Opening stock of raw materials	20,000	
Add Purchases of raw materials	70,000	
	90,000	
Deduct Closing stock of raw materials	40,000	
Raw materials used		50,000
Manufacturing labour		20,000
PRIME OR DIRECT COST OF GOODS MADE		70,000
Indirect manufacturing costs:		
Labour (supervisors and cleaning staff)	5,000	
Heat and light of factory or workshop	2,000	
Rent and rates of factory or workshop	10,000	
Depreciation of factory/workshop equipment and machinery	8,000	
General manufacturing expenses	3,000	28,000
		98,000
Add Opening work in progress (WIP)		3,000
		101,000
Deduct Closing work in progress (WIP)		1,000
Factory cost of goods made transferred		100,000

	£	£
Sales		180,000
Cost of sales (cost of goods sold):		
Opening stock of finished goods	5,000	
Add Factory cost of goods made transferred	100,000	
	105,000	
Deduct Closing stock of finished goods	45,000	
Cost of sales		60,000
Gross profit		120,000
Administrative and selling expenses:		
Wages	8,000	
Advertising	1,000	
Rates	2,000	
Light and heat	500	
General expenses	500	
Depreciation	1,200	
Bank charges	200	13,400
NET PROFIT BEFORE TAX		106,600

Corporation tax } These entries depend on the rate of corporation tax and necessary
Net profit after tax } adjustments.

Manufacturing Business Ltd
Balance sheet as at 30 November 19—

	Cost £	Depreciation £	Net book value (NBV) £
Fixed assets:			
Land and buildings	800,000	100,000	700,000
Plant and machinery	400,000	60,000	340,000
Fixtures and fittings	100,000	30,000	70,000
Motor vehicles	10,000	6,000	4,000
	1,310,000	196,000	1,114,000
Current assets:			
Stock			
Raw materials	40,000		
WIP	1,000		
Finished goods	45,000		
	86,000		
Debtors	4,000		
Bank	2,000		
Cash	500		
		92,500	
Deduct Current liabilities:			
Dividend due	5,000		
Creditors	41,500		
		46,500	
Working capital			46,000
NET CAPITAL EMPLOYED			1,160,000
Financed by:			
Authorized and issued share capital:			
900,000 £1 ordinary shares		900,000	
200,000 10 per cent preference shares		200,000	1,100,000
Reserves:			
General		40,000	
Profit and loss account		20,000	60,000
			1,160,000

4.1 PROFITABILITY RATIOS

Most businesses exist primarily to earn profits for their owners, which makes the ratio of profit to capital extremely important. This is so much the case that the expression:

$$\frac{\text{Net profit}}{\text{Capital}}$$

is often called the 'primary ratio'.

Unfortunately, profit and capital can be calculated in different ways, which makes comparison of the profitability of different businesses somewhat suspect. However, it is a good guide to general performance.

Profit to net capital employed

Net capital employed is equal to the total assets of a business *minus* its current liabilities.

Gross profit to net capital employed This ratio is useful as a means of control. The gross profit to net capital employed should not vary significantly from one accounting year to another. If it does vary management should be aware of the causes of the fluctuation. The ratio in our example is:

$$\frac{\text{Gross profit} \times 100}{\text{Net capital employed}} = \frac{120,000 \times 100}{1,160,000} = 10.34 \text{ per cent}$$

Net profit before tax to net capital employed (return on capital employed—ROCE) This ratio indicates the performance of the net assets of the company. It is an overall indicator of management performance and includes the effect of both operating efficiencies and financial efficiencies. The ratio in isolation is not very meaningful. It should be compared with the return that would be obtained from investing in the Post Office savings or building societies or in the banks. This will indicate whether or not you would be wise to discontinue your business, invest the proceeds and work for somebody else. The decision is never as clear-cut as that since many people prefer to work for themselves no matter how low the return on their investment. Trends over several years will show whether the result obtained is unusual or as expected for that business. Comparison with the industry average will show whether you are doing better or worse than the others. The ratio in our example is:

$$\frac{\text{Net profit before tax} \times 100}{\text{Net capital employed}} = \frac{106,600 \times 100}{1,160,000} = 9.19 \text{ per cent}$$

How does this compare with the return from the Post Office, bank, building society or the average figure for the sector in which your organization operates?

Profit on sales

Gross profit to sales This ratio expresses the gross profitability as a percentage of sales. Gross profit to sales must be healthy if the business is to survive. The figure on its own means little and it should be compared with that for the previous four years and with the average for the industry.

This will enable you to say whether or not it is an unusual result and also if you are doing better than the industry average. The ratio in our example is:

$$\frac{\text{Gross profit} \times 100}{\text{Net sales}} = \frac{120{,}000 \times 100}{180{,}000} = 66.67 \text{ per cent}$$

This seems a reasonable return but without the additional information mentioned above we are not able to comment. However, it does provide sufficient for the expenses to be met without using all the profit for the year.

Net profit to sales This ratio expresses the net profitability as a percentage of sales. It lets you know how much £1 of sales is contributing to profit. Trends and averages are more important than the figure in isolation. The ratio in our example is:

$$\frac{\text{Net profit} \times 100}{\text{Net sales}} = \frac{106{,}600 \times 100}{180{,}000} = 59.22 \text{ per cent}$$

That is each £1 of sales is contributing 59.22 pence profit.

4.2 SHORT-TERM LIQUIDITY RATIOS

Approximately 80 per cent of the companies that fail in the UK are profitable at the time that they do so. Lack of money with which to pay their way forces them into liquidation. The importance of the liquidity ratios lies in the fact that they can help to avoid this situation.

Current ratio

This is a measure of an organization's ability to pay its way in the medium term, that is, from about four to nine months in the future. The current ratio expresses the current assets as a ratio of the current liabilities. The ratio in our example is:

Current assets	: Current liabilities
92,500	: 46,500
1.99	: 1

This is not meaningful in isolation. The trend over the last four years might show that it has suddenly dropped from 5:1 to 1.99:1 in which case it would warrant further investigation. On the other hand it might have been 1.97:1 for the previous years in which case there would probably be no need for further investigation. The ratios should always be read in conjunction with the available balance sheet information. In this case it does appear that there might be a liquidity problem since £86,000 of the current assets are tied up in stock. Various ratios are stated as giving the required margin of safety for a company and 2:1 is often quoted as the minimum to allow for safe operation. This is nonsense, for if we look at the published accounts of three companies that do not seem to have any liquidity problems, i.e. Marks and Spencer Plc, J Sainsbury Plc, Tesco Plc, we will see that their current ratios are:

	Marks and Spencer Plc	J Sainsbury Plc	Tesco Plc
	£	£	£
Current assets	2,365,800,000	1,179,000,000	731,000,000
Current liabilities	1,363,800,000	2,519,000,000	2,002,000,000
Current assets : Current liabilities	1.7 : 1	0.5 : 1	0.4 : 1

I do not believe anyone would claim that any of these three companies was about to go out of business due to a liquidity shortage. You should remember, however, that this *does not mean* that all companies could operate on these ratios. What it does emphasize is the fact that different industries work on and need different working capital.

The figures for Simon Engineering Plc and Redrow Group Plc in their accounts are:

	Simon Engineering Plc	Redrow Group Plc
	£	£
Current assets	182,100,000	199,618,000
Current liabilities	132,200,000	54,327,000
Current assets : Current liabilities	1.4 : 1	3.7 : 1

A more sensitive ratio which will give us a better idea of whether or not the company has liquidity problems is shown below.

Quick ratio (acid test)

This is a measure of an organization's ability to pay its way in the short term, that is up to about four months in the future. It expresses the quick assets as a ratio of the current liabilities, that is, those assets which may readily be turned into cash, together with the cash and bank figures. The ratio in our example is:

Quick assets	: Current liabilities
6,500	: 46,500
0.14	: 1

This is not meaningful in isolation although it does seem rather low. The trend for the last four years will show whether it is unusually low as will the average for the industry. If we study the balance sheet it shows that we have creditors of £41,500 and debtors, bank and cash balances of only £6,500. This does indicate a quite serious liquidity problem and steps should be taken to alleviate it. It would be possible to raise a loan secured on the premises for £100,000, which would dramatically improve the liquidity of the company, or the bank may be prepared to provide overdraft facilities if it was convinced that the profitability of the company could be maintained or improved. The quoted safe ratio for the acid test is 1 : 1 but this again is rubbish. There is no ideal ratio since what is good for one business is bad for another. If we look at our five companies again we see:

	Marks and Spencer Plc £	J Sainsbury Plc £	Tesco Plc £
Quick assets	506,400,000	418,000,000	172,000,000
Current liabilities	1,363,800,000	2,519,000,000	2,002,000,000
Quick assets : Current liabilities	1.1 : 1	0.2 : 1	0.1 : 1

	Simon Engineering Plc £	Redrow Group Plc £
Quick assets	141,500,000	15,774,000
Current liabilities	132,200,000	54,327,000
Quick assets : Current liabilities	1.1 : 1	0.3 : 1

Two of these companies are running successfully on ratios of less than 1:1, other companies need ratios of over 1:1 depending on their industrial sector and methods of operation. Sainsbury and Tesco can operate on such low ratios because the bulk of their sales are for cash. In using these ratios it should be remembered that it is as bad to be too liquid as it is to have too little liquidity. There may be some concern over Redrow Group Plc, which is a building company in that it may need to generate more liquidity by selling some assets in order to pay its way.

4.3 LONG-TERM SOLVENCY RATIOS

Businesses can obtain the funds that they require by issuing shares, both ordinary and preference. The ordinary shareholders have the equity of the business and become the owners. Money can be borrowed by means of debentures, or bank overdraft facilities may be obtained. However the funds are obtained, there is a rule that it is wise to follow if you wish to avoid problems in the future. The rule is that you do not borrow short to invest long. The fringe banks ignored this rule in 1972 and some of them went out of existence, others were saved by larger banks. So far as the business in our example, or any other business is concerned, it means that the fixed assets should be bought out of long-term capital, that is equity, i.e. the owner's interest, or debentures. In our example we have fixed assets of £1,114,000 and share capital and reserves, i.e. equity interest, of £1,160,000 and so we are following the rule. Had we not done so we would have added an additional strain to the working capital.

Too much borrowing causes dramatic changes in the return to ordinary shareholders when profits fluctuate only slightly and puts the company at risk. Companies that have a high proportion of fixed interest loan capital to equity are said to be highly geared, and these companies may find that they cannot survive at all if profits fall or exchange rates alter. An example of this was Polly Peck which was extremely highly geared. The following illustrates the effect of gearing on profit available to ordinary shareholders:

	A Co. £'000s	B Co. £'000s
Capital structure		
Ordinary share capital £1 shares	1,000	250
Retained profits	500	500
Equity interest (due to ordinary shareholders)	1,500	750
10 per cent Debenture loan	250	1,000
	1,750	1,750
	Low gearing	High gearing

Let us suppose that profits before interest and tax earned by the two companies are exactly the same and they fluctuate between £100,000 and £400,000, then the impact on the ordinary shareholder may be traced as being:

	A Co. £'000s	£'000s	£'000s	B Co. £'000s	£'000s	£'000s
Profit before interest	100	200	400	100	200	400
Debenture interest	25	25	25	100	100	100
Profit after interest	75	175	375	0	100	300
Tax 52 per cent	39	91	195	0	52	156
Profit available to shareholders	36	84	180	0	48	144
Earnings per share	4p	8p	18p	0p	19p	58p

The earnings per share are calculated by dividing the available profit by the number of shares.

$$\text{For A Co. the first calculation is} \quad \frac{36,000}{1,000,000} = £0.04$$

$$\text{For B Co. the second calculation is} \quad \frac{48,000}{250,000} = £0.19$$

This clearly illustrates the fact that if profits are rising it is better to buy shares in a highly geared company and if they are falling you would be wise to be with a company that has low gearing. The earnings per share fluctuate greatly with profits in B Company, ranging from 0 to 58p, whereas in A Company they only fluctuate between 4p and 18p.

Capital gearing ratio

$$\frac{\text{Fixed investment borrowing} \times 100}{\text{Equity capital}}$$

There is no accepted relationship but you should remember the risk of high gearing (sometimes called leverage). In our example we have a ratio of infinity since we have no borrowing at all. It may be that the organization should seriously consider some borrowing to improve its liquidity, and, if the resources are properly employed, it should be possible to increase the earnings per share.

This ratio may be illustrated by using A Company and B Company:

		A Co.	*B Co.*
$\dfrac{\text{Fixed investment borrowing} \times 100}{\text{Equity capital}}$	=	$\dfrac{250,000 \times 100}{1,500,000}$	$\dfrac{1,000,000 \times 100}{750,000}$
	=	16.7 per cent	133.3 per cent

The practice of 'off balance sheet financing' has made it extremely difficult to assess how highly geared companies are simply by looking at the balance sheet. Concern has been increased by the collapse of Polly Peck among others, and the problems of organizations like Brent Walker, because lack of information in the balance sheet make it impossible for analysts to foresee the problems. Things have now reached such a state that many people are querying the value of income statements and balance sheets in their current form and demanding a complete revision of the way in which they are presented and the information that they contain.

Off balance sheet financing

This is the practice of showing what is often a liability of an organization in the balance sheet as an asset. It is not done intentionally in order to mislead would-be investors or suppliers but it is becoming a rather frequent occurrence. A company's balance sheet may show:

	£'000s	£'000s
Fixed assets:		
Land and buildings	900	
Plant and machinery	60	
Motor vehicles	10	
Investment in subsidiary undertakings	80	1050
Current assets:		
Stocks	40	
Debtors	80	
Bank	10	
	130	
Less Current liabilities	110	
Working capital		20
NET CAPITAL EMPLOYED		1070
Less Long-term loan		50
		1020
Financed by:		
Issued share capital		
4,000,000 ordinary shares		1000
Reserves		
Profit and loss account		20
		1020

This company would seem low geared and safe to deal with. What would not be revealed in the balance sheet is that the subsidiary company, for which it is responsible, is extremely highly geared with borrowings of £900,000. If this were shown it would present a very different picture indeed. You can see from this why balance sheets often have to be treated with utmost caution and further enquiries undertaken before any major decision is made.

Times interest earned

$$\frac{\text{Profit before fixed interest charges}}{\text{Fixed interest charges}}$$

This indicates the safety margin to allow the company to survive. If interest charges are equal to or greater than the earnings, then the company will not survive for long and there will be no surplus for shareholders/owners. The calculation is not relevant to our example since we have no borrowing. Again using the example of A Company and B Company and the middle case for both companies we have:

$$\frac{\text{Profit before fixed interest charges}}{\text{Fixed interest charges}} = \frac{200,000}{25,000} \quad \frac{200,000}{100,000}$$

$$8 \text{ times} \qquad 2 \text{ times}$$

4.4   EFFICIENCY RATIOS

It is essential for anyone running a business to know how efficiently it is being done. The following three ratios will enable you to keep an eye on the business without becoming too immersed in details.

Debtors' ratio

$$\frac{\text{Debtors} \times 365}{\text{Credit sales}}$$

This measures the average time to collect a debt and when more companies are failing daily because they cannot pay their way, it is an extremely important ratio. No business can survive today if it is failing to collect sums of money that are due to it within a reasonable period of time. In our example, if we assume that none of the sales are for cash and they have taken place evenly throughout the working year of, say, 365 days then the daily average is:

$$\frac{4,000}{180,000} \times 365 = 8.11 \text{ days' sales}$$

The company is taking approximately one week to collect moneys due to it, which is exceptionally good. Had the answer been four months, then there would have been cause for concern and action would have had to be taken to remedy the situation.

Creditors' ratio

$$\frac{\text{Creditors} \times 365}{\text{Credit purchases}}$$

This measures the average time taken to pay a debt. The answer in the present climate is to keep your supplier waiting as long as you decently can without impairing the relationship that you have built up. In our example, if we assume that all purchases are on credit and that they have taken place evenly throughout the year of 365 days, then the daily average is:

$$\frac{41,500}{70,000} \times 365 = 216.4 \text{ days' purchases}$$

The business is taking 31 weeks to pay its suppliers. This is far too long and may be a reflection of the liquidity problem that it has. Steps should be taken to correct the situation before suppliers lose confidence and refuse any further credit. Had payment been made in

14 days that would have been too short a period and more credit could have been safely taken.

Stock turnover

$$\frac{\text{Cost of goods sold}}{\text{Average stock of finished goods}}$$

This helps to ensure that you do not tie up large volumes of working capital in stocks. Within reason the faster you turn over your stock the better, as long as you avoid running round in circles and getting nowhere. This can help ensure that your stock does not increase without your being aware of it. In our example cost of goods sold is £60,000 and a rough average stock can be obtained from:

$$\frac{\text{Opening stock} + \text{Closing stock}}{2} = \frac{5,000 + 45,000}{2} = £25,000$$

so the calculation becomes:

$$\frac{\text{Cost of goods sold}}{\text{Average stock of finished goods}} = \frac{60,000}{25,000} = 2.4 \text{ times per year}$$

To convert this to days you simply divide it into the number of sales days in the year.

$$\frac{365}{2.4} = 152 \text{ days}$$

The stock is being turned over in 152 days. This ratio in isolation is not very meaningful and should be compared with the last three to four years' figures as well as the industry average. Stocks naturally increase as sales expand, or there would be nothing left to sell, and contract as sales fall. For companies such as wholesalers and some retailers a high turnover is essential if any profit is to be made at all. Obsolete stock lying in store would cause a low rate of stock turnover and should be immediately dealt with.

Mark-up

$$\frac{(\text{Selling price} - \text{Cost price}) \times 100}{\text{Cost price}}$$

This tells the owner or manager how much is being added to the cost price of the goods to arrive at the selling price. Having decided how much should be added it is important that it is maintained from period to period. If the mark-up is reduced profitability will suffer unless turnover can be increased sufficiently or fixed costs reduced. No change in mark-up should occur without you being fully aware of it.

In our example the cost of goods sold is £60,000 and the selling price is £180,000, so the mark-up is:

$$\frac{(£180,000 - £60,000) \times 100}{£60,000} = \frac{£120,000 \times 100}{£60,000} = 200 \text{ per cent}$$

Thus 200 per cent is being added to the cost price of the goods to arrive at the selling price. The management has decided that this is sufficient to meet all the fixed costs and leave a reasonable profit. The figure is not very meaningful in isolation but it is extremely helpful for control purposes when comparing one month or year with another.

There are a great many ratios that it is possible to use to help you control your business. Those mentioned above are some of the more useful but it should be remembered that in themselves they produce no answers. However, they do ask some relevant questions, and, when used in conjunction with other information, provide indicators that if properly used can help your business to avoid many pitfalls and may even prevent it going into liquidation.

SELF-TEST QUESTIONS

1. Why are trends important in ratio analysis?
2. Which are the most important—ratios or changes in ratios?
3. How is the primary ratio calculated?
4. What is the importance of the mark-up?
5. Sales £120,000, gross profit £40,000. Calculate the profit on sales ratio.

QUESTIONS

4.1 The following are the summarized balance sheets of Polytam Plc on 31 December 1997 and 31 December 1998. Polytam Plc is in the engineering field.

	1997 £'000s	1998 £'000s		1997 £'000s	1998 £'000s
Freehold property at valuation	180	180	Authorized and issued share capital	300	300
Equipment (cost less depreciation)	170	130	Fixed asset re-valuation reserve	80	80
Investment at cost	50	0	Income statement balance	70	85
				450	465
Current assets					
Stocks:			15% debenture loan		
Materials	90	60	redeemable 2008–09	180	180
Work in progress and finished goods	100	95	Current liabilities:		
Uncompleted long-term contracts	300	250	Creditors	300	240
Debtors	230	370	Bank overdraft	190	200
	1,120	1,085		1,120	1,085

The following are the summarized income statements for the years ending 31 December 1997 and 31 December 1998.

	1997 £'000s	1997 £'000s	1998 £'000s	1998 £'000s
Sales		1,700		1,300
Gain on sale of investment		—		60
Gain arising from change in basis of accounting for long-term contracts		—		190
		1,700		1,550
Deduct:				
Salaries and wages	420		380	
Materials	870		790	
General expenses	300	1,590	280	1,450
NET PROFIT		110		100

In the 1997 balance sheet contracts were shown at cost. The long-term contracts in the 1998 accounts include anticipated profit attributable to the work undertaken on them up to the date of the balance sheet.

The company has overdraft facilities of £210,000 secured by a floating charge on its assets. The facilities are fully utilized on 23 March 1999 and the Managing Director is considering what to do. He considers the accounts for 1998 and sends out the following note stating what he feels has happened:

> The year to December 1998 was bad. We suffered from the full weight of the recession. Our total sales fell with inevitable consequences for our trading results. The situation was made worse by staff changes in our accounting department where control has slipped. We have now engaged a first class person to get this side sorted out.
>
> There are obvious problems which have caused a temporary set-back but we are now overcoming them and have every confidence in producing good results this year.

Fully discuss the financial position of Polytam Plc using any ratios that you feel would be helpful.

4.2 Using the five-year summary calculate the following:
1. Return on equity
2. Return on capital employed
3. Interest cover
4. Fixed asset turnover
5. Percentage growth in sales year on year
6. Percentage growth in profit year on year

Company Plc — Five-year summary

	1998 £ million	1997 £ million	1996 £ million	1995 £ million	1994 £ million
Turnover					
Continuing operations (including acquisitions)	2,934.4	2,757.8	2,377.6	2,248.5	1,740.4
Discontinued operations			31.6	127.8	2.7
	2,934.4	2,757.8	2,409.2	2,376.3	1,743.1
Operating profit before exceptional items:					
Continuing operations (including acquisitions)					
Lubricants	181.2	153.9	127.2	122.5	120.8
Chemicals	48.9	36.6	34.0	34.1	10.7
Fuels	20.7	25.5	27.2	19.7	22.3
LNG Transportation	5.5	8.4	9.3	10.4	10.9
Energy Investments	4.5	6.1	7.9	7.6	6.8
Central Management	(11.1)	(11.3)	(9.8)	(7.5)	(9.0)
	249.7	219.2	195.8	186.8	162.5
Discontinued operations			0.9	6.8	5.5
	249.7	219.2	196.7	193.6	168.0
Interest	(30.2)	(37.5)	(39.8)	(47.0)	(19.3)
Profit before exceptional items and taxation	219.5	181.7	156.9	146.6	148.7
Exceptional items:					
Continuing operations	24.0	7.0	7.0	(26.7)	7.0
Disposal of discontinued operations		3.2			88.5
Profit before taxation	243.5	191.9	163.9	119.9	244.2
Taxation	(86.6)	(74.7)	(77.3)	(77.3)	(63.2)
Profit after taxation	156.9	117.2	86.6	42.6	181.0
Minority interests	(18.9)	(16.0)	(12.5)	(9.5)	(6.5)
Profit for the financial year attributable to shareholders	138.0	101.2	74.1	33.1	174.5

Balance sheet					
Fixed assets	921.6	941.0	886.1	845.8	830.8
Net current assets	357.8	299.6	374.1	200.8	75.7
Total assets less current liabilities	1,279.4	1,240.6	1,260.2	1,046.6	906.5
Long-term creditors and provisions	585.0	599.2	655.3	505.8	312.4
Minority interests	76.6	61.0	57.2	44.6	42.2
Shareholders' funds	617.8	580.4	547.7	496.2	551.9

4.3 Use ratios to analyse the performance of Portsdown Plc over the following five years:

(£millions)	1994	1995	1996	1997	1998
INCOME STATEMENT					
Sales	2,910.0	3,235.4	3,388.8	3,547.9	4,479.4
Operating profit	283.3	255.5	173.5	157.0	251.9
Other income	58.9	44.3	62.8	84.4	114.7
Profit before int.	342.2	299.8	236.3	241.4	366.6
Interest charge	(47.5)	(47.3)	(40.6)	(36.6)	(57.3)
Profit before tax	294.7	252.5	195.7	204.8	309.3
Tax charge	(63.3)	(63.7)	(61.5)	(56.9)	(77.4)
Minority interest					(1.8)
Preference div					
Earnings	231.4	188.8	134.2	147.9	230.1
Extraord. items	(5.8)	(4.4)			
Ordinary div.	(50.6)	(55.3)	(63.4)	(75.1)	(99.2)
Retained profit	175.0	129.1	70.8	72.8	130.9
BALANCE SHEET					
Properties	841.8	584.8	521.8	582.2	768.5
Other tangible FA	372.0	393.4	391.4	410.2	480.7
Investments	2.8	40.9	43.2	50.1	62.3
Other FA					
Total fixed assets	1,216.6	1,019.1	956.4	1,042.5	1,311.5
Stock & WiP	463.9	651.2	639.3	631.0	771.3
Debtors	124.2	121.9	155.5	139.0	250.0
Cash & securities	102.2	159.2	338.7	315.6	386.5
Creditors	(445.9)	(441.0)	(419.6)	(429.2)	(623.2)
Current tax due	(156.1)	(149.7)	(162.8)	(166.3)	(233.8)
Proposed dividend	(34.8)	(38.1)	(43.7)	(54.2)	(69.9)
Other working cap.	36.2	30.0	61.8	87.0	106.0
Total working cap.	89.7	333.5	569.2	522.9	586.9
Capital employed	1,306.3	1,352.6	1,525.6	1,565.4	1,898.4
CAPITAL & FINANCE					
Share capital	137.6	169.2	238.0	275.0	356.3
Reverves	824.2	805.4	844.3	882.8	734.8
Shareholders equity	961.8	974.6	1,082.3	1,157.8	1,091.1
Non-current tax	(11.6)	(12.7)	(14.6)	(15.2)	(16.6)
Deferred liabs.					82.0
Long & medium loan	301.3	274.7	233.0	132.3	384.9
Long-term capital	1,251.5	1,236.6	1,300.7	1,274.9	1,541.4
Short-term loans	54.8	116.0	224.9	290.5	357.0
Capital employed	1,306.3	1,352.6	1,525.6	1,565.4	1,898.4
Numbers employed	58,796	61,497	61,941	62,799	72,036

4.4 Critically assess the performance of Retail Plc over the following five years:

(£millions)	1994	1995	1996	1997	1998
INCOME STATEMENT					
Sales	3,593.0	4,119.1	4,717.7	5,401.9	6,346.3
Operating profit	154.5	210.3	273.6	351.8	417.1
Other income	31.0	36.1	41.1	56.3	72.3
Profit before int.	185.5	246.4	314.7	408.1	489.4
Interest charge	(9.6)	(20.8)	(38.7)	(46.5)	(53.2)
Profit before tax	175.9	225.6	276.0	361.6	436.2
Tax charge	(56.9)	(75.1)	(89.7)	(107.8)	(133.5)
Minority interest					
Preference div.					
Earnings	119.0	150.5	186.3	253.8	302.7
Extraord. items					
Ordinary div.	(31.0)	(42.1)	(53.8)	(67.3)	(97.3)
Retained profit	88.0	108.4	132.5	186.5	205.4
BALANCE SHEET					
Properties	598.9	876.8	1,033.3	1,321.7	1,585.9
Other tangible FA	401.0	538.9	683.0	837.7	1,280.0
Investments	0.2	0.2	0.3	1.9	1.6
Other FA					
Total fixed assets	1,000.1	1,415.9	1,716.6	2,161.3	2,867.5
Stock & WiP	182.5	179.0	192.2	212.8	231.5
Debtors	13.6	39.5	27.2	19.4	50.0
Cash & securities	60.5	35.3	85.5	26.3	501.9
Creditors	(324.8)	(370.6)	(475.9)	(577.5)	(688.8)
Current tax due	(86.6)	(44.6)	(104.6)	(111.2)	(192.1)
Proposed dividend	(20.2)	(27.4)	(35.8)	(45.4)	(69.6)
Other working cap.					
Total working cap.	(175.0)	(188.8)	(311.4)	(475.6)	(167.1)
Capital employed	825.1	1,227.1	1,405.2	1,685.7	2,700.4
CAPITAL & FINANCE					
Share capital	201.4	230.9	262.3	297.8	982.2
Reserves	488.7	636.5	769.0	956.3	1,177.7
Shareholders equity	690.1	867.4	1,031.3	1,254.1	2,159.9
Non-current tax	5.8	51.7	61.2	72.8	15.1
Deferred liabs.		5.0	10.8	15.9	
Long & medium loan	120.4	236.9	293.0	327.6	363.5
Long-term capital	816.3	1,161.0	1,396.3	1,670.4	2,538.5
Short-term loans	8.8	66.1	8.9	15.3	161.9
Capital employed	825.1	1,227.1	1,405.2	1,685.7	2,700.4
Numbers employed	62,652	71,262	75,658	83,224	87,691

CASH FLOW STATEMENTS

OBJECTIVE

To provide an understanding of cash flow statements and their application in assessing the profitability and liquidity of organizations.

At the end of this chapter you will be able to explain:

1. The purpose of the cash flow statement
2. The link of the cash flow statement with the income statement
3. The net cash flow from operations
4. The treatment of depreciation
5. The treatment of extraordinary items

Since 1991 funds flow statements have been replaced by cash flow statements because they are felt to be more useful to management and investors alike in trying to assess the profitability and liquidity of organizations. When used with the financial accounts (profit and loss account and balance sheet) the cash flow statement helps to give a better/more accurate guide to an organization's liquidity. The importance of this can hardly be overemphasized since the liquid organization can pay its way and survive while the organization that lacks liquidity cannot survive for long since it cannot pay its way. Used in conjunction with ratio analysis the cash flow statement becomes a useful managerial tool in assessing the financial position of the firm.

It is important for the organization to know whether or not it is generating sufficient cash to meet its operational requirements. If it is not doing so then corrective action must be taken before the situation becomes critical and the organization fails. The cash flow statement is designed to show a company's cash generation and cash absorption for a period under standardized headings which are operating activities, returns on investments, and servicing of finance, financing, taxation and investing activities. In order to prepare a cash flow statement you need access to the balance sheets at the beginning and end of the period under review as well as the income statement (profit and loss account) for the period. An example of a cash flow statement is given below using the accounts of Tops Plc.

Tops Plc
Balance sheet as at 30 June

(£'000s)	1996 Cost	1996 Dep.	1996 NBV	(£'000s)	1997 Cost	1997 Dep.	1997 NBV
Fixed assets:							
Buildings	90	36	54		190	50	140
Current assets:	—	—			—	—	
Stock	102				134		
Debtors	220				340		
Bank	4	326			2	476	
Less Current liabilities:							
Creditors	30				56		
Accruals	60				70		
Dividends	40	130			60	186	
Working capital			196				290
Net capital employed			250				430
Less Long-term loans			—				40
			250				390
Financed by:							
Ordinary share capital			200				300
Reserves			50				90
			250				390

Tops Plc
Income statement year ending 30 June 1997

	(£'000s)
Net profit before tax	170
Tax	70
Net profit after tax	100
Proposed dividend	60
	40
Profits brought forward	50
Profits carried forward	90

Notes
1. During the year 100,000 ordinary shares of £1 were issued for cash.
2. During the year £40,000 debenture stock was issued for cash.
3. Debenture interest paid £4,000.

Prepare the cash flow statement for the year.

In answering this and any subsequent questions on cash flow statements the following framework should be adopted and used as an *aide-mémoire*.

	£	£
Operating profit for the period		/
ADD		
Depreciation	/	
Losses on extraordinary items	/	
Bad debts written off	/	
Increase in provisions	/	
Decreases in current assets		
other than cash/bank	/	
Increases in current liabilities		
other than bank overdraft, taxation and dividends	/	/
DEDUCT		
Profit on extraordinary items	/	
Increases in current assets other than		
cash/bank	/	
Decreases in current liabilities other		
than bank overdraft, taxation and dividends	/	/
Balance net cash flow ±		/

We are now in a position to answer the question employing the above framework.

Tops Plc
Cash flow statement year ending 30 June 1997

	(£'000s)	(£'000s)
Net cash inflow from operations (1)		62
Interest paid	4	
Dividends paid	40	
Net cash outflow from investments, etc.		44
Corporation tax paid		60
Payments for fixed assets		100
Net cash outflow before financing		142
Financing		
Ordinary shares issued	100	
Debenture stock issued	40	
		140
Net cash flow		(2)

Notes

1. Reconciliation of operating profit to net cash flow from operations   (£'000s)

Operating profit		174
Depreciation		14
Increase in creditors		26
		214
Less Increase in stocks	32	
Increase in debtors	120	152
		62

The depreciation, creditors, stocks and debtors figures are arrived at by comparing the two numbers in the balance sheets at the beginning and end of the year.

SELF-TEST QUESTIONS

1. Why was it decided to replace the funds flow statement with the cash flow statement?
2. How is the operating profit adjusted to show the net cash flow from operations?
3. Are bad debts written off added to the operating profit or deducted from it?
4. What happens to losses on extraordinary items when operating profit is adjusted to show net cash flow from operations?

QUESTIONS

5.1 From the following information prepare the cash flow statement for the year ending 31 December 1997.

Sea Ltd
Balance sheet as at 31 December

	1996		1997	
	£'000s	£'000s	£'000s	£'000s
Fixed assets:				
Land		1,200		1,400
Current assets:				
Stock	200		240	
Debtors	400		500	
Bank	12		20	
	612		760	
Less Current liabilities:				
Creditors	360	252	440	320
		1,452		1,720
Financed by:				
Ordinary shares		1,400		1,600
Profit (all retained)		52		120
		1,452		1,720

5.2 Using the information given prepare Davies Ltd cash flow statement for the year ending 31 March 1997.

Income statement year ending 31 March 1997

	£'000s	£'000s
Gross profit		460
Fixed expenses	152	
Loss on sale fixed assets	6	
Increase in provisions	2	
Depreciation of vehicles	70	230
Net profit		230
Tax		130
		100
Dividends		50
Retained profit		50

Davies Ltd
Balance sheets as at 31 March

	1996 £'000s	1996 £'000s	1997 £'000s	1997 £'000s
Fixed assets:				
Plant and machinery at cost		300		400
Depreciation		150		200
		150		200
Current assets:				
Stock		120		100
Debtors	160		200	
Less Provision	8	152	10	190
Cash		12		16
		284		306
Less Current liabilities:				
Creditors	120		106	
Tax	104		130	
Dividend due	40	264	50	286
Working capital		20		20
Net capital employed		170		220
Financed by:				
Ordinary shares		150		150
Profit retained		20		70
		170		220

Notes
1. Additional plant and machinery was purchased during the year for £150,000.
2. During the year plant and machinery was sold for £24,000 cash. It had originally cost £50,000 and £20,000 had been charged for depreciation.

SIX
COSTING

OBJECTIVE

To provide an understanding of costing, its links to the financial accounts, and its use to the practising manager.

At the end of this chapter you will be able to explain:

1. The link between financial accounts and cost accounts
2. The purposes of costing
3. Prime cost
4. Production cost
5. Labour cost
6. Material cost
7. Overhead costing

We have seen that the financial accounts in the form of the income statement, balance sheet and cash flow statement provide much useful information that is made even more meaningful when the appropriate ratios are sensibly employed. In today's fast-changing environment, management requires even more detailed information in order to help facilitate decision making and control. It is for this reason that costing, the process of analysing the expenditure of a business unit into the separate costs for each of the products or services which the business supplies to its customers, came into being.

The cost accounts, while providing more detailed information than the financial accounts, do not stand alone. To be meaningful they must be reconciled with the financial accounts on a frequent basis, preferably monthly. The way in which the cost and financial accounts are reconciled may be illustrated simply as follows:

Financial accounts

	£'000s
Revenues	485
Expenses	300
PROFIT	185

Cost accounts

Product	£'000s A	£'000s B	£'000s C	£'000s TOTAL
Revenue	250	130	105	485
Expenses	200	90	10	300
PROFIT	50	40	95	185

Without the benefit of cost accounts management may have been unaware of the performance of product C. The accounts reconcile with one another; if they did not do so there would be little point in preparing them.

The aims of costing can be summarized as:

1. To provide information for effective decision making. However, it will not make the decision for you.
2. To provide the basis of pricing policies, estimates and tenders. It should be borne in mind that price is generally dependent on what the market will bear rather than on costs.
3. To maintain operational control over the activities of the organization and in particular its costs. This is considered by many to be the primary aim of costing and standard costing has been developed specifically for this purpose.
4. To enable valuations of work in progress and finished stock to be made for short-term and annual trading accounts.

Costs consist of three elements which are further divided into direct costs and indirect costs. The three elements are:

1. Labour costs
2. Material costs
3. Overhead costs or expenses

Direct labour costs are the wages of those employees who are actually building the product. Indirect labour costs are the wages of those employees who are not actually building the product, like cleaners or supervisors.

Direct materials costs are the costs of those materials actually consumed in the building of the product and which become a tangible part of the product. Indirect materials costs are those materials that are not incorporated in the product, such as oil for lubricating machinery and cleaning cloth.

Direct overhead costs are the costs of services applied directly to the product such as electroplating. Indirect overhead costs are all production, administration, distribution and selling expenses not specific to a unit of the product, e.g. rent and rates. The cost accounts are amalgamated in the financial accounts to enable their preparation in the following way:

>   Direct labour
>   + Direct materials
>   + Direct expenses
>   _____
>   = PRIME COST
>   + Factory overhead
>   _____
>   = PRODUCTION COST
>   + Selling and distribution overhead
>   + Selling and distribution direct expenses
>   + Administrative overhead
>   _____
>   = COST OF SALES taken from SELLING PRICE
>   = NET PROFIT
>   _____

Before the above information can be prepared the relevant costs have to be collected. In the case of labour and materials the collection of the data may be achieved fairly readily but so far as overhead costs for a period are concerned it is much more difficult to achieve.

Labour costs are recovered on the basis of the time used on an operation and this information is readily available from time sheets and job cards. Direct labour is charged to order numbers that refer to individual jobs so that the labour cost for each job may be collected. Indirect labour is charged to expense codes or standing order numbers which relate to a particular type and location of overhead expense.

Material costs are calculated from the material requisition or the bill of materials, copies of which are sent to the finance section. Material issues are most commonly priced using one of the following methods:

1. *Specific price*. This is used for material that has been bought for a specific job and sometimes in small concerns that hold little stock.
2. *First in first out (FIFO)*. This is used where it can be assumed that the stock is turned over regularly. The issues are always made from the stock that has been held for the longest time. The price charged is that of the longest held stock.
3. *Average price*. This is frequently used where accounts are computerized. Each time supplies are received an average price is calculated and employed until the next receipt of supplies. The price is calculated on the following basis:

$$\frac{(\text{Qty received} \times \text{Actual price}) + (\text{Qty in stock} \times \text{Previous average price})}{\text{Quantity received} + \text{Quantity in stock}}$$

4. *Standard price*. This prices stocks and issues at the predetermined standard, any difference is immediately charged to an account that contains the differences or variances called the material price variance account.

Direct materials are charged to the job order numbers while indirect materials go to expense code numbers.

There must be a physical reconciliation between the amounts received and issues from stock and the amounts paid for on invoices and charged to work done.

Overhead costing is concerned with charging the indirect expenses of production, administration, selling and distribution to the product or service provided by the business. The overhead cost is usually more significant than either direct wages or direct materials.

Where the level of overhead is considered to be sufficiently different in different parts of the business it is divided up into cost centres. Each cost centre has overhead costs built around it which can be separately totalled. A cost centre may be a whole factory, a department, a group of people, a specialized piece of equipment or a group of machines.

There are many ways of charging overheads to a cost centre and the following are some of them:

1. Actual—this is suitable for indirect wages
2. Floorspace—suitable for rent and rates
3. Number of employees—suitable for canteen costs
4. Horsepower of machinery—electricity
5. Wattage of equipment—electricity

The overhead cost of each cost centre can then be recovered on the products passing through the cost centre on the most appropriate basis.

6.1 COSTING METHODS

Absorption costing, which is fully discussed in Chapter 7, takes account of the full cost of providing the goods or services. There is another approach, which will be explored in Chapter 10 on marginal costing. This takes account of the variable cost of products and excludes fixed costs from the decision-making process.

Job and process costing are two other methods used to fill specific needs. The examples used in Chapter 7 are of job costing, employed when it is necessary to arrive at the cost of a job or operation. They can employ either the total cost or marginal cost approach, depending on the philosophy of the organization in which they are employed. Process costing is used where production goes ahead as a continuous flow and is not broken down into discrete units. Examples may be in chemical manufacture or petroleum products. There may well be separate processes or stages before the final product and each of these stages is treated as a separate cost centre around which costs may be collected. Job and process costing are very similar to one another and which is chosen depends entirely on the operation being undertaken by the organization.

The final costing system that will be discussed is *standard costing*. The job costing in Chapter 7 is based on actual labour and materials costs, whereas a standard costing system would be based on forecast or expected costs. This enables the actual costs to be compared with the expected costs and the differences (variances) analysed. Standard costing in an extremely effective system of control when correctly employed by management and is fully integrated with and reconcilable to the financial operating system. It is discussed in Chapter 8.

Whichever costing system is employed, actual or standard, and the costing method used in conjunction with them, it should be remembered that no two businesses are the same and what is suitable for one is unlikely to be suitable for another. Even the same business changes over time so the usefulness of the costing information that is being provided should be regularly and frequently reviewed.

SELF-TEST QUESTIONS

1. How do absorption costing and marginal costing differ in approach?
2. What is the main purpose of standard costing?
3. How frequently should cost information be provided?
4. What are the elements of cost?
5. What is the main purpose of absorption costing?

SEVEN

OVERHEAD COSTS

OBJECTIVE

To provide an understanding of the importance of overhead costs and the methods of allocating them to cost centres; to differentiate between absorption costing and activity based costing and discuss the situations in which they are applicable.

At the end of this chapter you will be able to explain:

1. Absorption costing
2. Activity based costing
3. The methods of allocating overheads to costs centres
4. Activity cost pools
5. Machine hour rate
6. Labour hour rate

Overhead/absorption costing, as has already been stated, takes account of the full cost of providing goods or services and ensures that the cost centres absorb the relevant costs. There are several ways of doing this and any of the following is quite acceptable.

7.1 PERCENTAGE METHODS

Percentage of direct wages

If, for example, the total direct wage bill for a period is expected to be £100,000 and the total overheads allocated to that cost centre for the same period is £500,000, then each £1 direct wages will also have to recover £5 of overheads if they are all to be recovered. That is, if a job takes 10 minutes and has a direct labour cost of £2 then £10 of overheads will also have to be charged to that job. Therefore, the overheads are 500 per cent of direct wages.

Percentage of direct materials

In this case the overheads of £500,000 would be expressed as a percentage of the expected cost of direct materials for the year. If this was £50,000 then the percentage would be 1,000 per cent of direct materials. Every £1 of direct materials would need to have £10 added to it to recover overhead costs.

Percentage of prime cost

The same process would be followed as before except that in this case the percentage would be added to the prime costs. That is, direct materials and direct labour.

7.2 HOURLY METHODS

Labour hour rate

If the total anticipated labour hours for a period are known and the total overhead cost for the cost centre has been calculated it is possible to arrive at a labour hour rate for the period. For example, if the total labour hours are 10,000 and the overheads to be recovered through that cost centre are £500,000 for the same period, then the labour hour rate will be £500,000 ÷ 10,000 = £50. That is to say the direct labour hour spent on an operation will have to recover £50 overheads.

Machine hour rate

This is calculated in exactly the same way as the labour hour rate, except machine hours replace labour hours.

7.3 UNIT METHOD

This is employed where only one product uses the cost centre. The total units that will be produced are estimated and divided into the overheads for the period, which gives the total overheads to be recovered by each unit. For example, if total units to be produced is 400 and the overheads are £500,000 each unit must recover £500,000 ÷ 400 = £1,250 of overheads.

To hasten the provision of information, labour and materials are normally charged at actual cost and overhead at a predetermined recovery rate. A periodical reconciliation between actual costs and overhead recovered is essential to ensure that the estimated and actual costs bear a close relation to one another.

7.4 ACTIVITY METHOD: ACTIVITY BASED COSTING (ABC)

Recent debates have accentuated the difference between the legal requirements of furnishing financial information for tax and reporting purposes, and the needs of management for accurate costs to aid good decision making. It is felt that the labour or machine hours methods of apportioning overheads to products may not be sufficiently relevant to provide good information for decision making and control. To provide information speedily a new approach to the allocation of overheads based on activity cost pools is advocated. The suggested approach may be compared with the absorption costing methods diagrammatically as shown in Figures 7.1 and 7.2. This is felt to give relevant information speedily to management thus helping decision making and control. Activity

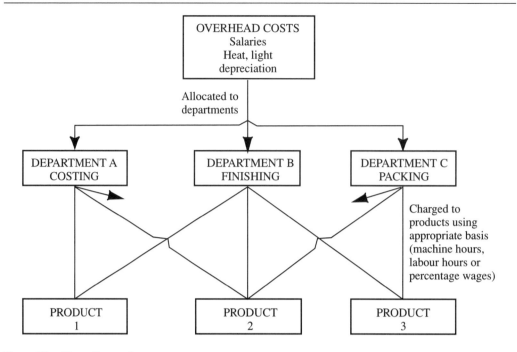

Figure 7.1   Absorption costing

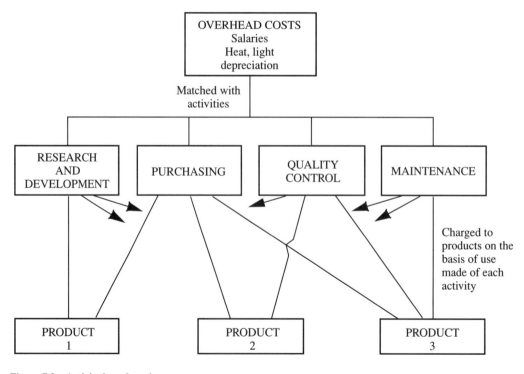

Figure 7.2   Activity based costing

based costing is already successfully employed in Europe, America and Japan and it is anticipated that it will replace the traditional method of absorption costing.

Cost calculations must be reviewed frequently. When a cost has been arrived at it is only true for further production under the same conditions, the same price levels and the same activity levels. Let us now work through an example illustrating some of the ways in which overhead costs may be recovered.

From the following information calculate the cost of Job No. 1:

Prime/direct costs of Job No. 1		*Machine hours*
Direct materials	£1,000	
Direct wages		
Press shop @ £12 per hr	10 hr	17
Machine shop @ £15 per hr	25 hr	90
Machine shop @ £11 per hr	8 hr	
Assembly shop @ £12 per hr	60 hr	6

The estimated total hours for the year are:

Direct labour		
Press shop 30,000 hr @ £12 per hr		60,000
Machine shop 45,000 hr @ £15 per hr		180,000
Machine shop 12,000 hr @ £11 per hr		
Assembly shop 113,000 hr @ £12 per hr		10,000

Estimated overheads for the year:

	£	*Basis of apportionment*
Indirect labour	500,000	Direct labour hours
Salaries	200,000	Direct labour hours
Depreciation	40,000	Plant valuation
Maintenance	20,000	As given (budget)
Rent, rates	60,000	Floor area

The following information relates to the respective shops:

	Press shop	*Machine shop*	*Assembly shop*
Plant valuation	£200,000	£150,000	£50,000
Floor area	6,000 sq.ft/	9,000 sq.ft/	5,000 sq.ft/
	557 sq.m.	836 sq.m.	465 sq.m.
Maintenance	£ 7,000	£ 5,000	£ 8,000

Calculate the cost of Job No. 1

In calculating the cost we first need to discover how much of the annual overhead it should carry. To do so we apportion the overhead between the three shops on the suggested basis. There is no set way of laying out this calculation but one method would be:

	Press shop £	Machine shop £	Assembly shop £
Indirect labour	75,000	142,500	282,500
Salaries	30,000	57,000	113,000
Depreciation	20,000	15,000	5,000
Maintenance	7,000	5,000	8,000
Rent and rates	18,000	27,000	15,000
TOTAL	150,000	246,500	423,500
Direct labour hr	30,000	57,000	113,000
Labour hr rate	£5	£4.32	£3.75
Machine hr	60,000	180,000	10,000
Machine hr rate	£2.50	£1.37	£42.35
Direct wages (£)	360,000	807,000	1,356,000
Direct wages (%)	41.67%	30.55%	31.23%

The prime or direct cost of Job No. 1 will be the same whichever method is employed to recover overheads.

Prime/direct cost of Job No. 1

Labour		£	£
Press shop 10 hr @ £12 per hr	=	120	
Machine shop 25 hr @ £15 per hr	=	375	
Machine shop 8 hr @ £11 per hr	=	88	
Assembly shop 60 hr @ £12 per hr	=	720	
		1,303	
Materials		1,000	
PRIME/DIRECT COST			2,303

Overhead cost

1. Using labour hr to recover overheads

Press shop 10hr @ £5 per hr	=	50.00	
Machine shop 33 hr @ £4.32 per hr	=	142.56	
Assembly shop 60 hr @ £3.75 per hr	=	225.00	
			417.56
TOTAL COST OF JOB NO. 1			£2,720.56

2. Using machine hr to recover overheads
   Press shop 17 hr @ £2.50   =   42.50
   Machine shop 90 hr @ £1.37   =   123.30
   Assembly shop 6 hr @ £42.35   =   254.10
                                         _____

   Total overhead cost   419.90
   Add Prime cost   2,303.00
                                                            _____

   TOTAL COST OF JOB NO. 1   £2,722.90
                                                            ════════

3. Using percentage of direct wages
   Press shop 41.67% of £120   =   50.00
   Machine shop 30.55% of £463   =   141.45
   Assembly shop 31.23% of £720   =   224.86
                                         _____

   Total overhead cost   416.31
   Add Prime cost   2,303.00
                                                            _____

   TOTAL COST OF JOB NO. 1   £2,719.31
                                                            ════════

Each different method of recovering overheads gives a slightly different answer, but they are all in the same region and will even out over the period. It is important to remember that the calculation gives the cost of the job and includes no profit element. If similar firms are charging £1,500 for this type of work you will have serious problems as it is extremely unlikely that anyone could be persuaded to pay you £3,000. The price that you charge will be very largely decided by what the market will bear and not what it costs you to make. In an expanding economy, if your production process is about right you might be able to charge £4,000 for the job and make a reasonable profit. In a poor economic climate you may be pleased to keep your workforce employed and charge £2,500, so that you cover your prime costs and get a contribution to your overhead cost. This concept will be further discussed in Chapter 11 on costing for decision making.

SELF-TEST QUESTIONS

1. What are the percentage methods of allocating overheads?
2. Does it matter which method of allocating overheads is employed?
3. When may the unit method of allocating overheads be used?
4. Why is it important to recover all overheads?
5. Why has activity based costing been introduced?
6. Are absorption costing and activity based costing the same thing?

QUESTIONS

7.1 An engineering company makes scale models in two types, standard and de luxe. Three departments are involved in manufacturing the product—casting, finishing and packing. Calculate the cost of one de luxe model and one standard model using the following information.

Costs and expenses incurred in quarter 1

	Casting £	Finishing £	Packing £	TOTAL £
Apportioned company admin.				3,000
Clerical and indirect wages				2,250
Maintenance of equipment				900
Management salaries				2,000
Depreciation of equipment				1,800
Rent and rates				480
Expense supplies				375
Direct materials	3,600	400	800	4,800
Direct wages	2,000	4,000	4,000	10,000
Labour hours	400 hr	800 hr	800 hr	2,000 hr

The total output for the quarter was 10,000 standard and 5,000 de luxe models. The division of direct costs between the two models was:

	Casting £	Finishing £	Packing £	TOTAL £
Direct wages—standard	1,200	2,000	2,400	5,600
Direct wages—de luxe	800	2,000	1,600	4,400
Direct materials—standard	2,000	240	480	2,720
Direct materials—de luxe	1,600	160	220	1,980
General information				
Floor area—sq.ft/sq.m.	2,000/186	2,000/186	4,000/372	8,000/744
Equipment at book value	50,000	15,000	15,000	80,000

7.2 Hit Limited has two production departments and one service department. The following information relates to January 1998:

	£
Allocated expenses	
Production department X	65,000
Production department Y	35,000
Service department	50,000

The allocated expenses shown above are all indirect expenses as far as individual units are concerned.

The benefit provided by the service department is shared among the production departments X and Y in the proportion 70 : 30.

Required:

Calculate the amount of overhead to be charged to specific units for both production department X and production department Y.

7.3 Scope Limited has several production departments. In the assembly department it has been estimated that £25,000 of overhead should be charged to that particular department. It now wants to charge for an order. The relevant information is:

Assembly department		Unit
Number of units	5,000	—
Direct material cost	£50,000	£ 7.00
Direct labour cost	£100,000	£28.00
Prime cost	£153,000	£42.00
Direct labour hours	10,000	3.2
Machine hours	2,500	0.7

The accountant is not sure which overhead absorption rate to adopt.

Required:
Calculate the overhead to be absorbed by a unit passing through the assembly department using each of the following overhead absorption rate methods:
1. Percentage of direct materials cost
2. Percentage of direct labour cost
3. Percentage of prime cost
4. Direct labour hours
5. Machine hours

7.4 The production department of Davies Limited produced the following results for September 1998

	Production department	Job no. 22
Direct materials consumed	£60,000	25 hrs
Direct wages	£90,000	30 hrs
Overhead chargeable	£70,000	—
Direct labour hours worked	£15,000	10 hrs
Machine hours operated	£ 5,000	4 hrs

The company adds 25 per cent to the total production cost of specific units to cover expenses and to provide a profit.

Required:
1. Calculate the selling price of job number 22 if overhead is absorbed using the following methods of overhead absorption:
   (a) Direct labour hours
   (b) Machine hours
2. State which of the two methods you would recommend for the production department.

EIGHT

STANDARD COSTING

OBJECTIVE

To provide an understanding of standard costing and its use by the manager in measuring performance.

At the end of this chapter you will be able to explain:

1. Standard costing
2. Standard costs
3. Variance analysis
4. Principal variances

Standard costing is based on expected costs and the first difficulty lies in deciding what costs should be expected. They will rarely if ever be 100 per cent accurate as nobody has perfect knowledge of the future. The second difficulty lies in comparing the actual with the expected costs and the third is what to do about the differences where they are found to exist.

In setting the standard or expected costs, existing businesses have advantages over entirely new businesses because it is a little easier to forecast what you think will happen in the future if you know what has happened over the last three or four years. For both existing and new businesses, however, the forecasts should be based on all the available relevant information. Market research surveys should be undertaken and balanced with views on the likely economic environment to arrive at the activity level. When this has been done, wherever possible there should be a spread of at least three outcomes—most optimistic, most pessimistic and most likely to be achieved.

The behavioural impact of a good standard costing system cannot be overemphasized. It is one of the few ways in which the performance of individuals may be measured. For this reason great care must be exercised in arriving at the standard or norm. It is of little use to either the organization or the individuals within it to set a standard that is too easily obtained as this will lead to underperformance and frustration. At first there will be a feeling of satisfaction at having achieved the targets, but as this is repeated period after period, with increasing ease, boredom will set in and staff concerned will become disillusioned and demotivated to the detriment of the organization.

The setting of a standard that is too difficult to attain will be equally detrimental to both staff and organization. Staff that have been carefully recruited will at first be highly motivated and make every effort to achieve the targets set. With each accounting period it will become more obvious that the targets cannot be achieved and, gradually, staff will become demotivated until they finally give up the unequal struggle. Once they become demoralized, it is difficult to restore people's faith in the management of the organization. In view of this it is better to avoid this situation altogether by setting targets that are obtainable, but only when people are working at a high level of efficiency.

This is easy to state but difficult to achieve. How do we set standards that are achievable only after the expenditure of effort and the use of initiative? To use last year's standards inflated by 5 per cent for the current year achieves little, since errors and slack in all probability were built into last year's figures. To employ a method study approach, and state that in perfect conditions an operation can be done in two hours, and set this as the standard will not work either. We have somehow to find ways of eliminating the errors and building in sufficient slack to allow for the abilities of the personnel who are carrying out the work. If this can be done with any degree of accuracy the organization will become more efficient, and the people in it obtain greater satisfaction from their work.

Costs, as we have seen, can be broken down into labour, materials and overheads. It is possible to set a standard for each of these elements and to compare it with the actual cost periodically, e.g. weekly or monthly. This enables action to be taken where the actual cost differs from the expected. For the standard costing system to be really useful it is necessary to analyse the costs a little further than labour, materials and overheads.

8.1 PRINCIPAL VARIANCES EMPLOYED IN COSTING

Materials

1. *Material price variance.* This is caused by changes in the purchase prices of the materials used. This variance is calculated by using the formula:

$$\text{Actual quantity (Standard price } - \text{ Actual price)}$$

2. *Material usage variance.* This is caused by using more or less material than the standard quantity and the formula used to calculate it is:

$$\text{Standard price (Standard usage } - \text{ Actual usage)}$$

Example
Standard—8 metres of material @ £2 a metre = £16 per unit
Actual—820 metres of material @ £2.10 a metre = £1,722 per 100 units
Price variance = (820 × 10p) = £82 adverse
That is, actual usage × price change. It is adverse because the price has increased. It is greater than standard. An adverse variance shows that costs are greater than expected whereas a favourable variance shows they are less than expected.

$$\text{Usage variance} = (20 \times £2) = £40 \text{ adverse}$$

That is, change in use × standard price. It is adverse because the use has increased. For 100 units you would have expected to use 800 metres (8 × 100 units) and have in fact used 820 metres. The total materials variance is £122 adverse which is (£82 + £40) and equals actual £1,722 − standard £1,600 (16 × 100 units).

Labour

1. *Labour rate variance.* This is caused by changes in the wage rates. The formula to calculate this is:

Actual hours (Standard wage rate per hour − Actual wage rate per hour)

2. *Labour efficiency variance.* This is caused by the speed of production being greater or less than the standard speed. The formula employed is:

Standard wage rate per hour (Standard hours worked − Actual hours worked)

Example

Standard—2 hr @ £5 per hour = £10 per unit
Actual—190 hr @ £5.40 per hour = £1,026 per 100 units
Rate variance = (£190 × 40p) = £76 adverse

That is, change in rate × actual hours. It is adverse because the rate has increased. It is 40p greater than standard.

Efficiency variance = (10 × £5) = £50 favourable

It is favourable because for 100 units you would expect to use 200 hours but have only used 190 hours.

Total labour variance is £26 adverse

This is (£76 − £50) and equals 1,026 − 1,000 (£10 × 100 units).

Overhead

1. *Expenditure variance.* This is caused by spending more or less than that allowed by the standard.
   To calculate this we use this formula:

(Actual hours at standard cost − Actual hours at actual cost)

2. *Efficiency.* This is caused by the speed of production being greater or less than the standard or expected speed.
   This uses the formula:

(Actual production − Standard production) Standard overhead per unit

3. *Capacity.* This is caused by working more or fewer hours than the standard working hours. The formula used is:

$$(\text{Actual hours} - \text{expected hours}) \text{ Fixed overhead per hour}$$

Example

Standard overhead cost is £4 per unit, based on a four week capacity of 600 units in 200 working hours with an allowed expenditure £2,400 on overheads, of which £800 is fixed and £1,600 is variable with the time worked. Actual results were 660 units produced in 240 hours at a cost of £2,600.

$$\text{Expenditure variance} = (£800 + £1,920) - £2,600 = £120 \text{ favourable}$$

That is, the expected expenditure for that level of activity of £800 fixed + (£8 variable with time × 240 hours = £1,920) less the actual cost of £2,600.

$$\text{Efficiency variance} = (720 \text{ units} - 660 \text{ units}) \times £4 = £240 \text{ adverse}$$

That is, the expected production of three units per hour × the 240 hours equals 720 units less the actual output 660. The difference is multiplied by £4 per unit standard overhead cost. Fewer units than expected have been produced so there is an adverse difference (variance) as we have fewer units over which to spread our costs.

$$\text{Capacity variance} = 40 \text{ hours} \times £4 = £160 \text{ favourable}$$

That is, the actual hours of 240 less the expected hours of 200 and the difference is multiplied by the fixed overhead cost per hour. More than the expected hours have been worked so we have a favourable variance.

$$\text{The total variance is } (£120 + £160) \text{ favourable} - £240 \text{ adverse} = £40 \text{ favourable}$$

This ties in with the total overhead variance which is:

Expected cost of 660 units (660 × 4)	= £2,640
Actual cost of 660 units	= £2,600
Total variance	£40 favourable

Having calculated these variances what use can we make of them? The materials variance is broken down into material price and material usage, each of which may be either controllable or non-controllable as far as the management of the undertaking is concerned.

Material price variance

If this is caused by a nationally agreed change in the price of the materials used in production or providing a service or because the original standard was wrong, management can only accept the price change and use it to explain the difference between the standard and actual. This is an explainable variance which will be repeated in each period until it is possible to set the new standard cost. Where the price variance is caused because material of a higher or lower quality than necessary is being used, action can be taken to ensure that material of the correct quality is purchased from the right supplier.

Material usage variance

If this is caused because the original estimate was wrong, management can only accept the usage variance and use it to explain the difference between the standard and the actual, in which case it will remain an explainable variance until the new standard can be established. Where it is caused by materials of the wrong quality, action can be taken to ensure that material of the correct quality is obtained. If the difference is caused because new staff are being trained, then it will be an explainable variance until the training is complete when the material usage should revert to normal.

The labour variance is broken down into labour rate and labour efficiency, each of which may be either controllable or non-controllable as far as management is concerned.

Labour rate variance

If this is caused by a nationally agreed change in the wage rate or because the standard was wrong, management can only accept it as an explainable variance until the standard can be altered. Where it is caused by using labour that is either too highly skilled or not yet skilled enough, management can take action to ensure that labour of the correct calibre is employed.

Labour efficiency variance

If this is caused by an incorrect standard, management can only accept it as an explainable variance until the new standard is established. Where it is caused by variances in the quality of material, making the work either more or less difficult, steps should be taken to ensure that material of the correct quality is obtained. Where it is caused by using staff who are more or less highly trained than is necessary to perform the task satisfactorily, the correct staff should be employed. Where it is caused through demotivated staff, then a serious problem exists that will have to be handled extremely carefully.

Overhead variances

These should be monitored in the same way as the other variances so that those concerned are aware of their existence. There is little that management can do, however, to correct them in the short term.

Before anything can be done about any of the variances, the organization has to be aware that they exist. This necessitates an efficient system of financial control and reporting that presents the required information promptly and in a readily understandable form. Providing the information serves no useful purpose unless it is acted upon vigorously and punctually. Failure to do so will allow the situation continually to deteriorate until it may become too late to correct it and save the organization.

Standard costing involves comparing actual costs with estimated, forecast or budgeted costs and refers to a small part of the organization which may be a job, a department, a factory or a machine. Budgetary control employs exactly the same principles as standard costing but relates it to the whole organization. Budgetary control is discussed in Chapter 9.

Example

Davies Production Company makes fuel packs which are sold in dozen packs to the retail trade at £6 per pack. The standard cost of a dozen packs is as follows:

Manufacturing		£
Materials 4kg @ 20p per kg	=	0.80
Labour 1 hr @ £3.00 per hr	=	3.00
Overhead (based on a 40 hr 10,000 production hr week with production set at 10,000 dozen and budgeted expenditure—£12,000)	=	1.20
Selling		
Salary and commission	=	0.40
		___
TOTAL STANDARD COST	=	5.40

The actual costs in period 10 (four-week period) were as follows:

		£
Material 220,000 kg @ 20.5p per kg	=	45,100
Labour 47,000 hours @ £3.10	=	145,700
Overhead	=	49,500
Selling costs	=	16,500
		___
TOTAL	=	256,800

In period 10 the sales and production totalled 50,000 dozen packs, all sold at the full wholesale price.

SUGGESTED SOLUTION

Normal profit and loss account—period 10

	£	£
Sales		300,000
Cost of sales:		
Materials	45,100	
Labour	145,700	
Manufacturing overhead	49,500	240,300
		59,700
Selling costs		16,500
NET PROFIT		43,200

Standard cost profit and loss account—period 10

	£	£
Sales		300,000
Standard cost of sales		270,000
Standard profit on sales		30,000
Add FAVOURABLE VARIANCES		
Labour efficiency	9,000	
Selling costs	3,500	
Overhead	10,500	23,000
		53,000
Less ADVERSE VARIANCES		
Material price	1,100	
Material usage	4,000	
Wage rate	4,700	9,800
NET PROFIT		43,200

			£
Labour efficiency variance			
3,000 hours × £3	=		9,000 favourable
Selling costs variance			
Expected 50,000 × 40p	=	20,000	
Actual	=	16,500	3,500 favourable
Material price variance			
220,000 kg × £0.005	=		1,100 adverse
Material usage variance			
20,000 kg × £0.2	=		4,000 adverse
Labour rate variance			
47,000 kg × £0.1	=		4,700 adverse
Overhead variance			
Expected (50,000 × £1.2)	=	60,000	
Actual	=	49,500	10,500 favourable

The variances are calculated in the manner shown. In each case the actual performance is compared with the expected performance and the differences reported. It is important that they are acted upon as well as reported. Modern business is complex and there is insufficient time to act upon every variance that occurs so some differences cannot be investigated. Once it has been decided what is an acceptable variance, say, up to 15 per cent deviation from standard, those that exceed it must be promptly investigated and acted upon. It is as bad to be underspent as it is to be overspent.

Information technology is a great help in the application of standard costing in that programs exist that will highlight variances that are outside the acceptable parameters. These will be drawn to the manager's attention on the daily, weekly or monthly report so that prompt corrective action can be implemented. It is important that the management information system (MIS) is designed to meet the needs of the organization and not simply purchased off the shelf. The needs of organizations differ as they do in the same organization over time and to provide the maximum benefit the system must provide the right information to the right people and at the right time.

SELF-TEST QUESTIONS

1. What are the difficulties of setting standard costs?
2. What would be the behavioural impact of a perfect standard?
3. On what should estimates be based?
4. What is the formula for calculating the labour efficiency variance?
5. Why is the labour rate variance important?
6. What is an explainable variance?

QUESTIONS

8.1 The Highways Department of a County Council has formulated the following standard costs per mile for white lining the centre of the road:

	£
Materials: 10 litres paint @ £20	200
Labour: 3 men for 10 hours each @ £7	210
	410

Four weeks' work, with 20 miles of lining, has cost:

	£
Materials: 210 litres paint @ £20.70	4,347
Labour: 590 hours @ £7.30	4,307
	8,654

Calculate the standard cost variance. How should they be dealt with?

8.2 A company engaged in wall insulation has formulated the following standard costs per 1,000 sq.ft of wall:

	£
Materials: 10 litres of foam @ £18.00	180
Labour: 2 men for 10 hours each @ £7.50	150
Overheads	100
	430

Four weeks' work, with an estimated wall area of 80,000 sq. ft, has cost:

	£
840 litres of foam @ £18.30	15,372
1,400 hours of labour @ £7.20	10,080
Overheads	8,500
	33,952

Calculate the standard cost variances. Give reasons for each variance separately and explain how you would, as a manager, deal with the information.

8.3 A county bus service has a standard cost of £88 per 100 miles, made up of 10 litres of diesel @ £1.80 per litre and 10 driver hours @ £7 per hour. In the month of September, 8,000 miles were run at a cost of 820 litres of diesel @ £1.85 per litre and 750 drivers' hours @ £7.20 per hour.

Analyse the costs by reference to standards.

NINE

BUDGETARY CONTROL

OBJECTIVE

To provide an understanding of the process of budgetary control and its application in the management of the organization.

At the end of this chapter you will be able to explain:

1. The budgetary process
2. The master budget
3. Long-term planning
4. Short-term planning
5. The relationship between the individual budgets
6. The purpose of the cash budget

We have seen that standard costing, when properly used, is an effective method of control that can be applied to small parts of an organization. Budgetary control uses exactly the same principles but applies them to the whole organization. In budgetary control, as in standard costing, expected levels of activity are arrived at and the actual performance is compared with the expected performance. The differences between the actual activity level and expected activity level, termed variances, are reported and, where it is felt to be necessary, investigated.

9.1 THE BUDGETARY PROCESS

The budgetary process is long drawn out, often taking nine to twelve months to prepare and can be illustrated as shown in Figure 9.1.

The corporate objectives may be to maximize profit, to maximize cash flow, to achieve greatest market share, to provide the best service, to have the best product, to have the

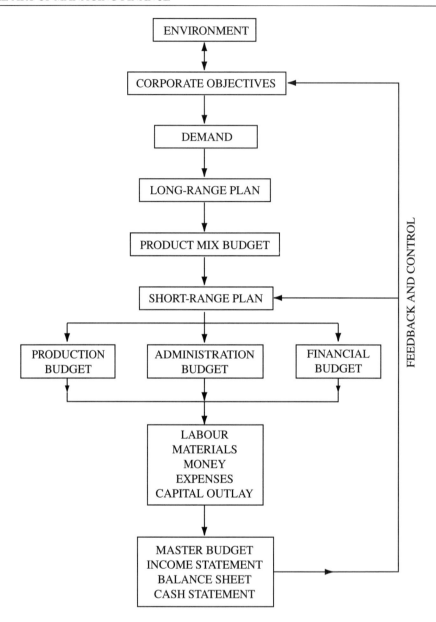

Figure 9.1 Total budgetary process

happiest employee relations, to enjoy a good public image, to provide the best possible working conditions or any combination of these or other objectives. Whatever they are they will not be arrived at instantaneously and the culture of the organization will have much to do with the final choice. It will generally be made by a small group of top executives. Existing organizations may find it difficult to change their objectives while new ones may find it hard to arrive at the objectives of the organization for the next ten years.

Once objectives have been set they should not be treated as sacrosanct. Conditions are changing at an ever-increasing rate, and if organizations are to survive they must be amenable to altering their objectives as the need arises. The personality of the dominant character in the group of executives will have a big impact on the decision. Generally, if the accountant is dominant, the approach will be more constrained than would be the case if a marketing person were to prevail. The objectives having been set, a long-range plan has to be prepared to try to ensure that they are achieved. This is often for ten years into the future, with annual reviews to see that the plan is kept under control and not allowed to become meaningless. The first year is firm, the next three years firm but subject to change, and the last six tentative. The plan is subject to change when it is five years or more into the future, but it is much better to have a plan than to drift with no sense of direction at all. To have no plan is an infallible recipe for disaster.

The sales plan should be derived from the long-term demand and the information obtained from marketing surveys and other research carried out by people in touch with existing and prospective customers. From this the product mix strategy will be decided upon and the plan for the year set, that is, the sales of each product that are expected to be achieved during the next 12 months, which will enable the individual budgets to be prepared that lead to the master budget. This will tell you how the cash situation will stand on a monthly or weekly basis over the next 12 months, what profit will be made or loss incurred, and the overall business position in the same period. Actual figures can be compared with the expected and, where necessary, the budget altered or corrective action taken. A computerized information system is an invaluable aid to a successful system of budgetary control. It can be programmed to ensure that people deal with information that is relevant to them and that items requiring immediate attention are flagged in some way that draws them to the notice of the person concerned. Care has to be taken in the design of the system as one of the problems faced by many organizations today is 'information overload'. People receive so much information that they do not have time to sort the essential from the irrelevant and so fail to use what is available effectively.

It is worth noting that while budgets are expressed in pounds (£) it is only at the very last stage that this occurs. The accountant does not prepare the budget, he or she simply expresses other people's ideas in terms that are universally accepted and understood. The process has to be fully integrated or it will not work. It is of little use to decide on a product mix strategy that asks for 10,000 units of A, 4,000 units of B, and 15,000 units of C if limited materials make it possible to produce only 10,000 units of A and nothing else; or to plan to make 10,000 units of A if only 2,000 units can be sold. For the budget to succeed it must be fully supported and integrated. The best way for this to be achieved is by involving as many of those who will have a role in the successful use of the budget in discussions as early as possible in the budget process.

People who have limits imposed upon them with no explanation are, generally speaking, not committed to making them work. The organization that obtains the best results from budgeting is the one that involves its people at an early stage and, so far as possible, ensures that their ideas are treated seriously and incorporated in the budget. However, there are those who do not wish to be involved in the budgetary process and resent efforts to involve them. To do so would be to court disaster. In this, as in every other case, it is dangerous to generalize and each occasion should be treated on merit. A good system of budgetary control is invaluable to any organization and even a bad one is better than none at all.

9.2 CASH BUDGET (Cash Flow Forecast)

OBJECTIVE

To provide an understanding of the preparation of the cash budget and its use to the manager in controlling the cash resources of the organization.

At the end of this section you will be able to explain:

1. The difference between cash in hand and a bank overdraft
2. The difference between cash transactions and credit transactions and their impact on the cash budget
3. The impact of depreciation on the cash budget
4. The place of the cash budget in the system of budgetary control

We have seen in Chapter 3 that profitability does not mean liquidity and that many profitable firms fail through lack of liquidity. In order to reduce the likelihood of this happening a cash flow forecast or budget should be prepared annually and carefully monitored, if possible on a weekly basis but certainly once a month. Many organizations monitor their cash on a daily basis.

A cash budget is a forecast of future cash requirements that is prepared one year in advance, broken down into monthly figures to show the anticipated surplus or deficit at the start of the month, plus cash receipts in the month less cash payments in the month, which will give the anticipated cash in hand at the end of the month. Collecting the figures to put into the cash budget is, however, rather more difficult, because to forecast accurately your activities for a year ahead is virtually impossible, but with a little practice forecasts can be made accurate enough to make them well worth while.

In the previous section we discussed the budgetary process and saw that, as part of the master budget, the cash budget comes right at the end of the process. It does not, as many people believe, start it. We have already discussed the importance of monitoring your forecast for each month during the year, then, if for some reason your forecast is wrong, you have the opportunity to take action to improve the cash situation before it becomes critical. This is an extremely useful tool in managing a business and many fail because they do not plan their cash needs. It will greatly increase your chances of success if you go to your bank manager with a well-prepared cash budget to ask for a loan or overdraft six months before you need the money, rather than waiting until the need has arisen and then wondering what to do about it. If you are aware of the situation far enough in advance, it may be possible to amend your plans and so avoid the cash deficit altogether. A good spreadsheet is an enormous help in the preparation and monitoring of the cash budget and there are several programs commercially available. You should always bear in mind, however, that whatever tools are available to help you in the process, in the final analysis they are dependent on the information that you provide.

A cash budget has been drawn up as an example of one of the ways in which it can be done. It is not the only way and you may prefer some other approach. The starting point is the cash position as it stands now and the rest of the information is inserted on your best estimate of the likely happenings of the next year. You may need more or less detailed descriptions of the items according to your requirements.

Example *Cash budget for six months, January to June*

	Jan £'000s	Feb £'000s	Mar £'000s	Apr £'000s	May £'000s	Jun £'000s
Opening cash balance (( ) = deficit)	(11)	17	53	60	(38)	(13)
Receipts:						
Cash receipts from cash sales	70	75	74	80	75	80
Cash receipts from credit sales	90	100	96	100	95	100
Miscellaneous cash receipts	—	5	—	—	—	—
TOTAL CASH AVAILABLE	149	197	223	240	132	167
Payments:						
Payment for wages	50	55	54	60	56	60
Cash purchases	20	20	22	25	24	25
Payments for previous credit purchases	60	65	64	65	60	64
Loan interest	—	—	20	—	—	—
Loan repaid	—	—	—	—	—	—
Rent paid	—	—	—	5	—	—
Rates paid	—	—	—	10	—	—
Electricity paid	—	—	—	5	—	—
Gas paid	—	—	—	3	—	—
Postage paid	1	2	1	3	2	2
Telephone paid	—	—	—	—	1	—
Miscellaneous	1	2	2	2	2	2
Capital payments	—	—	—	100	—	—
TOTAL PAYMENTS	132	144	163	278	145	153
TOTAL CASH − TOTAL PAYMENTS (( ) = deficit)	17	53	60	(38)	(13)	14

Thus £14,000 opening cash balance in hand would be carried forward for July.

In the example given April has a cash deficit of £38,000 shown by writing the figure in brackets, thus (£38,000). The owner of the business would have been aware of this some time before it occurred and, through preparing his cash budget and monitoring it regularly, would have been able to take the action necessary to overcome a potentially critical cash shortage. A suggested form for the preparation of a cash budget is given on page 80. Other styles may be used if preferred as the important thing is the preparation of the cash budget and not the form it takes.

In preparing the cash budget the opening balance would be known but all the other figures would be uncertain to a greater or lesser extent. The estimates would be prepared on the basis of the figures for the previous period adjusted for any changes that you think may take place. For example, if you anticipate a wage increase of 10 per cent as from April then you would increase your salary estimate accordingly. The same sort of approach is needed for all your estimates and, with experience, your forecasts will become more accurate.

Note The cash budget as the name implies refers only to *cash* and excludes non-cash items, like depreciation, which affect only profit, credit purchases and credit sales.

Answer the cash flow question (9.1) at the end of the chapter using the blank table below, compare your answer with the one provided at the back of the book.

Suggested form of cash budget for six months, July to December

	Jul £	Aug £	Sept £	Oct £	Nov £	Dec £
Opening balance						
Sales receipts						
Legacy						
	___	___	___	___	___	___
TOTAL CASH AVAILABLE						
	___	___	___	___	___	___
Payments:						
Labour						
Materials						
Variable expenses						
Fixed expenses						
Capital expenditure						
	___	___	___	___	___	___
TOTAL PAYMENTS						
	___	___	___	___	___	___
TOTAL CASH − TOTAL PAYMENTS						
Balance c/fwd						

9.3 OTHER BUDGETS

The other budgets that relate just to one year, normally called revenue budgets, are prepared in the same way as the cash budgets, that is every budget shown on the chart (Figure 9.2) except the capital budget, which is treated differently and will be described in a separate chapter. Once the corporate objectives and long-range plan have been prepared and the budgeting process starts in more detail, there is usually a part which is restricting the others. It may be that a shortage of material, skilled staff or money or the sales potential could be causing concern. Whichever it is, it restricts the operation of the organization and is called the limiting factor. In most organizations today there are two areas vying for this distinction, the cash situation and the sales potential. The one that is limiting activity is chosen as the starting point for the annual budget, which is then built around it. This process may be illustrated as shown in Figure 9.2.

Selling budget

The selling budget is built up from the forecasts of the sales that will be made of each of the products over the next 12 months. The sales manager will provide this from information obtained from the sales team. In smaller organizations the owner will decide on the basis of just what the sales are likely to be over the next year.

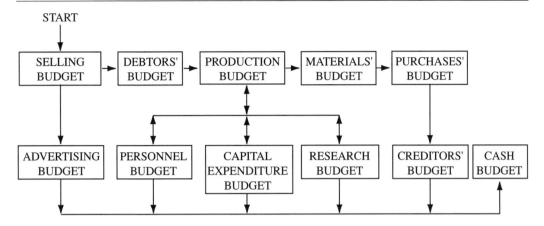

Figure 9.2 Revenue budgets

Debtors' budget

This will depend on the proportion of sales that are for cash. In a purely cash sales organization such as Tesco Plc there should be few people owing money to the business. If sales are low, one way to increase them may be to extend further credit facilities to customers. The debtors' budget should not be allowed to get out of control as it can lead to serious cash flow problems.

Advertising budget

The advertising budget will be set at the level believed to be necessary to obtain the required sales.

Production budget

This will be set to meet the sales levels of each product and the minimum stock requirement.

Materials' budget

This depends on the production budget and stock requirements.

Purchases' budget

This refers to the purchase of parts required in the production process and is directly dependent on the materials' budget.

Creditors' budget

This is related to the purchases' budget and the credit that suppliers are prepared to advance. Generally speaking it is good sense to keep your suppliers waiting for as long as possible before paying them. Care should be taken to ensure that payment is not withheld for so long that goodwill is lost and supplies become hard to obtain on any terms other than cash.

Personnel budget

The personnel budget is decided upon by the level of activity of the whole organization as the operations to be performed depend upon the availability of suitably qualified people.

Capital expenditure budget

This looks at the needs of the organization for accommodation and plant, machinery and equipment if it is to meet its goals. It forms a large part of the spending of most organizations that has an impact over many years.

Research budget

This budget depends on the availability of resources and the product range. If the organization is to survive it must be competitive and to be competitive means that the product is continually being updated and improved through research and development.

Example Davies plans to start a business making realistic model sailing dinghies from wood. He believes that he will need to keep a small stock of a dozen boats on hand and that he will be able to make ten boats per week working on his own. The wood he needs will have to be purchased four weeks in advance, and, until he is better known, he will receive no credit. His purchases will be for cash. Each boat will use a metre of wood at £10 a cubic metre, £2 of cloth for the sails, brass fitments costing £5 and miscellaneous items to the value of £2. Each boat he estimates will take him five hours to make. He considers it to be a superior product that will be very much in demand for window displays, and feels that once he becomes known there will be strong demand for his product. He hopes to market the boat at £63 to start with, which will cover the costs already mentioned together with fixed costs consisting of rates £400, electricity £200, miscellaneous £200 and salary £6 an hour. He feels that he could just survive for the first three years on an annual profit of £6,200 in addition to his private income of £15,000. His customers will be given two months' credit. He intends to start his business on 1 July and meet his production target in the first week. On 1 July he will have to pay £760 for his first four weeks' materials and this payment will be repeated each month. Rates are payable in two equal instalments on 1 July and 1 January. Electricity is payable quarterly, in equal amounts, on 1 April, 1 July, 1 October and 1 January. Miscellaneous expenses are paid weekly in equal amounts and salary is paid weekly according to hours worked, expected to be 50 hours per week. Sales are expected to be none in the first month, three in the second month, six in the third month and thereafter 80 per month.

Prepare for Davies his production, purchases, sales, stock and cash budgets for the first six months' operations, together with a statement of his projected profit and a projected balance sheet. Assume he starts business with £10,000 in the business bank account. What effect would the figures arrived at have on his original plan?

SOLUTION

Production budget (units)

	Opening stock	Made	Closing
July	—	40	40
August	40	40	77
September	77	40	111
October	111	40	71
November	71	40	31
December	31	40	—

Stock budget (units)

	Opening stock	Made	Sold	Balance
July	—	40	—	40
August	40	40	3	77
September	77	40	6	111
October	111	40	80	71
November	71	40	80	31
December	31	40	80	(Maximum 71)

Purchases budget (£)

July	760
August	760
September	760
October	760
November	760
December	760

Sales budget (units and £)

	Units	£
July	—	—
August	3	189
September	6	378
October	80	5040
November	80	5040
December	71	4473

Cash budget

	Jul £	Aug £	Sept £	Oct £	Nov £	Dec £
Opening	10,000	7,774	5,798	3,822	1,985	387
Sales receipts	—	—	—	189	378	5,040
	10,000	7,774	5,798	4,011	2,363	5,427
Payments:						
Purchases	760	760	760	760	760	760
Salary	1,200	1,200	1,200	1,200	1,200	1,200
Rates	200	—	—	—	—	—
Electricity	50	—	—	50	—	—
Miscellaneous	16	16	16	16	16	16
	2,226	1,976	1,976	2,026	1,976	1,976
Balance c/fwd	7,774	5,798	3,822	1,985	387	3,451

Projected profit statement for 6 months to 31 December

	£	£
Sales		15,120
Less Materials purchased		4,560
GROSS PROFIT		10,560
Less Expenses		
Salary	7,200	
Rates	200	
Electricity	100	
Miscellaneous	96	7,596
NET PROFIT		2,964

The figures for the income statement have been obtained from the cash budget except for the sales figure which is made up of the three amounts actually received in the cash budget (£189 + £378 + £5,040) = £5,607, together with November and December sales which have not yet been received (80 + 71) × £63 = £9,513. The addition of the £9,513 to the £5,607 gives the total sales figure for the six months of £15,120.

Projected balance sheet as at 31 December

	£		£
Current assets:		Capital	10,000
Debtors	9,513	RESERVES	
Bank	3,451	Net profit	2,964
	___		___
	12,964		12,964
	===		===

The capital is the money Davies originally brought into the business. The profit is as shown in the budgeted income statement. The bank balance is from the balance in the cash budget and the debtors are the moneys due for November and December sales as shown above. Davies's budgets reveal that he will require storage capacity for 111 boats at the end of month three which may cause him problems. He will be unable to meet demand by the end of December and could suffer a shortage of cash in November. If his sales forecast of 80 boats a month is realistic he will have to decide whether he wants to meet his demand or go for a smaller figure. His stock holding of 12 boats is unlikely to be met without increasing his rate of production which will probably entail capital expenditure as well as obtaining some help.

SELF-TEST QUESTIONS

1. How do you calculate a variance?
2. Why is it important to involve people in the budgetary process?
3. Who is generally responsible for preparing the budget?
4. How long a period does a long-range plan usually cover?
5. How long a period does the long-range plan cover in your organization?
6. What is the limiting factor?

QUESTIONS

9.1 Draw up the cash budget for Davies from the following information for the six months for 1 July to 31 December 19—:

1. Opening cash balance at 1 July 19— is £1,500.
2. Sales at £20 per unit (figures in units):

April	May	June	July	Aug	Sept	Oct	Nov	Dec
110	120	140	160	180	190	130	80	70

Debtors will pay two months after they have bought the goods.
3. £5 per unit direct labour is payable in the same month as production.
4. Raw materials cost £6 per unit and are paid for three months after the goods are used in production.

5. Production in units:

April	May	June	July	Aug	Sept	Oct	Nov	Dec
150	170	180	200	130	110	100	90	7060

6. Other variable expenses are £3 per unit. Two-thirds of this cost is paid for in the same month as production and one-third in the month following production.
7. Fixed expenses of £150 per month are paid one month in arrears.
8. Capital expenditure for September is £6,000.
9. Davies expects a legacy of £3,000 in December and will pay it into the business bank account.

9.2 *The balance sheet of Mary's delicatessen at 31 October*

	Cost £	Depn £	NBV £		£
Fixed assets:					
Premises	10,000	2,000	8,000	Capital	13,750
Fittings	8,000	4,000	4,000	Creditors	3,000
	18,000	6,000	12,000	Overdraft	1,050
Current assets:					
Stock		5,000			
Debtors		800	5,800		
			17,800		17,800

Sales are budgeted to be:

Nov	Dec	Jan	Feb	March	April
£6,000	£10,000	£7,000	£23,000	£4,000	£8,000

Some sales are on credit and the proportions are on average 10 per cent credit and 90 per cent cash.
Credit customers pay in the month following the sales.
The gross profit margin is 25 per cent of selling price.
Stocks are maintained at a constant level throughout the year.
Purchases are paid for in the following proportions: 50 per cent in the same month as they are purchased and 50 per cent in the subsequent month.
Wages and other running expenses are £2,000 per month paid in the month in which they are incurred.
Premises and fittings are depreciated at 10 per cent per annum on cost.

Required:
The preparation of a cash budget showing Mary's bank balance or overdraft for each month in the half year ending 30 April.

MARGINAL COSTING

OBJECTIVE

To provide an understanding of marginal costing and its use to management in the decision making process.

At the end of this chapter you will be able to explain:

1. Contribution
2. Break-even activity
3. Fixed cost
4. Marginal cost
5. Marginal costing
6. Gross margin

Marginal costing is not a complete costing system but a method of focusing the attention of management on those items that can most readily be controlled in the short term. Costs are divided into fixed costs and variable costs. Fixed costs are considered to be those that are unchanged by the level of activity while variable costs vary directly with the activity level. The behaviour of the two types of cost may be illustrated as shown in Figure 10.1 (a) and (b).

The fixed costs remain at £10,000 whether nothing is produced or 50,000 units, whereas the variable costs are nil when nothing is produced and £25,000 when 50,000 units are produced. The economies of scale are ignored for this purpose and a linear relationship is assumed between output and costs. The fixed costs are treated as fixed but this will apply only within limits. If, for example, demand increases above 50,000 units it may not be possible to meet it without obtaining additional buildings and machinery, in which case the fixed cost line becomes like that shown in Figure 10.2, which illustrates the changes that take place when full capacity is reached. Despite these limitations, marginal costing is an

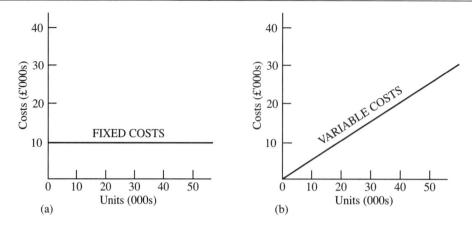

Figure 10.1   Marginal costing

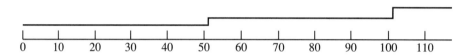

Figure 10.2   Marginal costing—fixed costs

extremely useful planning tool as it assists management to prepare a scale of charges that enable different costs to be recovered. It also enables a graphical presentation of the likely impact on the business of an increase (or decrease) of sales volume using the concept of contribution. Contribution is the surplus selling price that is available to meet the fixed costs once the variable costs have been covered. For example, if a product has a selling price of £100 and variable costs of £60, then every unit sold makes a contribution of £40 towards the fixed costs and, afterwards, profit.

	£
Selling price	100
Variable cost	60
Contribution	40

In engineering circles the contribution is referred to as the gross margin.

This concept can be used to arrive at the level of sales that is necessary for the organization to break even, i.e. for total income to equal level costs. Suppose the fixed costs of the organization mentioned above are £1,000,000, then the level of sales necessary for it to break even are given by the formula:

$$\text{Break-even point} \quad = \quad \frac{\text{Total fixed costs}}{(\text{Selling price} - \text{Variable cost}) \text{ per unit}}$$

$$= \frac{\text{Fixed costs}}{(SP - VC) \text{ per unit}}$$

$$= \frac{1,000,000}{(100 - 60)} = 25,000 \text{ units}$$

If 24,999 units are sold a loss of £40 is incurred.
If 25,001 units are sold a profit of £40 is made.
If no units are sold and made a loss of £1,000,000 is incurred.
If one unit is sold and made a loss of £999,960 is incurred.

So, it could be argued that in the short term it is better to work and sell one unit than to do nothing at all. This state of affairs could not be allowed to continue for too long but it may enable the organization to be slowly run down, or a new profitable product to be brought on line.

There is another formula which can be used to calculate the break-even point in £ (pounds) worth of sales as opposed to units sold. That is total fixed costs multiplied by the total value of sales and divided by the total contribution. Using the above example and assuming 25,001 units are sold we have:

$$\frac{F \times S}{C} = \frac{£1,000,000 \text{ x } £2,500,100}{1,000,040}$$

$$= \quad £2,500,000$$

This formula is useful when unit information is not available.

The concept of marginal costing is employed by, among others, the rail companies, bus companies, and electricity companies when they calculate their off-peak charges to customers. They all have enormous fixed costs, and, while there are times of the day at which they can hardly meet demand, there are other times when there is a great deal of spare capacity. They would like more use to be made of this and use marginal costing in their pricing in an effort to obtain some contribution to the fixed costs. The full return fare from Fareham to Cardiff by rail may be £31 whereas an off-peak return would be, say, £22 with children travelling free. This, it is hoped, would persuade more people to use the trains that are running two-thirds empty. The charges for electricity are less at night than during normal working hours as are those for using the telephone. All this is done in an effort to get a bigger contribution to fixed costs and, then, hopefully to profit.

Contribution or gross margin as the engineers describe it, has been discussed but an example will illustrate how it first of all covers fixed costs and then profit.

Example
Selling price £200 per unit. Variable cost £100 per unit. Total fixed costs £10,000.
The projected sales in units over the next four years are:

Year	1	2	3	4
Sales	50 units	70 units	100 units	200 units

Assuming all costs and the selling price for the period remain unchanged, calculate the profit or loss in each of the four years.

SOLUTION

Year	1	2	3	4
Fixed costs	10,000	10,000	10,000	10,000
Contribution (Selling price − variable cost) × units sold				
	£100 × 50	£100 × 70	£100 × 100	£100 × 200
	5,000	7,000	10,000	20,000
(Loss)/profit	(5,000)	(3,000)	—	10,000

The calculations show that in years 1 and 2 the contribution is insufficient to meet the fixed costs so a loss in incurred. In year 3 the contribution is exactly equal to the fixed costs so the organization breaks even, making neither a profit nor a loss. A profit of £10,000 is made in year 4 and the business may well continue in profit if it has carefully planned its course for the next ten years.

The marginal costing approach enables the break-even chart to be drawn. This is a useful planning tool as it illustrates, at a glance, the likely impact of increases or decreases in the level of sales. The axes are sales/costs in money terms against units sold, including the fixed cost line at £10,000 (see Figure 10.3).

The example may be shown graphically (see Figure 10.4). In constructing the graph it is necessary to decide where the lines are to finish. This can be achieved by dropping a perpendicular at the maximum potential capacity. In this case 200 units sold. All lines will be drawn to finish against the perpendicular. The fixed cost line is drawn parallel to the base at £10,000. The total cost line (that is, the fixed + variable costs) is drawn from fixed

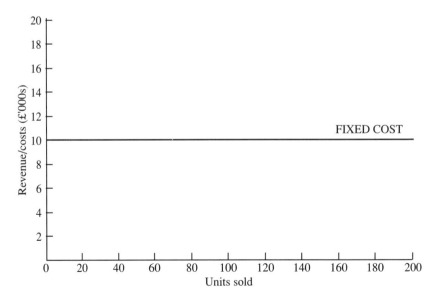

Figure 10.3   Fixed costs graph

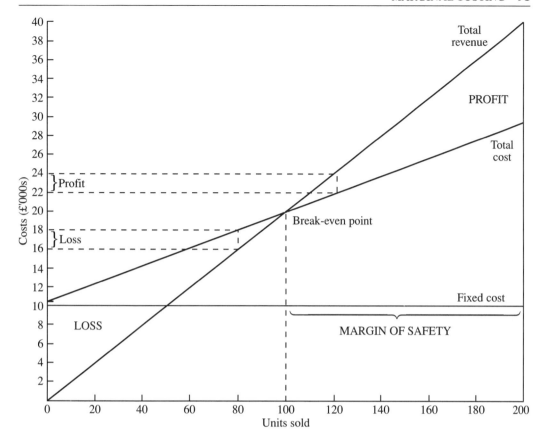

Figure 10.4   Break even graph

costs £10,000 up to total costs for 200 units, that is, £10,000 + (200 × £100 variable cost) = £10,000 + £20,000 = £30,000 total cost. The total revenue line is drawn from zero up to the total revenue for 200 units sold (200 × £200) = £40,000.

The break-even point is where the total revenue and total cost lines intersect. That is, at 100 units sold. Any sales below 100 will result in a loss and any above in a profit. The magnitude of the profit or loss is given by the vertical distance between the total revenue and total cost lines of that level of activity read on the vertical scale. Management often finds graphical presentation easier to assimilate than columns of figures. The difference between the break-even level of activity and the anticipated level of activity is called the margin of safety because that is the fall of sales in volume that the business can stand before it begins to make a loss. That is, sales can fall from 200 units to 100 units, a margin of safety of 100 units.

The concept of contribution is helpful when one factor restrains the level of activity in an organization. It may be that production is restricted by a shortage of labour in which case that is the limiting factor, or materials, or money. Whatever is in short supply is the limiting factor, and the concept of contribution can help ensure that the optimum use is made of available resources. This can be illustrated through the following example.

Example *Marginal costing—Limiting factor*

An organization has three products and available skilled labour that limits production. A sufficient supply of the other necessary factors of production exists. Sales demand is good and with labour as the limiting factor the following alternatives are available.

	Product 1	Product 2	Product 3
Alternative A	50,000 units	125,000 units	50,000 units
Alternative B	25,000 units	165,000 units	50,000 units
Alternative C	50,000 units	260,000 units	—
Alternative D	150,000 units	—	45,000 units
Alternative E	—	—	125,000 units

The results for the previous year are summarized below:

	Product 1		Product 2		Product 3	
	£	£	£	£	£	£
Sales		350,000		625,000		675,000
Prime cost	150,000		250,000		350,000	
Variable overhead	75,000		125,000		150,000	
Fixed overhead	54,000		200,000		110,000	
		279,000		575,000		610,000
Profit		71,000		50,000		65,000
Sales in units		50,000		125,000		50,000

Assuming that no changes are envisaged which of the alternatives A to E would you recommend to management?

SOLUTION

Product 1	£	£
Sales 50,000 units		350,000
Variable costs		
Prime cost	150,000	
Variable overhead	75,000	
		225,000
TOTAL CONTRIBUTION		125,000
		125,000
CONTRIBUTION PER UNIT SOLD		$\dfrac{125,000}{50,000} = £2.50$

Product 2	£	£
Sales 125,000 units		625,000
Variable costs		
Prime cost	250,000	
Variable overhead	125,000	
		375,000
TOTAL CONTRIBUTION		250,000
		250,000
CONTRIBUTION PER UNIT SOLD		$\dfrac{250,000}{125,000} = £2$

Product 3	£	£
Sales 50,000 units		675,000
Variable costs		
Prime cost	350,000	
Variable overhead	150,000	
		500,000
TOTAL CONTRIBUTION		175,000
		175,000
CONTRIBUTION PER UNIT SOLD		$\dfrac{175,000}{50,000} = £3.50$

Applying these contributions to the available product mixes we arrive at the most profitable alternative as shown below and see that it is alternative C which gives a total contribution of £625,000. However, management may prefer option B as, although it makes a smaller contribution, it maintains all three of the products and could in the long run prove the better choice. Customers, on finding that they can no longer obtain product 3, may turn to other suppliers for all three products and management must decide whether to risk this by taking option C or minimizing the risk and choosing option B.

Notes

Alternative

Product 1	£	Product 2	£	Product 3	£	TOTAL £
A 50,000 units @ £2.50 = 125,000		125,000 units @ £2 = 250,000		50,000 units @ £3.50 = 175,000		550,000
B 25,000 units @ £2.50 = 62,500		165,000 units @ £2 = 330,000		50,000 units @ £3.50 = 175,000		567,500
C 50,000 units @ £2.50 = 125,000		250,000 units @ £2 = 500,000		—		625,000
D 150,000 units @ £2.50 =375,000		—		45,000 units @ £3.50 = 157,500		532,500
E —		—		125,000 units @ £3.50 = 437,500		437,500

SELF-TEST QUESTIONS

1. What is the cost/volume/profit relationship?
2. How may the cost/volume/profit relationship be illustrated?
3. How are the CVP chart and the break-even chart related?
4. How is the break-even point calculated in units sold?
5. How is the break-even point calculated in £(pounds) worth of sales?

QUESTIONS

10.1 An organization has undertaken some market research and the sales forecast is:

Sales at £10 each—10,000 units total value of sales £100,000
Sales at £9.50 each—15,000 units total value of sales £142,500
Sales at £9 each—20,000 units total value of sales £180,000
Sales at £8.50 each—25,000 units total value of sales £212,500

The costs of production are variable cost per unit £8 and annual fixed costs £10,000.
   The company has the capacity to produce at any of the suggested levels but is at present selling 20,000 units at £9 each. Do you recommend any changes?

10.2 A personnel department provides a service for which it charges £65 per hour. The marginal cost of the service is £35 per hour and the departmental overheads for the relevant period are £15,000.

1. What is the break-even point in service hours sold?
2. How many hours must be sold in order to make a profit of £9,000?
3. What would the loss be if the hours sold fell to 300?
4. Draw a break-even chart. Maximum activity 900 hours.

10.3 Determine the most profitable sales mix for a company manufacturing products A, B and C. The budgeted profit and loss account reads:

	A	B	C	Total	
	£	£	£	£	£
Sales	40,000	35,000	45,000		120,000
Costs					
Prime	20,000	15,000	15,000	50,000	
Variable overhead	10,000	10,000	10,000	30,000	
Fixed overhead				30,000	110,000
NET PROFIT					10,000

The alternatives available to the company are:

1. To concentrate equally on all products as at present (A 20,000 units @ £2, B 10,000 units @ £3.50, C 15,000 units @ £3).
2. To concentrate on products B and C (B 20,000 units, C 21,000 units).
3. To concentrate on products A and C (A 30,000 units, C 24,000 units).
4. To concentrate on products A and B (A 30,000 units, B 20,000 units).

ELEVEN

DIFFERENTIAL COSTING
(Costing for Decision Making)

OBJECTIVE

To provide an understanding of differential costing and its application by the manager in the decision-making process.

At the end of this chapter you will be able to explain:

1. Differential costing
2. Differential costs
3. Relationship of differential and marginal costing

Marginal costing is applied over a period of time to a large number of problems. Differential costing applies the same techniques but accepts that each problem is unique and could well have different fixed costs over a period of time. It is important that managers have the correct information when decisions are being made because if the wrong figures are employed the organization will soon run into trouble or at the very least the manager's reputation will be tarnished. An organization that is considering discontinuing the provision of canteen facilities for its employees and buying from an outside caterer would be foolish to ignore the fixed charges outstanding on the current facility when comparing costs. The average cost per lunch provided internally might be £2.50 and that provided by the outside caterer £2.10, assuming the quality of the food was maintained there appears to be a saving of 40p per lunch. Further investigation might reveal that loan charges of £10,000 per annum and the business rate apportioned to the canteen of £1,000 per annum will still have to be met. The additional cost per meal if 25,000 meals were provided in each year would be (£11,000 ÷ 25,000) = 44p making the total cost per meal £2.54 not £2.10, or 4p per lunch in excess of the internal provision. The decision might still be to use the outside caterer for perfectly valid reasons but it will be made on the basis of full information.

In decision making it is essential to ensure that all the relevant costs are taken into account and irrelevant costs ignored. In deciding whether to close a school and transfer the

96

pupils to another one in a different area, the loan charges will have to be met whichever decision is made and so can be ignored but wages of teachers, secretaries and canteen staff will be reduced to some extent and will have to be considered in coming to an informed decision. It should always be remembered that very few decisions are made purely on the basis of the financial information. However, if the schools were run by different authorities the loan charges would become relevant to the decision as they would not be common to both authorities.

In calculating departmental or product costs it is difficult to apportion those costs which bear no clear relationship to the products or departments concerned. Examples are proportion of managing director's salary, of rates or of finance costs to be charged. We have already seen that absorption costing does not apportion overheads accurately and because of the concerns that have been expressed attempts have been made to improve the situation through activity based costing; but this too has its drawbacks.

The allocation of these costs can be made on an arbitrary basis that is true for one set of conditions only; because of this, cost figures that have been prepared for one purpose should be closely examined before they are used for any other purpose. Differential costs are the costs that will be altered by a change in an organization's scale, mix, place or method of operating. The financial effect of any such change can be estimated only by distinguishing between the fixed costs, i.e. those that will be unaltered by the change, and the differential costs which are affected by the change. Differential costing is the term used to describe cost investigations which are set up to determine the effect of such changes.

Example A manager who runs his car 10,000 miles a year has worked out the costs to be:

	Pence per mile
Depreciation £1,000 p.a.	10.0
Maintenance £120 service every 5,000 miles	2.4
Maintenance £240 service every 10,000 miles	2.4
Tyres new set £200 every 20,000 miles	1.0
Licence and insurance £400 p.a.	4.0
Petrol and oil at 35 mpg	7.3
Annual interest on £12,000 car is £1,440	14.4
	41.5

He moves his job and has to travel 20 miles to his new place of employment, in addition to the normal 10,000 miles p.a. that he travels in his car. There is a bus that stops outside his front door and goes by the most direct route to his place of work. Bus and car are equally convenient. Which do you recommend he should use on financial grounds if the bus fare is £5 per day?

SUGGESTED SOLUTION Using the differential costing approach the only additional costs of the car are servicing, tyres and fuel, the other costs are all fixed and have to be met. The car costs that are charged add up to:

	Pence per mile
5,000 miles service	2.4
10,000 miles service	2.4
Tyres	1.0
Fuel	7.3
	13.1

The costs for the bus are 40 miles at £5 = 12.5p per mile. On financial considerations alone the bus should be used.

Depreciation is normally charged on the age of the article rather than usage. However, it could be that heavy mileage would increase the annual cost of depreciation.

SELF-TEST QUESTIONS

1. How are fixed costs treated in differential costing or marginal costing?
2. Does the differential cost vary with changes in activity?
3. How may differential costs be described?
4. What are the 'relevant costs'?

QUESTIONS

11.1 A product costs £9 when purchased from outside suppliers. The annual production costs are:

	£
Salary of product manager	20,000
Depreciation of departmental machinery	6,000
Overhead from other departments allocated to the product	24,000
Variable overhead	30,000
Variable/prime/direct cost	60,000
TOTAL for 12,000 units	140,000

Cost per unit $\dfrac{140,000}{12,000}$ = £11.67. Working capital £15,000 at 12 per cent.

Do you recommend that the organization should buy in from the outside supplier or continue to produce the product itself?

11.2 An organization is considering the introduction of a new product which will sell at £10 and can be manufactured in either one of two ways:

1. Method X costs are:	Leasing of machine	£12,000 p.a.	Labour £5.00 unit
	Maintenance	£ 4,000 p.a.	Materials £2.00 unit
2. Method Y costs are:	Leasing of machine	£58,000 p.a.	Labour £2.00 unit
	Maintenance	£ 6,000 p.a.	Materials £2.00 unit

Estimated annual sales 14,000 units: Rent £8,000 p.a.
   Which method of manufacture should be used?

TWELVE
CAPITAL BUDGETING

OBJECTIVE

To provide an understanding of capital budgeting and its use to the manager in arriving at the best use of limited cash resources.

At the end of this chapter you will be able to explain:

1. The strengths and weaknesses of the capital budgeting process
2. The capital budget
3. Ranking competing schemes
4. Payback
5. Accounting rate of return
6. Discounted cash flow

The capital budgeting decision is extremely important to any organization because it generally involves incurring expenditure of large sums of money that will have an effect on the profitability of the organization for many years. The general budgeting process usually extends over ten years into the future and the capital budgeting process is part of this.

In all organizations the demand for funds for capital outlay exceeds the money available, so some means of ranking these competing schemes has to be devised. Capital expenditure gives rise to fixed assets like land and buildings, plant and machinery and motor vehicles and in assessing the order of priority the first step is to draw up a schedule of likely projects over the next ten years. This will be firm for the first and second years, flexible for the next three years, and tentative for the last five years.

One format for the capital budget may be:

SCHEME	Yr1 £'000s	Yr2 £'000s	Yr3 £'000s	Yr4 £'000s	Yr5 £'000s	Yr6 £'000s	Yr7 £'000s	Yr8 £'000s	Yr9 £'000s	Yr10 £'000s
A	200	500	50	—	—	—	—	—	—	—
B	500	—	80	—	—	—	—	—	—	—
C	40	80	—	—	—	—	—	—	—	—
D	50	60	—	—	—	—	—	—	—	—
E	20	40	—	20	—	—	—	—	—	—
F	—	—	—	—	20	100	60	50	100	60
G	60	10	30	—	—	—	—	—	—	—
H	—	—	—	60	40	10	80	—	—	—
I	10	40	100	—	—	—	—	—	—	—
TOTAL	880	730	260	80	60	110	140	50	100	60

This will tell you how much money is likely to be required for capital purposes over the next ten years. The budget is not all-embracing, however, and if other schemes arise they cannot be excluded but must be considered. Having established their needs for the next 12 months a method has to be derived to rank the schemes. Some of them will of course select themselves on grounds of pure necessity. This may be brought about by a technological advance making some new equipment essential, or a breakdown making replacement necessary. There are many ways of ranking the remaining schemes but three will be described here that are in common usage. They are payback, accounting rate of return, and discounted cash flow.

12.1 PAYBACK

Payback is frequently employed either alone or in conjunction with the net present value technique because managers are keen to know how quickly they are likely to recover their capital outlay. The sooner this can be achieved the better, so far as the organization is concerned, as the money is then available for other purposes. An example of a payback calculation would be if an organization were to consider installing a drink-dispensing machine in an office. The machine would cost £4,000 and be instrumental in generating an additional cash flow of £500 a year after the deduction of running costs. The payback would be eight years as it would take 4,000/500 = 8 years to recover the £4,000 capital outlay.

If the only criteria were financial and the organization was looking for a three-year payback the scheme would be rejected. If, on the other hand, a nine-year payback was required the scheme would be accepted *for further consideration*. It would not automatically go ahead but it would be grouped with the other schemes that met the payback criteria.

This basis is easy to understand and apply and recognizes that each £1 received earlier is more valuable than £1 received later, because the £1 received earlier can be invested at the going rate of interest which is denied to the person who receives the £1 later. However, it does not attempt to put a value on the £1 that is received earlier, neither does it consider the whole scheme. Cash flows generated after the payback period are completely ignored. Under this method all projects that meet the payback requirement go forward for further consideration and those that do not are rejected.

12.2 ACCOUNTING RATE OF RETURN

Under this method the average annual cash flow generated over the life of the asset is calculated and expressed as a percentage of the capital investment. This may be illustrated with the following example.

An organization is considering installing double glazing in its administrative offices. The cost is £40,000 and it is expected to result in savings on heating over the next 15 years of:

Year	£
1	1,000
2	2,200
3	2,500
4	2,600
5	2,800
6	3,000
7	3,200
8	3,200
9	3,200
10	3,300
11	3,300
12	3,400
13	3,400
14	3,500
15	3,500
Total	£44,100

$$\text{Average annual cash flow} = \frac{44,100 \text{ (total)}}{15 \text{ (years)}} = £2,940$$

This is expressed as a percentage of capital invested by multiplying by 100 and dividing by the sum invested

$$\frac{2,940 \times 100}{40,000} = 7.35 \text{ per cent}$$

If the organization were looking for a 15 per cent return on the capital invested this scheme would not go forward for further consideration. On the other hand if a 6 per cent return was the criterion then it would receive further consideration.

This method of assessing capital investment schemes is easy to understand and does use the whole life of the scheme in arriving at a figure. Its major drawback is that it ignores the time value of money.

12.3 DISCOUNTED CASH FLOW

Net present value

This is a discounted cash flow (DCF) approach to rank competing capital projects. It considers the whole life of the project and recognizes the time value of money. It is in common use, frequently in combination with the payback method. It may be illustrated by the following example.

There are two competing schemes, A and B, to produce a household good. Scheme A costs £80,000 to buy the necessary equipment which will last for eight years. The equipment is sophisticated and results in savings in material and labour over the eight years of:

Year	Savings £
1	9,000
2	18,000
3	20,000
4	20,000
5	20,000
6	15,000
7	10,000
8	4,000

Scheme B requires a capital investment of £60,000 on not such sophisticated equipment which will also last for eight years. It is expected to generate the following savings over its life:

Year	Savings £
1	6,000
2	9,000
3	10,000
4	10,000
5	10,000
6	9,000
7	5,000
8	5,000

Which of the two schemes should be chosen?

Scheme A costs £80,000. This is now, so the value of the money is now. Savings assume that they are achieved at the end of the year in question and the organization could invest money at 11 per cent. This means that the cost of capital is 11 per cent and any schemes introduced must be instrumental in earning or saving more than this. Tables are prepared to show how time affects the value of money and a set is included at the end of this book. In this case we will have to use the 11 per cent table.

Year		Factor £	Present value £
0	Outlay		80,000
1	Savings	9,000 × 0.9009	8,108
2		18,000 × 0.8116	14,609
3		20,000 × 0.7312	14,624
4		20,000 × 0.6587	13,174
5		20,000 × 0.5935	11,870
6		15,000 × 0.5346	8,019
7		10,000 × 0.4817	4,817
8		4,000 × 0.4339	1,736
		PRESENT VALUE	76,957
		NET PRESENT VALUE	−3,043

This tells us that the present value of all the future savings brought about by scheme A is £76,957 when the cost of capital is 11 per cent. This, when compared with the capital outlay of £80,000, gives a negative net present value (NPV) of £3,043 which would mean that the scheme would not be further considered as the 11 per cent criterion had not been met. The table used was the 11 per cent table under the third column title of 'Present value of £1'. From this you see that if you could invest money at 11 per cent, a pound received in ten years' time would be worth only 35p when compared with a pound that you hold now.

Using the same procedures for scheme B we have:

Year		Factor £	Present value £
0	Outlay		60,000
1	Savings	6,000 × 0.9009	5,405
2		9,000 × 0.8116	7,304
3		10,000 × 0.7312	7,312
4		10,000 × 0.6587	6,587
5		10,000 × 0.5935	5,935
6		9,000 × 0.5346	4,811
7		5,000 × 0.4817	2,409
8		5,000 × 0.4339	2,170
		PRESENT VALUE	41,933
		NET PRESENT VALUE	−18,067

Neither of these schemes would be accepted using the 11 per cent criterion, but if it was essential that one was chosen then scheme A is the better of the two since it has a NPV of − £3,043 compared with B which gives NPV of −£18,067.

An alternative approach to decide which of these two schemes should be chosen, if it had already been decided that one of them was essential, would be to use the differential approach:

				£
Additional cost of scheme A now (£80,000 − £60,000)				20,000
Additional savings generated by scheme A:				
Year	1	(£9,000 − £6,000)	£3,000 × 0.9009	2,703
	2	(£18,000 − £9,000)	£9,000 × 0.8116	7,304
	3	(£20,000 − £10,000)	£10,000 × 0.7312	7,312
	4	(£20,000 − £10,000)	£10,000 × 0.6587	6,587
	5	(£20,000 − £10,000)	£10,000 × 0.5935	5,935
	6	(£15,000 − £9,000)	£6,000 × 0.5346	3,208
	7	(£10,000 − £5,000)	£5,000 × 0.4817	2,408
	8	(£4,000 − £5,000)	− £1,000 × 0.4339	(434)
		PRESENT VALUE		35,023
		NET PRESENT VALUE		+15,023

This shows that the extra savings generated by scheme A, discounted to their present value, exceed the additional cost of scheme A by £15,023 and that, all other things being equal, scheme A would be chosen.

Internal rate of return

A second discounted cash flow approach to the ranking of competing capital projects is the internal rate of return. Like NPV it considers the whole life of the project, recognizes the time value of money, and is in common use, frequently in combination with the payback method. It will generally lead to the same decisions as those reached when the net present value approach is employed. This method requires the interest rate that will make the total of the future cash flows exactly equal to the original investment. This concept may be illustrated by returning to our example of two competing schemes on page 103.

Scheme A
Try 11%

Year			Factor	Present value	Present value
		£		£	£
0	Costs	80,000 × 1			80,000
1	Savings	9,000 × 0.9009		8,108	
2		18,000 × 0.8116		14,609	
3		20,000 × 0.7312		14,624	
4		20,000 × 0.6587		13,174	
5		20,000 × 0.5935		11,870	
6		15,000 × 0.5346		8,019	
7		10,000 × 0.4817		4,817	
8		4,000 × 0.4339		1,736	
		PRESENT VALUE			76,957
		NET PRESENT VALUE			−3,043

This has a negative NPV so we try to find an interest rate that will give a positive NPV and, by interpolation, arrive at the interest rate that gives a NPV of zero (0). That will be the internal rate of return (IRR). As 11 per cent gives a negative NPV, anything above 11 per cent will increase the size of the negative NPV as it will reduce further the present value of the future cash flows. It is necessary, therefore, to try a percentage below 11 per cent.

Scheme A
Try 7%

Year			Factor	Present value	Present value
		£		£	£
0	Costs	80,000 × 1			80,000
1	Savings	9,000 × 0.9346		8,411	
2		18,000 × 0.8734		15,721	
3		20,000 × 0.8163		16,326	
4		20,000 × 0.7629		15,258	
5		20,000 × 0.7130		14,260	
6		15,000 × 0.6663		9,994	
7		10,000 × 0.6227		6,227	
8		4,000 × 0.5820		2,328	
		PRESENT VALUE			88,525
		NET PRESENT VALUE			+8,525

We now have both a negative and a positive NPV and can arrive at the IRR by interpolation.

The percentage that gives the positive NPV plus the difference between the percentage that gives the positive NPV and the percentage that gives the negative NPV, multiplied by the value of the positive NPV and divided by the sum of the positive and negative NPVs, ignoring the sign.

$$\text{Positive NPV \%} + \left[\begin{array}{c} \text{Difference between} \\ \text{positive and negative} \\ \text{NPV \%} \end{array} \left(\frac{\text{Positive NPV}}{\text{Sum of NPVs ignoring signs}} \right) \right]$$

$$7\% + 4 \left(\frac{8,525}{11,568} \right) = 7\% + (4 \times 0.74) = 7\% + 2.96 \approx 10\%$$

We can test this by trying 10 per cent and seeing how close the result is to zero. You will have noticed that in the calculation of the IRR, 7 per cent is the percentage that gave a positive NPV, 4 per cent is the difference between 7 per cent and 11 per cent which gave the negative NPV, the numerator is the positive NPV of £8,525 at 7 per cent, while the denominator is the addition of the two NPVs ignoring their signs; that is (£3,043 + £8,525) = £11,568.

Test
Try 10%

Year		Factor	Present value £	Present value £
		£		
0	Costs	80,000 ×1		80,000
1	Savings	9,000 × 0.9091	8,182	
2		18,000 × 0.8264	14,875	
3		20,000 × 0.7513	15,026	
4		20,000 × 0.6830	13,660	
5		20,000 × 0.6209	12,418	
6		15,000 × 0.5645	8,467	
7		10,000 × 0.5132	5,132	
8		4,000 × 0.4665	1,866	
	PRESENT VALUE			79,626
	NET PRESENT VALUE			−374

This test confirms that interpolation has enabled us to arrive at the IRR which is 10 per cent. The slight difference of £374 can be accounted for by rounding up to 10 per cent the 9.96 per cent that the calculation gave.

The cost of funds is 11 per cent, that is the *opportunity cost* of the investment, and the return is 10 per cent so the scheme would not be considered any further. This agrees with the decision reached when the NPV method is used. Using the same approach for scheme B we have:

Scheme B
Try 11%

Year		£	Factor	Present value £	Present value £
0	Costs	60,000	×1		60,000
1	Savings	6,000	× 0.9009	5,405	
2		9,000	× 0.8116	7,304	
3		10,000	× 0.7312	7,312	
4		10,000	× 0.6587	6,587	
5		10,000	× 0.5935	5,935	
6		9,000	× 0.5346	4,811	
7		5,000	× 0.4817	2,409	
8		5,000	× 0.4339	2,170	
		PRESENT VALUE			41,933
		NET PRESENT VALUE			−18,067

The negative NPV means that we have to look for a lower rate of interest that gives a positive result and then arrive at the IRR by interpolation. Try 3 per cent.

Scheme B
Try 3%

Year		£	Factor	Present value £	Present value £
0	Costs	60,000	×1		60,000
1	Savings	6,000	× 0.9709	5,825	
2		9,000	× 0.9426	8,483	
3		10,000	× 0.9151	9,151	
4		10,000	× 0.8885	8,885	
5		10,000	× 0.8626	8,626	
6		9,000	× 0.8375	7,538	
7		5,000	× 0.8131	4,066	
8		5,000	× 0.7894	3,947	
		PRESENT VALUE			56,521
		NET PRESENT VALUE			−3,479

This is a negative NPV so we try 1 per cent.

Scheme B
Try 1%

Year		Factor	*Present value*	*Present value*
		£	£	£
0	Costs	60,000 ×1		60,000
1	Savings	6,000 × 0.9901	5,941	
2		9,000 × 0.9803	8,823	
3		10,000 × 0.9706	9,706	
4		10,000 × 0.9610	9,610	
5		10,000 × 0.9515	9,515	
6		9,000 × 0.9420	8,478	
7		5,000 × 0.9327	4,664	
8		5,000 × 0.9235	4,618	
		PRESENT VALUE		61,355
		NET PRESENT VALUE		+1,355

This gives a positive NPV and by interpolation the IRR may be found.

$$1\% + 2\% \left(\frac{1,355}{4,834} \right) = 1\% + (2 \times 0.28) = 1\% + 0.56 \approx 2\%$$

This scheme would be rejected, as it uses the NPV approach, where the 11 per cent criterion is imposed, but if it was essential that one was chosen it would be scheme A as it gives the higher return of 10 per cent as opposed to 2 per cent for scheme B.

The capital budgeting process is essential and some method of choosing between competing schemes must be used that is seen to be fair. If this is not done unrest will be fermented, as the dominant character or department in the organization will always obtain a lion's share of the monetary cake, which will often not be deserved. Even in the best run organizations the unexpected happens, like a technological advance making equipment obsolete or machinery breaking down. In these cases capital expenditure has to be incurred from pure necessity, but it does not mean that the capital budget should not be prepared, nor does it imply that it should be completely ignored.

The capital budgeting techniques are available to all managers but they are unfortunately all too often ignored. The vast majority of capital investment decisions are in my experience made on the basis of urgency, that is, money having to be spent to enable the organization to survive. This does not obviate the need for capital budget programmes, but it does mean that they very often have to undergo major adjustments, which is to be expected of any system of forecasting in conditions of uncertainty.

SELF-TEST QUESTIONS

1. What is the significance of the payback period?
2. How is the appropriate discount rate assessed when using discounted cash flow (DCF) techniques?
3. What does the internal rate of return (IRR) tell you?
4. Is the accounting rate of return a frequently used technique?

QUESTIONS

12.1 A machine costs £8,000 and the estimated after tax savings from its use over the next five years are:

Year 1	£ 1,000
Year 2	£ 2,000
Year 3	£ 4,000
Year 4	£ 2,000
Year 5	£ 1,000
	£10,000

Should it be purchased if the company's profit target is 10 per cent per annum?

12.2 An investment project will need £25,000. If the net revenue over the next ten years will be £5,000 p.a. and the company's profit objective is 12 per cent, is this project advisable?

12.3 A company is considering whether to borrow £20,000 on a 7 per cent debenture for an extension which will earn £5,000 per annum (gross) over the next five years. What is your opinion?

12.4 Overfull has a problem with space that is expected to last for seven years. A cheap prefabricated building is available that will last seven years and be removed after that time. Enquiries reveal that heating costs will be £10,000 p.a. This seems rather high and the question of heating is investigated further. Heat loss from this type of building is very great. If insulation was carried out for £24,000, the heating costs would be reduced to £5,000 p.a.

Overfull's cost of capital is 9 per cent. State whether the building should be insulated.

12.5 Suppliers are making a special component and require a new machine. It is available in the standard model which costs £15,000, lasts five years and has a scrap value of £2,000. The raw material costs will be £10,000 a year.

A more advanced model costs £30,000, lasts five years and has a scrap value of £4,000. Its greater efficiency will reduce raw material costs to £6,000 a year. If all other costs will be the same and supplier's cost of capital is 14 per cent which machine should be purchased?

THIRTEEN

RAISING PERMANENT AND LONG-TERM FINANCE

OBJECTIVE

To provide an understanding of the need for permanent and long-term finance, the sources from which it might be obtained and the role of the manager in raising the money.

At the end of this chapter you will be able to explain:

1. Permanent capital
2. Long-term capital
3. Capitalization issue
4. Share premium account
5. Placing

Sources from which finance may be raised have been discussed in Chapters 1 and 2 but the processes by which it can be raised were not considered. The purpose of this chapter is to explore the ways in which permanent and long-term capital or money may be raised. Permanent capital is provided by the owners of the business either by introducing money from their own resources or by retaining profits in the business instead of distributing them as dividends. The retained profits are shown as reserves in the balance sheet. Long-term capital is obtained by borrowing money that will have to be repaid at some time in the future. The borrowing may be from individuals, financial institutions or others with money to invest. We will now investigate each of these types of capital in turn.

14.1 PERMANENT CAPITAL

Permanent capital can be raised by the issue of shares that are either 'ordinary' or 'preference'. Ordinary shares carry voting rights and enable the shareholders to vote on matters of importance affecting the business. The ordinary shareholders are the owners of the business and appoint directors to act on their behalf in running the business. The directors having been appointed by the ordinary shareholders could in theory be removed by them. In practice this is extremely difficult to achieve and rarely happens. This is because the directors themselves hold large numbers of shares. You should view with suspicion any organization whose directors hold few or no shares. It means that the directors do not believe in the organization that they are running, and if they have no faith in it why should the general investor?

Each ordinary share carries a voting right so that the more shares you own the greater your say in what should be done. Anyone who owns more than 50 per cent of the ordinary share capital normally controls the business. The ordinary shareholders are the equity holders. They take the biggest risk and can, if things go badly, as with Polly Peck, lose virtually everything. Consequently when things go well, they expect the biggest return in terms of income by way of dividend received and capital growth through an increase in the market price of a share. The capital is permanent because the business is under no obligation to buy back the shares that it has sold. If a shareholder wishes to recover the money that has been invested in shares then he or she has to do so by selling the shares to a purchaser through the mechanism of the Stock Exchange. If the share price has risen, more will be obtained for the shares than was originally invested in them and a capital gain realized. On the other hand, if the price has fallen, less will be obtained than was originally paid and a loss incurred. The dividend paid to the ordinary shareholders is at the discretion of the directors but it will not normally vary much from year to year. It has to be paid out of after-tax profits but may be paid out of previously unused profits if the directors so decide. If at all possible directors will maintain dividends and not withhold them. It is interesting to note that in the difficult climate of the early 1990s many organizations were asking shareholders if they would like to receive their dividends in the form of additional shares instead of money; and some even talked of withholding the dividend altogether.

Preference shares generally carry no voting rights and as the name implies holders receive their dividends before the ordinary shareholders. The rate of dividend is stated on the face of the share, e.g. 9 per cent preference share. The 9 per cent is based on the nominal value of the share and not on profits earned or the market value of the share. The nominal value of any share is shown on the face of the share certificate and it is normally 25p. There are other nominal values and 50p and £1 are often seen. The nominal value is employed to show the value of the issued share capital in the balance sheet. Shares are usually issued for more than the nominal value and the difference between the nominal value and the amount actually received is shown in the share premium account under reserves.

Example

If a company issues 10,000 ordinary shares of 25p for £1 and 5,000 9 per cent preference shares of 25p for 50p the balance sheet will show:

	£
Issued share capital	
10,000 ordinary shares	2,500
5,000 9 per cent preference shares	1,250
Reserves	
Share premium account	8,750
	12,500

The total amount raised is		
10,000 × £1	=	£10,000
+ 5,000 × 50p	=	£ 2,500
		£12,500

but only £3,750 of this is shown in the issued share capital section. The balance of £8,750 is shown under reserves as share premium account. In practice shares would not normally be issued to raise such small sums of money. The smallest amount raised by a general issue of shares would usually be £1,000,000.

The preference shareholders receive their dividend before the ordinary shareholders and if the company fails they are paid what is due to them before the ordinary shareholders receive anything. The risk is smaller than that of the ordinary shareholders and because of this the ordinary shareholders expect a bigger dividend and a greater capital gain than the preference shareholders if things go well. In other respects the ordinary and preference shareholders are treated in the same way.

There are four ways in which ordinary shares are normally issued but only two of these result in additional finance for the issuing company.
1. Capitalization issue (also known as a 'scrip', 'free' or 'bonus' issue)
2. Rights issue
3. Placing
4. Vendor consideration

Capitalization issue

The purpose of a capitalization issue is to bring the issued capital into closer relationship with the capital employed in a business. It raises no additional money for the business and no money changes hands. Shares are normally issued to the existing shareholders in proportion to their existing holdings by capitalizing reserves. This reduces the reserves and increases the number of ordinary shares in issue which makes the market value of each ordinary share fall. Each individual shareholder is no better or worse off than he or she was previously because the additional shares have gone to existing shareholders. A person who previously had one share with a market value of £3 may now have three shares each of which has a market value of £1.

The relevant section of a business's balance sheet before and after a capitalization issue may be illustrated as follows:

	£
Issued share capital	
100,000 ordinary shares	25,000
Reserves	
Share premium account	175,000
Profit and loss account	100,000

After capitalization of £100,000 of the reserves by the issue of 400,000 25p shares

	£
Issued share capital	
500,000 ordinary shares	125,000
Reserves	
Share premium account	75,000
Profit and loss account	100,000

The total of the issued share capital and reserves remains at £300,000 but it has been adjusted to bring the issued share capital into a closer relationship with the capital employed in the business.

Rights issue

The purpose of a rights issue is to raise additional finance to allow a business to expand or prepare for a more competitive market situation. A rights issue is normally made at a price which is below the current market value of the shares. If it were not there would be no incentive for the existing shareholders to take up the offer. It cannot be made below the nominal value of the shares less a maximum commission of 10 per cent. The shares must be offered to the existing shareholders first because if they were offered to the public at large there would be a dilution of the existing holders' rights and benefits. In view of this a company in making a new issue of ordinary shares for cash must allot such rights to existing holders if its shares are quoted on the Stock Exchange. The term *rights* issue refers to the rights of the existing shareholders to maintain their relationship with the business.

When a rights issue takes place the issued share capital of the business and the bank balance will both increase as will the reserves if the issue is made at above the par value. This may be illustrated using the following balance sheet.

	£'000s	£'000s
Fixed assets:		
Land and buildings		400
Plant and machinery		100
Fixtures and fittings		50
		550
Current assets:		
Stock	60	
Debtors	10	
Bank	5	
	75	
Deduct		
Current liabilities	65	
Working capital		10
Net capital employed		560
Financed by:		
Issued share capital		
1,800,000 ordinary shares		450
Reserves		
Share premium account		80
Profit and loss account		30
		560

If the business now makes a rights issue of one new share for every nine shares already held then an additional 200,000 (1,800,000/9) shares will be issued and the issued share capital will become £500,000 (£450,000 + £50,000). Issuing the shares for £1, which is above their nominal value of 25p and below their assumed current market value of £1.30p, will have a twofold effect. Firstly, the share premium account will be increased by £150,000 (200,000 × £0.75) to £230,000 (£80,000 + £150,000) and, secondly, the bank balance will be increased by £200,000 to £205,000 (£5,000 + £200,000). The discount of 30p between the current market value of £1.30 and the issue price of £1 would help to ensure that the rights issue was taken up.

Placing

The purpose of a placing is to raise money for a business as cheaply as possible. It is only allowed where there is unlikely to be significant public demand for the shares and is usually restricted to a share value of £1.5 million at the placing price. The placing involves the sale of shares by an issuing house or broker through the market to its own clients. The advantages of placings are that they are relatively cheap to effect because they avoid much of the marketing and administrative expenses usually incurred and that the shares can be quickly and efficiently sold.

Placings will only normally be allowed in the following circumstances:

1. Where existing shareholders wish to dispose of shares which they have because of a rights issue or a vendor consideration issue (vendor consideration will be discussed next).
2. Where ordinary shares in a company not previously listed on the Stock Exchange are to be issued.
3. Where an already listed business wishes to issue additional shares. If the existing shareholders object this can only be done by way of a rights issue.

The effect on the balance sheet of issuing shares by means of a placing is the same as that for a rights issue which was previously illustrated.

Vendor consideration

The purpose of the issue of vendor consideration shares is to enable one business to acquire another business purely by issuing shares. It enables the acquiring business to keep its cash resources intact while at the same time giving the acquired business the opportunity to raise money by selling some of the shares it has been given. Where a part equity and part cash settlement is required by the vendor it is achieved by splitting the shares issued into two parts. The first comprises those shares the vendors intend to retain. The second comprises those shares that will later be sold by vendors for cash in the market place. The business issuing the shares does not receive any cash at all. The effect on the balance sheet will be for the issued share capital and reserves to increase and for a subsidiary company of the same value to appear among the fixed assets. This may be illustrated as follows:

	£'000s	£'000s
Fixed assets:		
Land and buildings		400
Plant and machinery		100
Fixtures and fittings		50
Investment in subsidiary co (1)		200
		750
Current assets:		
Stock	60	
Debtors	10	
Bank	5	
	75	
Deduct		
Current liabilities	65	
Working capital		10
Net capital employed		760

Financed by:
 Issued share capital
  2,000,000 ordinary shares   500
 Reserves
  Share premium account   230
  Profit and loss account   30

            760

The following example using Green Designs Plc further illustrates the effects of using vendor consideration shares.

Green Designs Plc
Balance sheet as at 30 November 1998

	£'000s	£'000s
Fixed assets:		
Land and buildings		400
Plant and machinery		150
Fixtures and fittings		80
Motor vehicles		20
		650
Current assets:		
Stock	100	
Debtors	80	
Bank	30	
	210	
Deduct		
Current liabilities	180	
Working capital		30
Net capital employed		680
Financed by:		
Issued share capital		
2,000,000 ordinary shares		500
Reserves		
Share premium account		100
Profit and loss account		80
		680

If another business is purchased for £300,000 by using 100,000 vendor consideration shares at £3 each then the balance sheet will be altered in three respects. The issued share capital becomes 2,100,000 ordinary shares valued at £525,000 (£500,000 + (£100,000 ×

25p)). The share premium £375,000 (£100,000 + (£100,000 × £2.75p)). The fixed assets increased by £300,000, being the value of the subsidiary business acquired, and the balance sheet will become:

Green Designs Plc
Balance sheet as at 30 November 1998

	£'000s	£'000s
Fixed assets:		
Land and buildings		400
Plant and machinery		150
Fixtures and fittings		80
Motor vehicles		20
Subsidiary undertaking		300
		950
Current assets:		
Stock	100	
Debtors	80	
Bank	30	
	210	
Deduct		
Current liabilities	180	
Working capital		30
Net capital employed		980
Financed by:		
Issued share capital		
2,100,000 ordinary shares		525
Reserves		
Share premium account		375
Profit and loss account		80
		980

The permanent capital of a business comes only through the owners either directly by means of new money that they invest or indirectly through profits that they allow to remain in the business. The methods by which it is raised do differ, however, as we have seen in this chapter.

13.2 LONG-TERM CAPITAL

Long-term capital can be raised by borrowing from the money market but the amount is restricted by the Articles of Association of the business. The borrowing will also be affected by the market's perception of the management and its record over recent years. A successful business will find it easier to borrow and obtain a lower rate of interest than a badly managed organization. Long-term loans are normally obtained through the issue of debentures in £100 stock units. The debenture is a piece of paper which states the number of £100 units and the dates over which it may be repaid. The holder of debenture, or loan stock as it is sometimes called, is a creditor of the company and has a right to an annual return, regardless of whether or not profits are made, with the promise of the repayment of a fixed sum of money by a set date in the future.

Debentures may be secured or unsecured but unsecured loan stock can only be raised by large safe companies such as ICI or Microsoft. It carries a rate of interest of about 0.5 per cent higher than that for a secured debenture. Secured debentures have either a floating charge or a fixed charge on the assets of the borrowing organization. An example of a fixed charge would be a debenture which is issued against the security of the buildings. Such a debenture is called a mortgage debenture and gives the lender the right to sell the buildings and recover the amount loaned should the business default on payment of interest or fail to repay the principal by the due date. A floating charge does not relate to any specific asset but 'floats' over all assets until such time as the business defaults. Should this happen the charge would cease to float and descend on the assets so that they could only be sold in order to repay the debenture holders.

The debenture stock may be issued at par, that is, £100 cash for each £100 stock or at slightly below par, which is a way of manipulating the effective rate of interest payable and making the stock more attractive to lenders. If, for example, it is issued at £100 with a rate of interest of 11 per cent then the rate is obviously 11 per cent. If, however, it is issued at £95 this means that every £95 invested will secure £100 worth of stock and the interest rate becomes 11.58 per cent. Not only this but when the loan is redeemed the lender will receive £100 for each £95 invested.

The debenture can normally be redeemed during any one of a number of years at the discretion of the borrower. This increases the possibility that the businesses will be able to obtain the money necessary to repay the loan on reasonable terms. Most businesses do not generate sufficient cash from their own activities to repay the borrowings as they fall due. They either issue additional shares or take fresh borrowings, and a spread of dates on which this can be done enables the directors to choose a favourable time to do so. The effect on the balance sheet of raising long-term capital by the issue of debentures would be for the bank balance to increase among the current assets and for the long-term liabilities also to increase. This may be illustrated using the following example. A debenture loan of £200,000 is raised with a 11 per cent debenture redeemable 2010–2014 which will result in the original balance sheet of Green Designs Plc becoming:

Green Designs Plc
Balance sheet as at 30 November 1998

	£'000s	£'000s
Fixed assets:		
Land and buildings		400
Plant and machinery		150
Fixtures and fittings		80
Motor vehicles		20
		650
Current assets:		
Stock	100	
Debtors	80	
Bank	230	
	410	
Deduct		
Current liabilities	180	
Working capital		230
Net capital employed		880
Less		
Long-term liability		200
(Creditors repayable after more than one year)		
11% Debenture		
		680
Financed by:		
Issued share capital		
2,000,000 ordinary shares		500
Reserves		
Share premium account		100
Profit and loss account		80
		680

The money would not of course remain in the bank for very long but would be employed in the purchase of new fixed assets or in other ways to enable the business to run more effectively.

Whenever businesses need finance, managers have to consider carefully whether it should be long term or permanent, and always have to bear in mind prevailing market conditions.

SELF-TEST QUESTIONS

1. Does a scrip issue affect the cash available to an organization?
2. Why is a rights issue usually priced below the current market price?
3. How may vendor consideration shares be used to acquire a business?
4. What is the effect of a capitalization issue on the balance sheet?

FOURTEEN

GEARING—COST OF CAPITAL

OBJECTIVE

To provide an understanding of gearing and the impact that the financial manager can have on the cost of financing the organization.

At the end of the chapter you will be able to explain:

1. Gearing
2. Cost of capital
3. Weighted average cost of capital
4. Optimal gearing level
5. Cost of equity
6. Cost of debt

There are two points of view about the way in which an organization obtains its money and the cost of that money. The traditional approach is that there is a relationship between equity moneys and borrowed moneys at which the weighted average cost of capital will be minimized. Modigliani and Miller put forward the idea that in the long term the cost of raising money would be the same, whether through borrowed moneys or equity moneys raised by the issue of shares. The gearing of an organization is the relationship between share capital and borrowed funds; as borrowings increase the gearing is raised. No empirical evidence has yet been found to support the Modigliani and Miller approach so the traditional view will be taken for the rest of this chapter.

Under the traditional view the weighted average cost of capital may be said to vary in relation to the gearing of the organization as shown in Figure 14.1. This indicates that the way in which an organization obtains its capital is important and financial managers should strive to obtain the level of gearing that minimizes the weighted cost of capital. Equity holders take the greatest risk, in that if the business fails they are the last to be paid and if profits are low they will receive little or no dividend. In view of this they look for a high return on their investment by way of dividends. Lenders are normally secured so that if the business fails they will recover their money; interest is a business expense that has to be paid whether or not profit is being generated, unlike dividends which can only be paid out

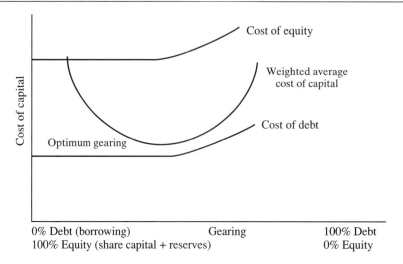

Figure 14.1   Cost of capital graph

of profits. This means that lenders are satisfied with a lower return than shareholders as they perceive that they are taking a smaller risk. This holds good as borrowing increases so far as the lenders are concerned, but the equity holders require larger and larger returns as they see increased risk that they will receive no dividends. The borrowing will reach a point at which lenders believe that there is a risk that interest payments may not be met in full and so demand a higher return on their loans. At this point the cost of borrowing and the weighted average cost of capital will both start to increase. The problem facing financial managers is to know this point and to endeavour to achieve it.

The impact of gearing on the profits that are available to the ordinary shareholders can best be illustrated as follows:

	A Company	B Company
	£	£
Share capital £1 ordinary shares	1,000,000	700,000
Loan 10 per cent debenture	400,000	700,000
Net capital employed	1,400,000	1,400,000

The two companies are employing the same net capital but A Company has relatively low gearing and B Company is relatively highly geared. Suppose now they each made the same profit of £70,000 before interest:

	£	£
Profit	70,000	70,000
Interest	40,000	70,000
Available for ordinary shareholders	30,000	NIL
Possible dividend per share	3p	NIL

The dividend per share is calculated by dividing the available profits by the numbers of shares issued. In this case it is £30,000 divided by 1,000,000 shares giving 3p per share. When profits are low there is a high risk that shareholders in highly geared organizations will receive no dividend.

If the profit before interest increases to £210,000 we have:

	£	£
Profit	210,000	210,000
Interest	40,000	70,000
Available for ordinary shareholders	170,000	140,000
Possible dividend per share	17p	20p

When profits are high, shareholders in highly geared organizations receive greater dividends because there are fewer shares to receive dividends. Dividends have an effect on share prices so those of highly geared organizations fluctuate more widely than those of less highly geared businesses. Generally, investors do not like too great a fluctuation in either earnings per share or share prices, unless they are always upwards, so financial managers aim to obtain satisfactory gearing. Another reason is that if you borrow so much that you cannot afford the interest payments you will go out of business altogether. Examples of this are Coloroll and Brent Walker and more recently Eurotunnel has faced serious problems.

The effect of gearing on the weighted average cost of capital of an organization may be illustrated by the following example of two organizations that employ the same net capital but have different structures:

Source of capital	£	Proportion of total capital %	Cost of capital %	Weighted cost of capital %
A Company				
Ordinary shares	2,000,000	41.7	12	5.00
12% Preference shares	1,000,000	20.8	12	2.50
Reserves	1,500,000	31.3	12	3.76
10% Debentures	300,000	6.2	10	0.62
	4,800,000	100.0		11.88
B Company				
Ordinary shares	1,500,000	31.3	12	3.76
12% Preference shares	1,000,000	20.8	12	2.50
Reserves	300,000	6.2	12	0.74
10% Debentures	2,000,000	41.7	10	4.17
	4,800,000	100.0		11.17

It can be seen that B Company, the more highly geared, has a lower weighted average cost of capital than A Company; 11.17 per cent as opposed to 11.88 per cent. This may not seem much but it ignores the impact of corporation tax. Interest on debenture loans is charged to profits before the liability to corporation tax is computed. Therefore, it reduces the corporation tax payable by the organization while the other sources of capital have no impact on corporation tax. If we assume that both A and B Companies are paying corporation tax at 50 per cent, then the cost of the loans to the organization (in terms of the net impact on profits) is not the 10 per cent payable to the lenders but only 5 per cent because of the tax allowance. The comparison between the two companies then becomes:

Source of capital	£	Proportion of total capital %	Cost of capital %	Weighted cost of capital %
A Company				
Ordinary shares	2,000,000	41.7	12	5.00
12% Preference shares	1,000,000	20.8	12	2.50
Reserves	1,500,000	31.3	12	3.76
10% Debentures	300,000	6.2	5	0.31
	4,800,000	100.0		11.57
B Company				
Ordinary shares	1,500,000	31.3	12	3.76
12% Preference shares	1,000,000	20.8	12	2.50
Reserves	300,000	6.2	12	0.74
10% Debentures	2,000,000	41.7	5	2.09
	4,800,000	100.0		9.09

We now have a weighted average cost of capital of 9.09 per cent for the highly geared company compared with 11.57 per cent for the company with lower gearing—a quite significant difference—and from this it can be seen that the way in which an organization obtains its funds is important.

The criteria employed in deciding whether to employ equity or borrowed funds may be said to be:

1. The effect of each option on profitability. The earnings per £1 share of equity, i.e. the after-tax profit divided by the number of ordinary shares.
2. The risk inherent in the borrowing option. Whether or not sufficient profits will be made to meet the interest charges and leave some over.
3. The effect of issuing further equity on the existing control of the organization. The holders of the greatest number of ordinary voting shares, i.e. in excess of 50 per cent, have control.
4. The effect of issuing further equity on the asset value per share. Issuing more shares generally reduces the asset value per share as the assets do not normally increase proportionally at once.

The decision will be made as a balancing of these factors together with what the markets will allow the business to do.

SELF-TEST QUESTIONS

1. How does the Modigliani and Miller approach differ from the classical approach to the cost of financing the firm?
2. How is the weighted average cost of capital calculated?
3. State with reasons whether you would prefer to hold shares in a highly geared company or one with lower gearing at a time of increasing profitability.
4. How would you calculate the impact of the 'tax shield' on interest charges?

QUESTIONS

14.1 An extract from Slim Plc balance sheet shows:

		£
Share capital		
500,000 £1 ordinary shares		500,000
Reserves		400,000
		900,000

The company is financed entirely by equity capital and has just paid a dividend for the year of 50p per share, a level which it is expected to maintain indefinitely. The current market value of a share is £2.50.

An opportunity has now arisen which, for an investment of £500,000 in plant and equipment, would increase the company's annual net cash flow by £200,000. To fund this expansion the directors propose to issue £500,000 18 per cent debenture stock. The interest on this stock has not been deducted in arriving at the net cash flow of £200,000 above. Although the expansion would not alter the business (or operating) risk it is anticipated that the increased financial risk to the ordinary shares would cause their required rate of return to rise to 25 per cent.

Required
1. Calculate whether the expansion should be accepted.
2. Discuss the implications of the above in relation to the proposed capital structure.

14.2 Evans Plc is estimated to have a current cost of capital of 17.27 per cent per annum which has been computed from the following figures:

	Market value	*Cost*
Equity	£10,000,000	18 per cent
Debt	£ 1,000,000	10 per cent
	Weighted average 17.27 per cent	

The Managing Director argues that the overall cost of capital could be sharply reduced by increasing the amount of debt employed. Discuss using simple illustrations to clarify your argument.

Your answer should include a graphical comparison of the 'traditional view' and the 'Modigliani/Miller theory'.

FIFTEEN

MANAGEMENT OF WORKING CAPITAL

OBJECTIVE

To provide an understanding of the importance of working capital and the dangers of 'overtrading'.

At the end of this chapter you will be able to explain:

1. The difference between liquidity and profitability
2. The working capital cycle.
3. The importance of stock control
4. The danger inherent in having too little working capital

The working capital of an organization is invested in its stock, debtors and cash. Working capital is calculated as current assets minus current liabilities and its management is highly significant to the survival of any organization. Of the organizations that fail in the UK, 75–80 per cent are profitable at the time that they do so. The problem stems from the fact that the relationship between cash flow and profitability is not fully understood. It may best be illustrated through the following example.

Example

Mr Brown of B Ltd started his financial year in an optimistic frame of mind. He manufactured cheap kitchen aids for which there was a buoyant demand. He sold them for £4 and manufactured them for £3 each. Stock was kept at 30 days, he paid his bills promptly and billed his customers on the basis of 30 days net. Sales were as expected with steady increases predicted and things began well.

1 April	Cash £28,000	Stock £12,000	Debtors £4,000

In April he made and sold 4,000 aids, dispatched them at a cost of £12,000 and collected the money due to him (receivables). He made £4,000 profit and his books showed:

1 May	Cash £20,000	Stock £12,000	Debtors £16,000

In May sales jumped as expected to 6,000 units. Production was increased to maintain the 30-day stock. He made 8,000 units at a cost of £24,000. The money due for the April sales was received. Total profit for the two months £10,000 (£6,000 + £4,000) and his books now showed:

1 June   Cash £12,000   Stock £18,000   Debtors £18,000

June sales increased even more to 8,000 units. He collected the money due to him on time and to maintain the 30-day stock policy 10,000 units were produced. Profit for the month was £8,000 making the total to date £18,000. The books showed:

1 July   Cash £6,000   Stock £24,000   Debtors £32,000

July sales continued the increase to 10,000 units. He collected the money due to him on time and to maintain the 30-day stock policy 12,000 units were produced. Profit for the month was £10,000 making the total to date £28,000. The books showed:

1 August   Cash £2,000   Stock £30,000   Debtors £40,000

August sales increased to 12,000 units. He collected the money due to him on time and produced 14,000 units to maintain the 30-day stock policy. Profit for the month was £12,000 making the total to date £40,000. The books showed:

1 September   Cash £0   Stock £36,000   Debtors £48,000

Calculations are shown below:

Balance of stock expressed in £

	April £	May £	June £	July £	August £
Opening	12,000	12,000	18,000	24,000	30,000
Made	12,000	24,000	30,000	36,000	42,000
	24,000	36,000	48,000	60,000	72,000
Sold	12,000	18,000	24,000	30,000	36,000
Closing	12,000	18,000	24,000	30,000	36,000

Cash statement

	April £	May £	June £	July £	August £
Opening balance	28,000	20,000	12,000	6,000	2,000
Add Receipts from sales	4,000	16,000	24,000	32,000	40,000
	32,000	36,000	36,000	38,000	42,000
Deduct Manufacturing/ distribution costs	12,000	24,000	30,000	36,000	42,000
Balance c/fwd	20,000	12,000	6,000	2,000	0

As can be seen, the business is overtrading which results in the cash balance being reduced from £28,000 to £0 between April and the end of August. Drastic action is required to control the working capital and prevent the business going into liquidation.

The working capital needs of a business can be illustrated as a cycle since it represents a net investment in short-term assets which are essential to pay for day-to-day operations; and are continually flowing into and out of the organization. Thus we have the working capital cycle (Figure 15.1).

Generally speaking the faster the money flows through the cycle the better since it minimizes the amount required in working capital. The cycle has been reduced by many organizations in recent years through the introduction of the Just in Time system of stock control. This, as has been previously discussed, involves the holding of little or no stock at all. The working capital cycle can be calculated in the following way:

Hughs Plc, a manufacturer of board games, has the following items of working capital for a year during which sales were £100,000 and the cost of sales £60,000.

	1 September	31 August
Stock of finished goods	£11,000	£13,000
Debtors	£6,000	£8,000
Creditors	£7,000	£9,000

Firstly we calculate the number of times each of the items is turned over in the year.

$$\text{Finished stock turnover} = \frac{\text{Cost of sales}}{\text{Average stock of FG}} = \frac{60,000}{12,000} = 5 \text{ times}$$

$$\text{Debtors' turnover} = \frac{\text{Sales}}{\text{Average debtors}} = \frac{100,000}{7,000} = 14.3 \text{ times}$$

$$\text{Creditors' turnover} = \frac{\text{Cost of sales}}{\text{Average creditors}} = \frac{60,000}{8,000} = 7.5 \text{ times}$$

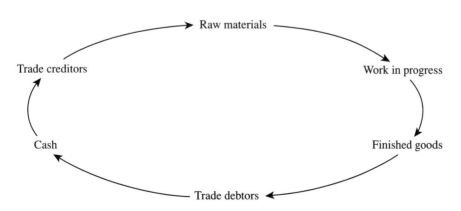

Figure 15.1 Working capital cycle

Secondly we divide the answer into 365 to give the average number of days for which each item is held.

$$\text{Stock of finished goods} = \frac{365}{5} = 73 \text{ days}$$

$$\text{Debtors} = \frac{365}{14.3} = 25.5 \text{ days}$$

$\left.\begin{array}{c}\\\\\end{array}\right\}$ 98.5 days

$$\text{Creditors} = \frac{365}{7.5} = \qquad 48.7 \text{ days}$$

$$\text{Cash operating cycle} = \qquad 49.8 \text{ days}$$

The cash operating cycle is given by adding the stock days and debtor days together and then subtracting the creditor days. This is because the creditors effectively allow us to save cash. In order to speed up the cycle we turn the stock over faster, i.e. sell it more quickly; collect the money from our customers faster, i.e. extend less credit; or pay our suppliers more slowly, i.e. take more credit. We may in fact adjust each of the items to ensure that the working capital cycle is minimized.

The less money organizations have tied up in stock and debtors the better, but the economic climate makes it difficult to keep these items down as far as most businesses would wish. Stock levels during the 1980s fell as the result of destocking brought about by the recession so there is less working capital tied up here than was previously the case. Unfortunately the same is not true of debtors. In the 1990s, businesses, desperate to obtain sales in a highly competitive environment, have been forced to extend credit facilities to customers. This as we have seen gives rise to cash flow problems. One way of dealing with this is to use the services of a factor as mentioned previously on page 4. This enables quicker collection of a large percentage of the money due so that it can be used in running the business. The service has to be paid for but is worth its weight in gold for many organizations.

SELF-TEST QUESTIONS

1. Illustrate the working capital cycle for a manufacturing business.
2. Why is the working capital cycle important?
3. What is 'overtrading'?
4. How can the danger of overtrading be minimized?

QUESTION

15.1 Lump Ltd manufactures lapel badges using a machine that turns out 2 million badges in a working year of 2,500 hours, i.e. 6,400 in an eight-hour working day or 800 per hour. Raw material costs are estimated at 5 pence per unit and the total cost is 20 pence per unit. The badges sell for 25 pence each.

The following is the projected balance sheet for the end of the year.

	£		£
Fixed assets			58,000
Current assets:			
Stock raw material	9,000	(i)	
Stock finished goods	42,000	(ii)	
Debtors	36,000	(iii)	
	87,000		
Less Current liabilities:			
Creditors	6,000	(iv)	
			81,000
			139,000
Share capital			110,000
Reserves			29,000
			139,000

Using the above information calculate the working capital cycle for Lump Ltd.

SIXTEEN

CHANGING PRICE LEVELS

OBJECTIVE

To provide an understanding of the impact of inflation on reported profits and the balance sheet. The main areas on which inflation has an effect and the steps that can be taken to correct the situation are explained.

At the end of this chapter you will be able to explain:

1. The gearing adjustment
2. The depreciation adjustment
3. The cost of sales adjustment
4. The Hyde approach

During the late 1980s and early 1990s a great deal has been written about the impact of changing price levels on company profits and liquidity. The accounting bodies as well as individuals have suggested methods of dealing with the problem but no method has been officially recognized by the government. Many organizations carried current cost accounts in their annual report alongside the traditional historical cost reports. In recent years inflation has been kept well under control so that the impact on reported profits is much less significant than it was and it is on the historical cost accounts that organizations are taxed. In this chapter the Hyde approach to dealing with changing price levels will be discussed and the impact of inflation on profits and liquidity illustrated.

16.1 INFLATION

Inflation has its greatest impact in three main areas, they are:

1. Stock value.
2. Borrowing referred to as gearing. The higher the borrowing the greater the gearing.
3. Replacement costs of assets in the balance sheet and through them the charge for depreciation.

Stock value

Changes in stock value are recorded in the cost of sales adjustment calculated by the average method.

(a) Cost of sales calculated on the historical cost basis:

	£'000s
Opening stock	350
Add Stock purchased	2,300
	2,650
Deduct Closing stock	540
Cost of sales historical basis	2,110

Index numbers for cost of stock:

Start of period	100
End of period	120
Average	110

These numbers would be obtained from an index relevant to the organization such as the Retail Price Index.

(b) Revise the opening and closing stock to the average current cost for the year, that is 110:

$$\text{Opening stock } 350 \times \frac{110}{100} = 385$$

$$\text{Closing stock } 540 \times \frac{110}{120} = 495$$

This has the effect of increasing the value of the opening stock and reducing the value of the closing stock to allow for the inflationary impact.

(c) Calculate the current cost of sales using the figures that have just been calculated:

	£'000s
Opening stock	385
Add Stock purchased	2,300
	2,685
Deduct Closing stock	495
Cost of sales current cost	2,190

You will see that when the inflationary element is adjusted, the cost of sales increases by £80,000. That is to say, the gross profit was previously overstated by that sum and the cost of sales adjustment is:

	£'000s
Cost of sales current cost basis	2,190
Cost of sales historical cost basis	2,110
Cost of sales adjustment	80

If the sales had been £4,000; gross profit would be:

	£'000s
Historical cost basis	
Sales	4,000
Cost of sales	2,110
Gross profit	1,890
Current cost basis	
Sales	4,000
Cost of sales	2,190
Gross profit	1,810

It could be argued that by ignoring the cost of sales adjustment the Inland Revenue is taxing the organization on £80,000 too much profit. The profit is being overstated in real terms by £80,000.

Gearing

Where the total liabilities exceed the total monetary assets after the fixed assets and stock have been adjusted for the difference between current values and historical costs, using a company balance sheet in which the total liabilities are:

	£'000s
Equity share capital plus reserves	684
Long-term liabilities	350
Current liabilities	406
	1,440
Fixed assets	600
Stock	540
Monetary assets (e.g. debtors and cash)	300
	1,440

The table is a balance sheet in vertical form of a hypothetical organization; it could just as easily be shown as:

Assets	£'000s	Liabilities	£'000s
Fixed assets	600	Equity share capital and reserves	684
Stocks	540	Long-term liabilities	350
Monetary assets	300	Current liabilities	406
	1,440		1,440

(a) The net balance of monetary liabilities is calculated as:

	£'000s
Long-term liabilities	350
Current liabilities	406
	756
Deduct Monetary assets	300
Net balance of monetary liabilities to outside interests	456

(b) The net balance of monetary liabilities plus equity share capital plus reserves is in this case:

	£'000s
Net balance of monetary liabilities	456
Add Equity share capital and reserves	684
	1,140

(c) The gearing proportion, designed to reduce the benefit organizations derive from net borrowings in times of inflation, is then shown to be:

	£'000s
Net balance of monetary liabilities	456
Divided by the net balance of monetary liabilities plus equity share capital and reserves	1,140
Expressed in percentage terms to calculate the gearing proportion we have	

$$\frac{456 \times 100}{1,140} = 40 \text{ per cent}$$

The cost of sales adjustment and the depreciation adjustment, which we have yet to calculate, work in favour of the organization as they reduce the reported profit on which tax has to be paid. This is because inflation works to overstate the profits made when accounts are prepared on the basis of historical costs. The gearing adjustment works the other way since the benefits derived by organizations that borrow in times of inflation are not shown in accounts that have been prepared on an historical cost basis. This is compensated for by the gearing adjustment which tends to increase profits reported on the historical cost basis.

Depreciation

The depreciation adjustment is calculated in the following way:

(a) From the hypothetical balance sheet we have fixed assets of £600,000 shown at cost.
(b) The replacement cost of the assets is obtained by pricing them (or their nearest equivalent) at today's costs. It may be that they would cost £1,300,000 to replace. That is to say that they are undervalued in the balance sheet on the replacement cost basis by £700,000.
(c) The depreciation adjustment is calculated as illustrated

	£'000s
Fixed assets on historical cost basis	600
Fixed assets on replacement cost basis	1,300
	700

Depreciation on additional value at 10 per cent (or whatever the appropriate rate of depreciation is for the assets in question)

$$\frac{10}{100} \times 700{,}000 = £70{,}000$$

This shows that the profits have been overstated by £70,000, because of the inflationary impact on the fixed assets, and by £80,000, because of the impact on stocks. Reported profits for tax purposes would be reduced by both these sums. The gearing adjustment works the other way and is, therefore, used to reduce the benefit gained from the stock and depreciation adjustment.

Gearing adjustment	£'000s
Depreciation adjustment	70
Cost of sales adjustment	80
	150
Multiply by gearing proportion	40%
Gearing adjustment	60

The overall impact on the profit of an organization can be illustrated as:

	£'000s	£'000s
Profit before tax		355
Less Adjustments:		
Depreciation	70	
Cost of sales	80	150
		205
Add Gearing adjustment		60
Adjusted profit before tax		265

This shows that many organizations are being taxed on inflated rather than on true economic profits but no agreement has yet been reached on what should be done about it.

The impact of inflation on the liquidity of an organization should never be ignored. It is highlighted in the following example which gives a good impression of its effect:

Example *1986–96 10 years of rising prices*

Balance sheet: 1 January

	Cost £000s	Depn £000s	1986 £000s	1996 £000s		1986 £000s	1996 £000s
Factory	100	—	100		Capital	300	
Plant	300	150	150		Reserves	100	
Vehicles	200	100	100		Debentures	100	
	600	250	350			500	
Stock		200			Creditors	113	
Debtors		100			Taxation provision	21	
Cash		5	305		Dividend provision	21	
					Bank overdraft	—	
		655				655	

Information 1986–96   General

Indices of capital replacement costs

	January 1986	*January 1996*	*Increase %*
Industrial buildings	336	508	51
Industrial plant	377	549	46
Commercial vehicles	293	404	38

Retail Price Index—increase 50 per cent (approx.)

Information 1986–96   Specific to above company
Depreciation of plant—straight line basis with estimated life of 10 years.
Depreciation of vehicles—straight line basis with estimated life of 5 years, i.e. plant replaced once, vehicles replaced twice during the decade.

Profit 1986   (10 per cent on capital employed)   50
Corporation tax 42.5 per cent   21.25
‾‾‾‾
28.75
Dividend 7 per cent   21.00 (cover 1.4)
‾‾‾‾
Retained profits   7.75
‾‾‾‾

Assumptions
1. Corporation tax levied at 42.5 per cent throughout the decade.
2. Stock costs rose at similar rate to Index of Retail Prices.
3. Company raised its prices at a similar rate, i.e. maintained the real value of its profits.
4. Dividends raised at same rate.

Required:
Trace the effects of rising prices on the company in the above model in which the physical level of activity remains constant throughout the ten-year period. The only change occurring is the change in prices.

How has the liquid position of the company changed? Approximate where necessary.

SOLUTION *1986–96   10 years of rising prices*

Balance sheet: 1 January

	Cost £000s	Depn £000s	1986 £000s	1996 £000s		1986 £000s	1996 £000s
Factory	100	—	100	100	Capital	300	300
Plant	300	150	150	219	Reserves	100	196
Vehicles	200	100	100	138	Debentures	100	100
	‾‾‾	‾‾‾	‾‾‾	‾‾‾		‾‾‾	‾‾‾
	600	250	350	457		500	596
	‾‾‾	‾‾‾					
Stock		200		300	Creditors	113	169.5
Debtors		100		150	Taxation provision	21	31.5
Cash		5	305	7.5	Dividend provision	21	31.5
		‾‾‾			Bank overdraft	—	86
			‾‾‾	‾‾‾		‾‾‾	‾‾‾
			655	914.5		655	914.5

SOLUTION (shown above) is derived as follows:

Factory   As this has not been replaced in the period, there is no change and so remains at £100,000.

Plant   This was five years old in 1986 and so will have been replaced. The effect is to increase its cost by 46 per cent to £219,000.

Vehicles   These were half-way through their life in 1986 and will have been replaced. The effect is to increase their cost by 38 per cent to £138,000.

Stock   Constantly replaced. The effect is to increase its value to £300,000, i.e. 50 per cent.

Debtors   Constantly replaced. The effect is to increase their value to £150,000, i.e. 50 per cent.

Cash Always circulating. Its value is increased to £7,500 from £5,000; £305,000 is the total of current assets in 1986.

Capital This will not have been replaced in the period and remains at £300,000.

Reserves These will be constantly increasing by the retained profits. The retentions may be roughly calculated as follows:

	1986 £'000s		1996 £'000s
Profit (10 per cent on capital employed)	50	50% inc.	75
Less Corporation tax 42.5 per cent	21.25	50% inc.	31.875
	28.75		43.125
Dividend 7 per cent	21	50% Inc.	31.5
Retained profits	7.75		11.625

The difference in the retained profits is £3,875; 50 per cent of the difference is £1,937.50. If £1,937.50 is deducted from the new retained profits of £11,625 it gives a rough average increase of £9,600 per annum, which over ten years becomes £96,000 and makes the reserves £100,000 + £96,000 = £196,000.

Debentures These have not been replaced and so remain constant at £100,000.

Creditors Constantly renewed. The effect is to increase their value to £169,500, i.e. by 50 per cent.

Taxation provision Constantly updated and so increased by the change in the Retail Price Index of 50 per cent to £31,500.

Dividend provision Constantly updated and so increased by 50 per cent to £31,500.

Bank overdraft This is put in as a balancing figure. It can be seen that the cash balance has changed from £5,000 in hand to a bank overdraft figure of £86,000. The liquidity of an apparently successful company has been reduced by £91,000 by the effect of inflation. This helps to explain why so many organizations are suffering with liquidity problems.

16.2 PROBLEMS CREATED FOR FINANCIAL MANAGERS

Having examined the adjustments caused by inflation we can investigate some of the problems created for financial managers. We will do this by discussing the three main areas.

Stock value

Changes in the value of stock make it difficult to arrive at the charge that should be made against income for the stock that has been used in achieving that income. When too small a charge is made, profits are overstated and too much may be withdrawn from the business by way of dividends, making it hard for the company to maintain its trading position when stocks have to be replaced.

Take an organization that has sales of £100,000 and profits of £10,000. It could be tempted, if it had enough cash, to distribute £8,000 of the £10,000 profit. This may be reasonable in some circumstances, but what if the cost of goods sold calculation (that is opening stock + purchases − closing stock) resulted in a charge of £10,000 while the cost of replacing those goods sold was £15,000. Profit should be reduced by half to £5,000 and the owners persuaded to take far less out of the business or it will not be possible for the organization to purchase enough stock to meet demands for the goods. The financial manager has to tread a careful line between being overcautious and allowing the business to fail through an inability to compete in the market place. Good communication skills are essential to the accountant/manager who has to make others understand the problem and cooperate in overcoming it.

Gearing

The problem for the financial manager is not only in arriving at the optimum level of borrowing to minimize costs but also in the maintenance of sufficient cash flow. Should decisions be taken to maximize borrowing when times are good, then a combination of inflation and poor trading conditions can cause insurmountable problems. In a stable environment an organization could be making profits regularly in the region of £200,000 and generating cash flow of £250,000. This could enable borrowings of £500,000 and interest payments of £50,000 to be easily supported. Changed conditions might cause profits to fall to £150,000 but inflation and the need to extend credit in order to maintain sales in a highly competitive market would have far greater impact on cash generated and could reduce it to £70,000. This would make it difficult for the business to survive, as insufficient money would be available to meet its expenses including interest on borrowing. The financial manager has some very difficult problems to overcome in trying to allow the business to expand while at the same time endeavouring to ensure that it is not vulnerable when conditions change.

Fixed assets

Changes in the value of fixed assets cause problems in arriving at the charge that should be included in each financial period for their use. This charge is made through depreciation and in times of inflation it is all too easy to under-depreciate which gives rise to problems of cash flow. The financial manager is in a quandary as he or she has to conform with the principle of consistency while at the same time ensuring that a sufficiently large charge is made for depreciation. One way of doing this is to create reserves which reduce profit and by so doing lower the amount available for distribution to the owners of the business.

To make this possible the rest of the management team has to be convinced that the transfer to reserves is a sensible thing to do and not just more trickery on the accountant's behalf. The impact on the business and on the individuals concerned of failing to do so must be clearly explained. This should help to secure cooperation and one way of doing this may be to explain the problem this way:

Asset cost end 1991 £12,000, life ten years, estimated scrap value £2,000
Book value end 1996 £7,000, replacement cost end 1996 £15,000
Total depreciation to date £5,000
Book value end 2001 £2,000, estimated replacement cost end 2001 £18,000
Total depreciation £10,000

In 2001 the organization will need to find £16,000 to replace the asset. That is the replacement cost of £18,000 less the scrap value of £2,000 but it will only have retained profits of £10,000 through depreciation provision. The depreciation will have helped to strengthen the business but it is doubtful if it will have done so sufficiently for it to generate the cash flow of £16,000 required. The financial manager has somehow to make up that shortfall, either by borrowing or else by internally generated funds. The best way of doing so is by using the business's own resources, but for this to be possible sufficient profits must be retained and not distributed by way of dividends or otherwise. This may be done by transferring an additional £1,200 to reserves in each of the years 1997 to 2001. The cooperation of all concerned must be obtained before anything of this nature can be achieved.

SELF-TEST QUESTIONS

1. Why is there no longer an urgent need to adjust accounts for inflation?
2. How is the net balance of monetary liabilities calculated?
3. Where would you go to find index numbers for the retail trade?
4. How is the gearing proportion calculated?

SEVENTEEN

PRICING

OBJECTIVE

To provide an understanding of pricing, the strategies that can be adopted and their likely impact on profits.

At the end of this chapter you will be able to explain:

1. Pricing strategies
2. Market skimming
3. Market penetration
4. Product pricing

The pricing decision is one of the most important made by the firm in that if you get it right the firm will prosper and grow; get it wrong and the business will fail. The decision is a complex one that cannot be made in isolation because the price competitors charge for similar products will affect the price that you are able to charge for your product. This holds good for all organizations unless they are in the happy position of having a monopoly when competitors do not exist. Even then the producer cannot charge what it likes as much will depend on whether the good is essential or a luxury and, if it is essential, ethical considerations will have to be taken into account. The price elasticity of demand is also important in that for some products small price changes result in large changes in demand while for others larger price changes bring little or no change in demand.

In pricing a product it is a good idea to avoid becoming involved in a price war with your competitor(s) unless the strategy has been carefully thought through and you are confident of your strengths. This is because price wars invariably lead to a fall in profits and usually result in casualties through redundancies, restructuring and sometimes bankruptcy. They can lead to a period of profitless prosperity as happened to the supermarkets in the UK. For example if the margin on goods is 10 per cent and you turn them over 5 times in a year you will make 5 × 10 per cent = 50 per cent. A price war breaks out and the margin is reduced to 0.05 per cent and the goods are turned over 30 times in a year you will make 30 × 0.05 per cent = 1.5 per cent, a drop of 48.5 per cent. This is a situation that nobody would want to last for too long a period but price wars have been successfully pursued over a number of years by large organizations such as Caterpillar.

Price is regarded by many to be a guide to quality so that if you bring your product to the market at too low a price the public will often shun it as they do not want to be seen to be buying shoddy goods. An example of this is the 'After Eight mint' which was first brought to the market unpackaged and at the lower end of the price range with disastrous effect. It was perceived to be a poor product which was the reason for its low price. The company withdrew the product from the market and repositioned it through good packaging and an effective marketing campaign with the result that it sold extremely well on its reintroduction as a quality product.

Your organization has come to the market with a new product that is protected by patents and has the following costs per unit:

	£
Labour	20
Materials	40
Overheads	100

What options are open to you in pricing the product? Presumably you are in business to make a profit (the primary objective of the firm is to maximize shareholders' wealth) so you will charge more than £160. There are two main strategies available to you and you have to decide which is the more appropriate.

17.1 MARKET SKIMMING

Here you set as high a price as possible to allow you to profit by skimming the luxury end of the market and then gradually reduce the price so that each segment of the market is skimmed in turn. An example of an organization that used this approach is Biro. When it invented the ballpoint it brought it out at an extremely high price and skimmed the top of the market and gradually reduced its price over the years until the patents ran out. Now there are innumerable competitors and the product is keenly priced in each market sector with ballpoint pens available in each price range. This can only be successfully carried out when there is sufficient demand in each market segment to make the approach profitable.

17.2 MARKET PENETRATION

The objective of this approach is to set a price that is low enough to capture a large market share in as short a time as possible. This is the policy of the discount stores that have recently arrived from America but there is a danger that the low price will be perceived to mean that the product or service is of a poor quality. This strategy can be extremely effective but for it to work successfully price sensitivity of demand is essential and the competition must be deterred by the low price.

What if your product is not covered by patents and similar products already exist in the market? You will still have to charge more than £160 or you will not make a profit and then decide on the strategy that you are to follow. There are nine strategies that are available to you and they can be ranked on price and quality as shown in the grid below. You could have a high quality product and charge a high price or at the other extreme low quality for which a low price is asked. The strategy chosen will depend on you and the business in which you are operating.

			PRICE		
			High	Medium	Low
P Q R U O A D L U I C T T Y		High	Premium	High value	Excellent value
		Medium	Overcharging	Medium value	Good value
		Low	Conning	Apparent value	Economy

Once a product has been priced it does not mean that the price has to remain unchanged for the whole of its life cycle. Circumstances alter and when they do different strategies can be adopted to take account of the new environment in which the business is operating. It may be felt necessary to cut prices because there is excess capacity and the organization has to generate more business, or aggressive pricing by competitors could be causing loss of market share. Rising costs can lead to price increases and although they may be resented by customers in the short term, many lost customers are recovered over a period of time. Over-demand can also lead to price increases as a way of regulating the sales of the product but the organization has to avoid pricing the product out of the market altogether.

Pricing then is extremely important to all organizations and many factors impinge on the decision. It is generally not a good idea to price a product at below cost unless it is part of a carefully thought out strategy that usually lasts a short time. Since price is a guide to quality, price increases can sometimes lead to increased sales and profits while reductions lead to reduced sales and profits. This is by no means always the case and each price must be reached after careful research and planning as part of the total business strategy.

SELF-TEST QUESTIONS

1. Why is pricing important?
2. How would you go about pricing a new product protected by a patent?
3. How would you go about pricing a new product that was not protected by a patent?
4. What might cause a firm to reduce the price of its product?

QUESTIONS

17.1 An organization employs cost-plus pricing to arrive at the cost of its products. Using the following information calculate the price to be charged for each unit of its product.

Total fixed costs	£600,000	Variable cost per unit £30	
Anticipated sales	60,000 units	The company wants a 25 per cent mark-up	

17.2 A firm wishes to employ break-even pricing. Using the information given in question 17.1 calculate the number of units that would have to be sold if the business wished to break even.

17.3 In a normal competitive market what is the main factor that influences the charges an organization can make for its goods or services?

EIGHTEEN
PERFORMANCE ANALYSIS

OBJECTIVE

To provide an understanding of the ways in which financial information can be organized in order to make it more useful to management.

At the end of this chapter you will be able to:

1. Employ financial information to aid decisions
2. Explain the ratio tree
3. Use the operating level ratios
4. Explain the purpose of the supporting ratios
5. Explain the importance of the debtors' ratio

In Chapter 4 we looked at some of the ways in which financial information can be used and interpreted by managers. This will be put on a more formalized basis in this chapter with the introduction of a 'ratio tree' for the manufacturing industry (Figure 18.1)

The ratio tree can be used as a useful diagnostic tool. If your primary ratio of operating profit to net capital employed is giving the desired return of, say, 18 per cent then there is no need for any investigation. If, on the other hand, the return is 5 per cent when 18 per cent was expected, something has gone seriously wrong and further investigation is necessary. The supporting ratios will be explored next to see if either or both are giving unexpected results. When the ratio of operating profit to sales is satisfactory it is not necessary to investigate any of the ratios that lead up to it, that is (3-1), (3-2), (3-3), (4-1), (4-2), (4-3), (4-4); should the ratio of sales to net assets employed figure be unsatisfactory then ratio (3-4) will be calculated. If it is unsatisfactory, attention will have to be concentrated on sales as little can be done with fixed capital in the short term. It may be that sales have fallen dramatically so that a drive is necessary to build them up or, if the product mix is wrong, it may be necessary to market an entirely new product. Should the sales to fixed capital ratio be unsatisfactory, then the sales to working capital ratio will be calculated, followed by the ratios (4-5), (4-6), (4-7), (4-8) and (4-9), whichever of the ratios

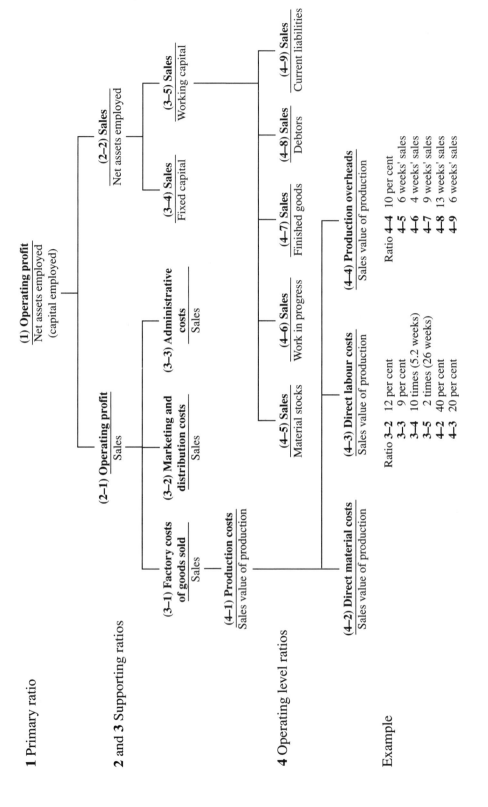

Figure 18.1 Accounting ratios manufacturing industry (ratio tree)

(3-2) $\dfrac{\text{Marketing and distribution costs} \times 100}{\text{Sales}} = $ Percentage of sales

(3-3) $\dfrac{\text{Admin. costs} \times 100}{\text{Sales}} = $ Percentage of sales

(3-4) $\dfrac{\text{Sales}}{\text{Fixed capital}} = $ Times turned over $\qquad \dfrac{52 \text{ weeks}}{\text{Times turned over}} = $ Weeks to turn over the fixed capital

(3-5) $\dfrac{\text{Sales}}{\text{Working capital}} = $ Times turned over $\qquad \dfrac{52 \text{ weeks}}{\text{Times turned over}} = $ Weeks to turn over the working capital

(4-2) $\dfrac{\text{Direct material costs} \times 100}{\text{Sales value of production}} = $ Percentage of the sales value of production made up of the direct material costs

(4-3) $\dfrac{\text{Direct labour costs} \times 100}{\text{Sales value of production}} = $ Percentage of the sales value of production made up of the direct labour costs

(4-4) $\dfrac{\text{Production overheads} \times 100}{\text{Sales value of production}} = $ Percentage of the sales value of production made up of the production overheads

(4-5) $\dfrac{\text{Sales}}{\text{Material stocks}} = $ Times material stocks are turned over $\qquad \dfrac{52 \text{ weeks}}{\text{Times turned over}} = $ Weeks' sales held in stock

(4-6) $\dfrac{\text{Sales}}{\text{Work in progress}} = $ Times work in progress turned over $\qquad \dfrac{52 \text{ weeks}}{\text{Times turned over}} = $ Weeks' sales held in WIP

(4-7) $\dfrac{\text{Sales}}{\text{Finished goods}} = $ Times finished goods are turned over $\qquad \dfrac{52 \text{ weeks}}{\text{Times turned over}} = $ Weeks' sales held in finished goods

(4-8) $\dfrac{\text{Sales}}{\text{Debtors}} = $ Times debtors turned over $\qquad \dfrac{52 \text{ weeks}}{\text{Times turned over}} = $ Weeks taken to collect money from your customers

(4-9) $\dfrac{\text{Sales}}{\text{Current liabilities}} = $ Times current liabilities turned over $\qquad \dfrac{52 \text{ weeks}}{\text{Times turned over}} = $ Weeks taken to cover your current liabilities in sales

are showing warning signals. Once the cause of the problem has been discovered the action necessary to correct it can be instigated or, if that is not possible, the business may have to be sold.

If, on the other hand, the problem is shown to be on the operating profit to sales side of the tree then the investigation will follow the ratios (3-1), (3-2), (3-3) and if these do not explain the cause of the problem the operating level ratios (4-1), (4-2), (4-3) and (4-4) will be calculated. This should reveal the cause of the problem and enable corrective action to be taken. The example at the foot of the tree illustrates the terms in which the ratios are expressed. It is *not* a guide to the magnitude of the ratio. No such guide can be issued as each sector has its own rule of thumb measure. Tracing the ratios through we see that they are expressed in the terms shown on p. 147.

SELF-TEST QUESTIONS

1. How is the primary ratio calculated and what is its importance?
2. Why are ratios important (a) to management (b) to employees and (c) to investors?
3. Why are some ratios expressed as percentages and others as weeks?
4. Which are the balance sheet ratios?
5. Why do ratios have little or no value when considered in isolation?

QUESTIONS

18.1 Electronic Appliances Ltd

Mr Wright, the Managing Director of Electronic Appliances Ltd, manufacturers of electronic control equipment, is reviewing the progress of his company which he established ten years ago in London. It is a public company and he has plans to obtain a Stock Exchange quotation in about two years' time. In view of this Mr Wright believes he should increase his dividend as much as possible; no interim dividends are paid, only the final dividend.

He is an inventive man, and a first-class engineer. He has an excellent and rapidly growing development and design department, and in the last three years he has produced some very sophisticated equipment. This increase in range has not only been through increasing the size range of each item, but also the number of new items now is four times what it was three years ago. He prides himself that his company could design almost anything of the highest quality that a customer would require in electronic controls. This viewpoint is well founded, for the company has a high reputation for inventive skills and is often consulted by private and government agencies.

His sales force has more than doubled over the last three years, and he now has seven technical representatives covering the UK and abroad. His customers are widely spread, both geographically and in the range of industries served.

His manufacturing plant is becoming very efficient, and two years ago a high degree of automation was introduced into the factory. He has doubled the output of his company but has only increased his total staff by 50 per cent over the last three years. The stock figures in the balance sheet represent materials, components and bought out sub-assemblies; none represents finished work.

Yet despite all this success his bank manager, who has just received the company's latest profit and loss account and balance sheet, has asked Mr Wright to call at the bank at 4.00 pm on Wednesday 12 March, as the bank is seriously concerned with the state of his company, and requires a substantial reduction in the overdraft, which has now risen to £180,000 at close of bank business on Monday 10 March. In September last year the overdraft limit was raised from £100,000 to £160,000.

The accounts and operating data of Electronic Appliances Ltd for the last three years of operation are shown on pages 149–153. Analyse these figures and relate them to the above information known about the company and its Managing Director.

1. Assume you are Mr Wright and marshal the facts, figures, plans and ideas in the most favourable light to persuade the bank to keep (or even raise) the current overdraft limits.
2. Assume you are the bank manager and critically assess the company's performance before deciding what action you believe is appropriate.

Electronic Appliances Ltd
Balance sheet—31 December 1995

CAPITAL EMPLOYED	£	£	£
Issued capital and reserves			
340,000 50p ordinary shares			170,000
General reserves			300,000
Share premium account			30,327
Balance profit and loss account			30,217
			530,544
EMPLOYMENT OF CAPITAL			
Fixed assets:			
Buildings		182,054	
Plant		120,265	
Vehicles		8,162	310,481
Current assets:			
Work in progress	106,203		
Stocks of finished goods	71,019		
Debtors	105,001		
Bank	1,050	283,273	
Current liabilities:			
Creditors	32,546		
Tax	30,664	63,210	220,063
			530,544

Electronic Appliances Ltd
Balance sheet—31 December 1996

CAPITAL EMPLOYED	£	£	£
Issued capital and reserves			
540,000 50p ordinary shares			270,000
Share premium account			405,000
General reserves			300,000
Balance profit and loss account			51,018
			1,026,018
EMPLOYMENT OF CAPITAL			
Fixed assets:			
Buildings		215,056	
Plant		463,472	
Vehicles		9,890	688,418
Current assets:			
Work in progress	176,321		
Stocks of finished goods	110,984		
Debtors	154,968		
Bank	1,283	443,556	
Current liabilities:			
Creditors	43,625		
Tax	35,331		
Dividends 10 per cent	27,000	105,956	337,600
			1,026,018

Electronic Appliances Ltd
Balance sheet—31 December 1997

CAPITAL EMPLOYED	£	£	£
Issued capital and reserves			
540,000 50p ordinary shares			270,000
Share premium account			405,000
General reserves			300,000
Profit and loss account			60,643
			1,035,643
EMPLOYMENT OF CAPITAL			
Fixed assets:			
Buildings		235,125	
Plant		456,684	
Vehicles		11,034	702,843
Current assets:			
Work in progress	246,105		
Stocks of finished goods	171,864		
Debtors	216,031	634,000	
Current liabilities:			
Creditors	53,201		
Tax	44,852		
Dividends 15 per cent	40,500		
Bank overdraft	162,647	301,200	332,800
			1,035,643

Profit and loss account for year ended 31 December

	1995 £	1995 £	1996 £	1996 £	1997 £	1997 £
SALES		500,607		699,231		899,698
PRODUCTION COSTS—DIRECT						
Materials	115,321		153,875		186,436	
Labour	70,653		87,487		103,502	
		185,974		241,362		289,938
PRODUCTION COSTS—INDIRECT						
Salaries	27,000		31,800		35,000	
Wages	38,200		68,500		100,200	
Indirect materials	13,500		29,500		45,500	
Tools	6,500		8,500		10,500	
Other expenses	12,280		17,568		22,940	
Depreciation	14,300		34,000		57,000	
Heating	19,000		23,000		24,000	
		130,780		212,868		295,140
TECHNICAL DEPARTMENT (including inspection)						
Salaries	20,820		33,700		51,490	
Wages	4,840		8,860		10,400	
Materials	1,800		4,770		5,200	
Other expenses	7,684		11,201		13,267	
Depreciation	960		1,590		2,100	
		36,104		60,121		82,457

	1995 £	£	1996 £	£	1997 £	£
SALES DEPARTMENT						
Technical representatives	7,185		11,108		17,863	
Representatives' expenses	2,835		4,682		6,947	
Exhibitions	6,243		9,235		15,386	
Advertising	3,820		6,461		7,010	
Sales office salaries	4,187		6,914		8,964	
Other expenses	6,600		10,350		13,100	
Depreciation	212		240		415	
		31,082		48,990		69,685
GENERAL ADMINISTRATION						
Managing Director	17,500		20,100		21,800	
Accounts department	11,890		15,040		17,740	
Other admin. costs	10,072		17,031		16,637	
Depreciation	545		587		912	
Bank interest	—		—		10,412	
		40,007		52,758		67,501
TOTAL COSTS		423,947		616,099		804,721
PROFIT		76,660		83,132		94,977

18.2 The following financial statements (pages 154–182) have been copied from the published accounts of Marks and Spencer Plc and are included for you to read and analyse using as many of the ratios as you think necessary to give a good feel for the organization. Compare the results with those of other organizations in the same field and draw your own conclusions using the information that you consider relevant, including the five-year record which provides trends and cash flow statement.

MARKS AND SPENCER PLC
CONSOLIDATED PROFIT AND LOSS ACCOUNT
For the year ended 31 March 1995

	Notes	1995 52 weeks £m	1994 53 weeks £m
Turnover	2, 3	**6,806.5**	6,541.2
Cost of sales	3	**(4,417.1)**	(4,247.0)
Gross profit		**2,389.4**	2,294.2
Other expenses	3	**(1,492.9)**	(1,439.7)
Operating profit	2, 3	**896.5**	854.5
Loss on sale of property and other fixed assets	4	**(5.4)**	(17.3)
Net interest income	5	**33.2**	14.3
Profit on ordinary activities before taxation	2	**924.3**	851.5
Tax on ordinary activities	6	**(299.5)**	(272.2)
Profit on ordinary activities after taxation		**624.8**	579.3
Minority interests (all equity)		**(1.0)**	(1.1)
Profit for the financial year	7	**623.8**	578.2
Dividends	8	**(288.2)**	(255.5)
Undisturbed surplus	22	**335.6**	322.7
Earnings per share	9	**22.4p**	20.9p

CONSOLIDATED STATEMENT OF TOTAL RECOGNISED GAINS AND LOSSES
For the year ended 31 March 1995

	Notes	1995 52 weeks £m	1994 53 weeks £m
Profit for the financial year		**623.8**	578.2
Exchange differences on foreign currency translation	22	**8.3**	(4.0)
Total recognised gains and losses relating to the year		**632.1**	574.2

BALANCE SHEETS
At 31 March 1995

	Notes	The group 1995 £m	1994 £m	The company 1995 £m	1994 £m
Fixed assets					
Tangible assets:					
Land and buildings		**2,736.4**	2,618.9	**2,446.6**	2,352.2
Fixtures, fittings and equipment		**521.8**	455.1	**395.4**	352.8
Assets in the course of construction		**38.8**	21.4	**23.4**	14.5
	12	**3,297.0**	3,095.4	**2,865.4**	2,719.5
Investments	13	**43.3**	15.5	**774.5**	742.0
		3,340.3	3,110.9	**3,639.9**	3,461.5
Current assets					
Stocks		**377.0**	354.6	**255.6**	234.9
Debtors – receivable within one year	14	**577.6**	480.0	**1,194.1**	963.6
– receivable after more than one year	14	**482.3**	404.4	**53.6**	47.3
Investments	15	**193.2**	263.9	**—**	3.3
Cash in bank and in hand	16	**735.7**	550.8	**56.8**	67.6
		2,365.8	2,053.7	**1,560.1**	1,316.7
Current liabilities					
Creditors: amounts falling due within one year	17	**1,363.8**	1,181.0	**982.2**	874.6
Net current assets		**1,002.0**	872.7	**577.9**	442.1
Total assets less current liabilities		**4,342.3**	3,983.6	**4,217.8**	3,903.6
Creditors: amounts falling due after more than one year	18	**568.7**	599.3	**250.0**	265.0
Provisions for liabilities and charges	19	**37.9**	40.9	**35.0**	35.1
Net assets		**3,735.7**	3,343.4	**3,932.8**	3,603.5
Capital and reserves					
Called up share capital	21	**699.0**	696.2	**699.0**	696.2
Share premium account		**190.1**	162.3	**190.1**	162.3
Revaluation reserve		**455.4**	457.0	**464.0**	465.6
Profit and loss account		**2,370.4**	2,008.5	**2,579.7**	2,279.4
Shareholders' funds	22	**3,714.9**	3,324.0	**3,932.8**	3,603.5
Minority interests (all equity)		**20.8**	19.4	**—**	—
Total capital employed		**3,735.7**	3,343.4	**3,932.8**	3,603.5

Approved by the Board
22 May 1995

Sir Richard Greenbury, Chairman
J K Oates, Deputy Chairman and Joint Managing Director

CONSOLIDATED CASH FLOW STATEMENT
For the year ended 31 March 1995

	Notes	1995 52 weeks £m	£m	1994 53 weeks £m
Operating activities				
Received from customers		**6,665.0**		6,401.3
Payments to suppliers		**(4,426.3)**		(4,232.1)
Payments to and on behalf of employees		**(782.8)**		(768.5)
Other payments		**(547.1)**		(515.5)
Net cash inflow from operating activities	24		**908.8**	885.2
Returns on investments and servicing of finance				
Interest received		**80.5**		42.8
Interest paid		**(49.9)**		(25.3)
Dividends paid	29	**(248.9)**		(215.1)
Net cash outflow from returns on investments and servicing of finance			**(218.3)**	(197.6)
Taxation				
UK corporation tax paid		**(257.3)**		(221.0)
Overseas tax paid		**(16.1)**		(10.8)
			(273.4)	(231.8)
Investing activities				
Purchase of tangible fixed assets		**(379.4)**		(284.2)
Sale of tangible fixed assets		**9.8**		2.1
Purchase of fixed asset investments	13	**(37.2)**		(23.0)
Sale of fixed asset investments	13	**9.4**		26.9
Increase in shareholding in subsidiary		**—**		(4.0)
Sale of subsidiary	29	**—**		2.6
Net cash outflow from investing activities			**(397.4)**	(279.6)
Net cash inflow before financing and treasury activities			**19.7**	176.2
Financing and treasury activities				
Shares issued under employees' share schemes	21	**32.0**		38.2
Redemption of cumulative preference shares	21	**(1.4)**		—
(Repayment)/increase in long-term borrowings		**(15.0)**		125.0
Increase/(decrease) in non-cash equivalent bank loans, overdrafts and commercial paper		**16.8**		(76.9)
(Purchase)/redemption of non-cash equivalent deposits and short term investments		**(140.6)**		8.1
Net cash (outflow)/inflow from financing and treasury activities	27		**(108.2)**	94.4
(Decrease)/increase in cash and cash equivalents	26		**88.5**	270.6
increase in net funds	28		**48.6**	205.5

This cash flow statement should be read in conjunction with notes 24 to 29.

ACCOUNTING POLICIES

The financial statements are prepared in accordance with applicable accounting standards in the United Kingdom. A summary of the more important Group accounting policies, which are applied consistently, is given below.

Basis of accounting
The financial statements are drawn up on the historical cost basis of accounting, modified to include the valuation of certain United Kingdom properties at 31 March 1988.

Basis of consolidation
The Group financial statements incorporate the financial statements of Marks and Spencer p.l.c. and all its subsidiaries for the year ended 31 March 1995.

Current asset investments
Current asset investments are stated at market value. All profits and losses from such investments are included in Net Interest Income or in Financial Activities turnover as appropriate.

Deferred taxation
Deferred taxation is accounted for at anticipated tax rates on differences arising from the inclusion of items of income and expenditure in taxation computations in periods different from those in which they are included in the financial statements. A deferred tax asset or provision is established to the extent that it is likely that an asset or liability will crystallise in the foreseeable future.

Fixed assets
a Capitalised interest
Interest is not capitalised in the cost of land and buildings.

b Depreciation
Depreciation is provided to write off the cost or valuation of tangible fixed assets by equal annual instalments at the following rates: Freehold and leasehold land and buildings over 50 years—1% or nil (see (i) below); Leasehold land and buildings under 50 years—over the remaining period of the lease; Fixtures, fittings and equipment—6⅔% to 33⅓% according to the estimated life of the asset.

(i) Given that the lives of the Group's freehold and long leasehold properties are so long and that they are maintained to such a high standard, it is the opinion of the directors, that in most instances the residual values would be sufficiently high to make any depreciation charge immaterial. The directors have based their estimates of residual values on prices prevailing at the time of acquisition or revaluation. Where residual values are lower than cost or valuation, depreciation is charged to the profit and loss account. Any permanent diminution in value is also charged to the revaluation reserve or the profit and loss account as appropriate.

(ii) Depreciation is charged on all additions to depreciating assets in the year of purchase.

c Repairs and renewals
Expenditure on repairs, renewals and minor items of equipment is written off in the year in which it is incurred.

Certain major items of fixed plant and structure are incorporated within the cost of the buildings when purchased. When replaced, these are fully expensed as repairs and renewals in the profit and loss account.

Foreign currencies
The results of overseas subsidiaries are translated at average exchange rates for sales and profits. The balance sheets of overseas subsidiaries are translated at year end exchange rates or, where appropriate, at the rate of exchange in a related forward exchange contract. The resulting exchange differences are dealt with through reserves, and reported in the consolidated statement of total recognised gains and losses.

Transactions denominated in foreign currencies are translated at the exchange rate at the date of the transaction. Foreign currency assets and liabilities held at year end are translated at year end exchange rates or the exchange rate of a related forward exchange contract where appropriate. The resulting exchange gain or loss is dealt with in the profit and loss account.

Goodwill
Goodwill arising on consolidation is written off to reserves on acquisition. Goodwill attributable to businesses disposed of is written back to reserves brought forward, and charged through the profit and loss account.

Pension contributions
Funded pension plans are in place for the Group's UK employees and the majority of staff overseas. The assets of these pension plans are managed by third party investment

managers and are held separately in trust.

Regular valuations are prepared by independent professionally qualified actuaries so as to determine the level of the Group's contributions required to fund the benefits set out in the rules of the plans and to allow for the periodic increase of pensions in payment. The values of these and any variations from regular cost arising from the actuarial valuations are charged or credited to profits on a systematic basis over the estimated remaining service lives of the employees.

Scrip dividends

The amount of dividends taken as shares instead of in cash under the scrip dividend scheme is added back to reserves. The nominal value of shares issued under the scheme is funded out of the share premium account.

Stocks

Stocks and work in progress are valued at the lower of cost and net realisable value using the retail method.

Trading results

The trading results include transactions at stores up to and including the nearest Saturday to 31 March. All other transactions are included up to 31 March each year.

NOTES TO THE FINANCIAL STATEMENTS

1   Trading period

The results for the year comprise store sales and related costs for the 52 weeks to 1 April 1995 (last year 53 weeks to 2 April 1994). All other activities are for the year to 31 March 1995. All results arise from continuing operations.

2   Segmental information

(a) Classes of business

Retailing—Turnover represents goods sold to customers outside the group, less returns and sales taxes.

Financial Activities—Turnover represents the interest and other income attributable to these activities. The turnover attributable to Financial Activities arises wholly within the United Kingdom and the Channel Islands.

	Turnover		Operating profit		Operating assets	
	1995	1994	1995	1994 Restated	1995	1994 Restated
	£m	£m	£m	£m	£m	£m
Retailing	6,670.8	6,418.4	847.6	813.1	3,228.7	2,879.4
Financial activities	135.7	122.8	48.9	41.4	165.0	136.6
Total	**6,806.5**	6,541.2	**896.5**	854.5	**3,393.7**	3,016.0
Loss on sale of property and other fixed assets			**(5.4)**	(17.3)		
Net interest income			**33.2**	14.3		
Profit on ordinary activities before taxation			**924.3**	851.5		
Unallocated assets					**342.0**	327.4
Net assets					**3.735.7**	3,343.4

Profit before taxation is £874.6m (last year £809.2m) for retailing, and £49.7m (last year £42.3m) for Financial Activities.

(b) Geographical segments	Turnover		Operating profit		Operating assets	
	1995	1994	1995	1994 Restated	1995	1994 Restated
	£m	£m	£m	£m	£m	£m
United Kingdom	5,831.7	5,622.8	845.5	790.2	2,981.7	2,678.7
Europe (excluding UK)	359.9	309.4	20.7	27.9	239.9	165.6
Rest of the World	614.9	609.0	30.3	36.4	172.1	171.7
Total	**6,806.5**	6,541.2	**896.5**	854.5	**3,393.7**	3,016.0
Loss on sale of property and other fixed assets			**(5.4)**	(17.3)		
Net interest income			**33.2**	14.3		
Profit on ordinary activities before taxation			**924.3**	851.5		
Unallocated assets					**342.0**	327.4
Net assets					**3,735.7**	3,343.4

2 Segmental information (continued)

	Turnover	
	1995	1994
		Restated
	£m	£m
Retailing	**5,596.2**	5,412.8
Export sales outside the Group	**99.8**	**87.2**
Financial activities	**135.7**	122.8
	5,831.7	5.622.8

UK retail turnover comprises Clothing and Footwear £3,009.8m (last year £2,888.4m). Home Furnishings £211.9m (last year £211.3m) and Foods £2,374m (last year £2,313.1m). Export sales outside the Group comprise sales to Europe £69.4m (last year £66.8m) and to the Rest of the World £30.4m (last year 20.4m).

The value of goods exported from the UK, including shipments to overseas subsidiaries, amounted to £339.8m (last year £280.8m).

Turnover and operating profits for the Rest of the World comprise:

	Turnover		Operating profit	
	1995	1994	**1995**	1994
	£m	£m	**£m**	£m
USA				
Brooks Brothers (including Japan)	**258.4**	252.1	**5.9**	14.8
Kings Super Markets	**211.6**	217.5	**8.6**	8.0
Corporate expenses	**—**	—	**(1.1)**	(1.2)
	470.0	469.6	**13.4**	21.6
Canada	**73.9**	82.8	**(0.6)**	(0.4)
Far East	**71.0**	56.6	**17.5**	15.2
	614.9	609.0	**30.3**	36.4

The results for the Republic of Ireland and MS Insurance have been reclassified so that Ireland is shown within Europe and MS Insurance within the United Kingdom. The net effect of the restatement is to reduce last year's United Kingdom turnover by £62.5m, reduce operating profit by £0.8m and increase operating assets by £8.3m. Last year's operating profit has also been restated to include the charge for the UK employees' profit sharing scheme by £18.9m with a corresponding decrease in the UK operating assets. In addition, the operating assets of the Rest of the World last year have been restated to exclude a borrowing of £55m which is now included within unallocated assets.

The results of overseas subsidiaries have been translated using average rates of exchange ruling during the financial year. When expressed at constant rates of exchange, sales increases on last year are affected as follows:

	Inc/(Dec)
	%
Europe (excluding UK)	12.7
Brooks Brothers (including Japan)	4.8
Kings Super Markets	1.5
Canada	(2.1)
Far East	31.0

Overall there has been no material effect on operating profits.

3   Operating profit

	1995		1994 Restated
	£m	£m	£m
Turnover		6,806.5	6,541.2
Cost of sales		(4,417.1)	(4,247.0)
Gross profit		2,389.4	2,294.2
Staff costs (see note 10)	776.1		756.7
Occupancy costs	233.4		234.2
Repairs, renewals and maintenance of fixed assets	74.1		74.7
Depreciation	150.7		136.3
Other costs	258.6		237.8
Total other expenses		(1,492.9)	(1,439.7)
Operating profit		896.5	854.5

The directors consider that the nature of the business is such that the analysis of expenses shown above is more informative than that set out in the formats of the Companies Act 1985.

Staff costs now include the cost of UK profit sharing of £19.4m (last year £18.9m). To reflect this, the comparative for last year has been restated.

Included in total other expenses are rentals under operating leases, comprising £10.0m for hire of plant and machinery (last year £10.7m) and £82.4m of other rental costs (last year £84.0m).

Included in other costs is the remuneration of the auditors for the Group audit of £0.8m (last year £0.8m) and for the Company audit of £0.3m (last year £0.3m). Also included in other costs is the remuneration of the auditors for the provision of non-audit services to the Group of £0.7m (last year £0.9m) and for the Company of £0.3m (last year £0.5m).

4   Loss on sale of property and other fixed assets

This year the loss on sale of property and other fixed assets is £5.4m (last year £17.3m). Last year's figure included the disposal of certain UK satellite stores.

5   Net interest income

	1995		1994	
	£m	£m	£m	£m
Bank and other interest income	180.5		148.8	
Less amounts included in turnover of Financial Activities	(118.5)		(104.0)	
		62.0		44.8
Interest expenditure	(65.8)		(64.4)	
Less amounts included in cost of sales of Financial Activities	37.0		33.9	
		(28.8)		(30.5)
		33.2		14.3

5 Net interest income (continued)	1995 £m	1994 £m
Interest expenditure comprises:		
Amounts repayable within five years:		
Bank loans, overdrafts and commercial paper	(31.0)	(29.5)
Debenture loans	(1.0)	(1.3)
8¼% Guaranteed bonds 1996	(5.3)	(5.4)
7⅜% Guaranteed notes 1998	(8.1)	(6.1)
US$ Promissory note 1998	(20.4)	(20.9)
Amounts repayable in more than five years:		
Debenture loans	—	(1.2)
	(65.8)	(64.4)

Income from listed investments during the year was £5.5m (last year £3.0m).

6 Tax on ordinary activities	1995 £m	1994 £m
The taxation charge comprises:		
Current taxation		
UK corporation tax at 33% (last year 33%)		
Current year	304.6	261.8
Prior years	(6.6)	(7.6)
	298.0	254.2
Double taxation relief	(10.6)	(1.4)
	287.4	252.8
Overseas taxation	13.3	14.3
	300.7	267.1
Deferred taxation (see note 20)		
Current year	(1.7)	5.2
Prior years	0.5	(0.1)
	(1.2)	5.1
	(299.5)	(272.2)

7   Profit for the financial year

As permitted by section 230 of the Companies Act 1985, the profit and loss account of the Company is not presented as part of these financial statements.

The consolidated profit for the financial year of £623.8m (last year £578.2m) includes £570.5m (last year £522.2m) which is dealt with in the financial statements of the company.

8 Dividends	1995 £m	1994 £m
Cumulative preference shares (see note below)	0.2	0.1
Ordinary shares		
—Interim paid of 2.8p per share (last year 2.5p)	78.1	69.2
—Proposed final of 7.5p per share (last year 6.7p)	209.9	186.2
	288.2	255.5

Included in this year's cumulative preference dividend charge of £0.2m is £0.1m which relates to the premium paid on redemption of these shares (see note 21).

Under the scrip dividend scheme, £11.8m of the 1993/94 final dividend and £4.6m of the 1994/95 interim dividend were paid by way of shares, and have been added back to the profit and loss account reserve (see note 22).

9   Earnings per share

The calculation of earnings per ordinary share is based on earnings after tax, minority interests and preference dividends of £623.6m (last year £578.1m), and on 2,786,909,407 ordinary shares (last year 2,767,913,633), being the weighted average number of ordinary shares in issue during the year ended 31 March 1995.

At 31 March 1995, directors, senior employees and retired staff held unexercised options in respect of 10,157,476 ordinary shares (last year 10,729,192). There were options outstanding under the Savings-Related Share Option Scheme in respect of 49,472,373 ordinary shares (last year 47,041,710). If all outstanding options had been exercised, the dilution of earnings per share would not have been material.

10   Employees

The average weekly number of employees of the Group during the year was:

		1995	1994
UK stores	Management and supervisory categories	3,660	3,753
	Other	45,334	44,292
UK head office	Management and supervisory categories	1,929	1,872
	Other	1,448	1,510
Financial Services	Management and supervisory categories	144	126
	Other	603	569
Overseas		10,213	9,998
		63,331	62,120

If the number of part-time hours worked was converted on the basis of a full working week, the equivalent average number of full-time employees would have been 41,535 (last year 41,386).

The aggregate remuneration and associated costs of Group employees were:

	1995 £m	1994 Restated £m
Wages and salaries	604.3	587.7
UK profit sharing (see note 10C)	19.4	18.9
Social security costs	50.1	47.7
Pension costs (see note 10A)	70.7	68.3
Staff welfare and other personnel costs	44.9	49.6
	789.4	772.2
Classified as:		
Staff costs (see note 3)	776.1	756.7
Manufacturing cost of sales	13.3	15.5
	789.4	772.2

a   Pension costs

The Group operates a number of funded defined benefit pension schemes throughout the world.

The total pension cost for the Group was £70.7m (last year £68.3m) of which £6.3m (last year £6.0m) relates to overseas schemes.

The latest actuarial valuation of the UK scheme was carried out at 1 April 1992 using the projected unit method. The assumptions which have the most significant effect on the results of the valuation are those relating to the rate of return on investments and the rates of increase in salaries and pensions. It has been assumed that the investment return is 2% higher per annum than future salary increases, with a further 2% differential between salaries and pension increases.

At the date of the latest actuarial valuation. the market value of the assets of the UK scheme was £1,405.8m and the actuarial valuation of these assets represented 106% of the benefits that had accrued to members, after allowing for expected future increases in earnings. The surplus of the actuarial valuation of assets over the benefits accrued to members was £77.8m. At that time, it was decided that this should be spread over six years from 1 April 1992, being

10   Employees (continued)

the remaining estimated service lives of the existing members. by a reduction in the annual contribution made to the scheme.

Since this valuation, the Government has changed the rules concerning Advance Corporation Tax. As this has adversely affected the income of the UK scheme the directors have decided, on actuarial advice, that it would be prudent to suspend, with effect from 1 April 1993, the reduction in annual contributions described above.

An actuarial valuation of the UK scheme as at 1 April 1995 is currently being carried out.

The pension costs relating to overseas schemes have been determined in accordance with the advice of independent qualified actuaries.

As shown in note 14, the Company has pre-paid a contribution of £66.9m to the UK scheme.

b   Post-retirement health benefits
The Company has a commitment to pay all or a proportion of the health insurance premiums for a number of its retired employees and their spouses. the last of whom retired in 1988. There is no commitment in respect of current employees or those who have retired since 1988.

At 1 April 1993, the Company assessed this liability in accordance with the advice of an independent qualified actuary and, at 31 March 1992. the discounted present value was £34.7m which was fully provided. The valuation assumed a premium inflation of 8.5% and an after-tax rate of discount of 5.36%. In addition, a deferred taxation asset was established at 31 March 1992 of £11.5m.

A further actuarial valuation will be carried out as at 1 April 1996.

c   United Kingdom employees' profit sharing schemes
The charge for the United Kingdom profit

sharing is now included within staff costs. Last year's figures have been restated accordingly.

The Trustees of the United Kingdom Employees' Profit Sharing Schemes have been allocated £19.4m (last year £18.9m) with which to subscribe for ordinary shares in the Company. The price of each share is 414p, being the average market price for the three dealing days immediately following the announcement of the results for the year ended 31 March 1995.

d   United Kingdom employees' savings-related share option scheme
Under the terms of the scheme the Board may offer options to purchase ordinary shares in the Company once in each financial year to those employees who enter into an Inland Revenue approved Save As You Earn (SAVE) savings contract. The price at which options may be offered is 80% of the market price for three consecutive dealing days preceding the date of offer. The options may normally be exercised during the period of six months after the completion of the SAYE contract, either five or seven years after entering the scheme.

Outstanding options granted under the UK Employees' Savings-Related Share Option Scheme are as follows:

Options granted	Number of shares 1995	1994	Option price
Jan 1988	**621,089**	2,341,892	182p
Jan 1989	**2,168,736**	2,467,340	143p
Jan 1990	**4,724,745**	8,113,039	151p
Jan 1991	**6,756,239**	7,087,259	182p
Jan 1992	**9,415,990**	9,873,495	229p
Jan 1993	**8.195.550**	8,682,860	257p
Jan 1994	**7,602,281**	7,891,868	319p
Jan 1995	**9,987,743**	—	322p

10   Employees (continued)

e   Senior staff share option schemes

Under the terms of the 1984 and 1987 schemes, following the announcement of the Company's results, the Board may offer options to purchase ordinary shares in the Company to executive directors and senior employees at the higher of the nominal value of the shares and the average market price for three consecutive dealing days preceding the date of the offer. The 1977 scheme has now expired and no further options may be granted or excercised under this scheme. Although options may be granted under each of the 1984 and 1987 schemes, the Maximum Option Value that can be exercised under both schemes is limited to four times earnings. Outstanding options granted under all senior schemes are as follows:

Options granted	Number of shares 1995	1994	Option price	Option dates
(1984 Scheme)				
May 1985	**60,388**	110,387	137.000p	May 1988–May 1995
May 1986	**36.145**	67,423	211.000p	May 1989–May 1996
May 1987	**148,722**	218,749	232.333p	May 1990–May 1997
October 1987	**312,755**	378,986	202.000p	Oct 1990–Oct 1997
May 1988	**650,575**	680,920	176.000p	May 1991–May 1998
October 1988	**22,424**	22,424	158.000p	Oct 1991–Oct 1998
May 1989	**857,604**	958,655	175.000p	May 1992–May 1999
May 1990	**1,204,881**	1,592,105	206.000p	May 1993–May 2000
May 1991	**2,979,433**	3,383,786	254.000p	May 1994–May 2001
May 1992	**2,962,692**	3,219,123	329.000p	May 1995–May 2002
May 1993	**1,678,839**	1,684,117	341.000p	May 1996–May 2003
October 1993	**61,026**	75,812	399.000p	Oct 1996–Oct 2003
May 1994	**2,247,521**	—	404.000p	May 1997–May 2004
October 1994	**21,541**	—	402.000p	Oct 1997–Oct 2004
(1987 Scheme)				
May 1988	**556,895**	1,190,915	176.000p	May 1991–May 1995
May 1989	**1,023,685**	1,109,398	175.000p	May 1992–May 1996
October 1989	**4,038**	4,038	188.000p	Oct 1992–Oct 1996
May 1990	**2,084,354**	2,480,777	206.000p	May 1993–May 1997
May 1991	**2,305,058**	2,691,374	254.000p	May 1994–May 1998
May 1992	**1,729,824**	1,816,449	329.000p	May 1995–May 1999
May 1993	**1,543,755**	1,734,535	341.000p	May 1996–May 2000
October 1993	**61,026**	75,812	399.000p	Oct 1996–Oct 2000
May 1994	**1,366,302**	—	404.000p	May 1997–May 2001
October 1994	**17,288**	—	402.000p	Oct 1997–Oct 2001

11 Directors

a Emoluments

The number of directors of the Company performing their duties mainly within the United Kingdom, whose emoluments (including bonus but excluding pension contributions) were within the following ranges, are:

Gross Emoluments £	1995	1994	Gross Emoluments £	1995	1994	Gross Emoluments £	1995	1994
805,001–810,000	1	—	255,001–260,000	—	1	180,001–185,000	—	1
685,001–690,000	—	1	250,001–255,000	—	1	175,001–180,000	1	1
520,001–525,000	1	1	240,001–245,000	—	1	165,001–170,000	—	1
445,001–450,000	—	1	235,001–240,000	1	—	140,001–145,000	—	1
300,001–305,000	1	—	225,001–230,000	—	1	60,001– 65,000	1	—
295,001–300,000	3	—	220,001–225,000	—	3	55,001– 60,000	—	1
290,001–295,000	1	—	205,001–210,000	1	—	35,001– 40,000	3	—
275,001–280,000	2	—	200,001–205,000	1	—	30,001– 35,000	—	2
265,001–270,000	—	1	195,001–200,000	1	—	25,001– 30,000	—	1
260,001–265,000	1	—	190,001–195,000	1	—	5,001– 10,000	—	1

b Directors' interests in shares

The beneficial interests of the directors and their families in the shares of the Company, together with their interests as trustees of both charitable and other trusts, are shown below in sections i to iii. These include shares held under the Delayed Profit Sharing Scheme. Options granted under the Savings-Related Share Option and Senior Staff Share Option Schemes are shown in section v. Further information regarding employee share option schemes is given in note 10.

There have been no changes in the directors' interests in shares or options granted by the Company and its subsidiaries between the end of the financial year and one month prior to the notice of the Annual General Meeting.

i Ordinary shares in the Company—beneficial and family interests

	At 31 March 1995	At 1 April 1994		At 31 March 1995	At 1 April 1994
Sir Richard Greenbury	27,184	21,934	B S Morris	2,962	122
J K Oates	41,733	24,862	J T Rowe	17,276	12,988
P G McCracken	41,045	24,002	S J Sacher	311,060	329,130
P L Salsbury	30,477	27,648	The Hon David Sieff	311,577	304,157
A Z Stone	23,505	24,990	P P D Smith	7,868	7,737
R Aldridge	23,334	18,974	D G Trangmar	202,945	189,006
J R Benfield	11,482	12,075	Sir Martin Jacomb	13,552	6,671
N L Colne	315,668	73,997	D G Lanigan	4,470	4,015
R W C Colvill	16,072	18,485	Sir Ralph Robins	2,110	2,061
D K Hayes	10,931	10,900	The Rt Hon The Baroness Young	5,827	5,443
C Littmoden	34,937	17,926			

ii Ordinary shares in the Company—trustee interests

	At 31 March 1995		At 1 April 1994	
	Charitable Trusts Shares	Other Trusts Shares	Charitable Trusts Shares	Other Trusts Shares
S J Sacher	85,000	148,095	85,000	151,368
The Hon David Sieff	12,000	75,899	12,000	75,533

iii Cumulative preference shares

At 31 March 1994 Mr N L Colne owned 500 4.9% cumulative preference shares and Mr C Littmoden owned 10 4.9% cumulative preference shares and 10 7.0% cumulative preference shares. Thre cumulative preference shares were redeemed during the year. Further information is given in note 21.

No director had any interests in any subsidiary at the beginning or the end of the year.

iv Transactions with directors

Interest-free loans were made under the employees' loan scheme by the Company to the following, prior to their appointment as directors:

	Dates of loan advances	At 31 March 1995	At 1 April 1994
D K Hayes	1985–1992	—	41,544
B S Morris	1987–1991	—	8,408

The balances at 1 April 1994 were the highest balances during the year.

During the year there was no contract of significance to which the Company or one of its subsidiaries was a party and in which a director of the Company was materially interested.

v Options

Particulars of the Company's share option schemes are given elsewhere.

Options which have been held for less than the minimum periods mentioned elsewhere are indicated in the following table as 'Not yet excercisable': options in excess of Maximum Option Value are shown as 'Not exercisable (exceed MOV)'.

Options under the Senior Schemes are granted in consideration of a £1 payment. The market price of the shares at the end of the financial year was 417p: the highest and lowest share prices during the financial year were 441p and 396p respectively.

The Register of Directors' Interests (which is open to shareholders' inspection) contains full details of directors shareholdings and options to subscribe for shares.

	At 1 April 1994	Granted during the year	Exercised during the year	At 31 March 1995	Option Price (pence)	Exercise Price (pence)	Option Period
Sir Richard Greenbury							
Exercisable	4,986			**53,324**	254.0		May 94–May 01
Not yet exercisable	Nil			**Nil**			
Not exercisable							
(exceed MOV)	897,112			**974,584**	320.0*		May 94–May 04
		166,826			404.0		May 97–May 04
			40,016		206.0	434.5	
J K Oates							
Exercisable	394,943			**552,887**	212.0*		May 91–May 01
Not yet exercisable	130,976			**15,907**	209.0*		Jan 97–Jun 02
Not exercisable							
(exceed MOV)	281,882			**269,549**	331.0*		May 94–May 04
		50,659			404.0		May 97–May 04
		3,633**			322.0		Jan 02–Jun 02
			23,750		176.0	417.5	
P G McCracken							
Exercisable	Nil			**173,279**	254.0		May 94–May 01
Not yet exercisable	50,637			**10,909**	244.0*		May 95–Jun 02
Not exercisable							
(exceed MOV)	289,339			**239,897**	358.0*		May 95–May 04
		87,128			404.0		May 97–May 04
		1,211**			322.0		Jan 02–Jun 02
			2,384**		151.0	385.5	
		1,846**		182.0	396.5		

b   *Directors' interests in shares (continued)*

v   *Options (continued)*

	At 1 April 1994	Granted during the year	Exercised during the year	At 31 March 1995	Option Price (pence)	Exercise Price (pence)	Option Period
P L Salsbury							
Exercisable	131,877			**192,913**	217.0*		May 93–May 01
Not yet exercisable	11,347			**72,643**	309.0*		May 95–May 02
Not exercisable							
(exceed MOV)	263,067			**246,757**	364.0*		May 95–May 04
		106,022			404.0		May 97–May 04
A Z Stone							
Exercisable	83,813			**154,506**	240.0*		May 93–May 01
Not yet exercisable	11,457			**24,984**	265.0*		Jan 95–Jun 02
Not exercisable							
(exceed MOV)	290,810			**259,670**	364.0*		May 95–May 04
		105,658			404.0		May 97–May 04
		2,422**			322.0		Jan 02–Jun 02
			55,000		206.0	435.0	
R Aldridge							
Exercisable	Nil			**109,678**	254.0		May 94–May 01
Not yet exercisable	101,640			**13,567**	217.0*		May 97–Jun 02
Not exercisable							
(exceed MOV)	183,009			**227,952**	322.0*		May 94–May 04
		66,433			404.0		May 97–May 04
		2,422**			322.0		Jan 02–Jun 02
			2,307**		182.0	375.5	
J R Benfield							
Exercisable	90,776			**98,438**	223.0*		May 93–May 01
Not yet exercisable	27,625			**13,567**	217.0*		Jan 97–Jun 02
Not exercisable							
(exceed MOV)	226,396			**228,668**	311.0*		May 94–May 04
		23,761			404.0		May 97–May 04
		2,422**			322.0		Jan 02–Jun 02
			3,000		206.0	410.5	
			5,000		206.0	406.0	
			10,000		206.0	398.0	
			10,000		206.0	416.0	
			2,307**		182.0	398.0	
N L Colne							
Exercisable	551,469			**251,145**	203.0*		May 91–May 01
Not yet exercisable	40,817			**16,241**	205.0*		Jan 96–Jun 02
Not exercisable							
(exceed MOV)	182,398			**194,665**	334.0*		May 94–May 04
		44,263			404.0		May 97–May 04
		1,211**			322.0		Jan 02–Jun 02
			27,372		137.0	378.5	
			23,696		211.0	378.5	
			36,585		232.3	378.5	
			270,454		176.0	418.0	

b   *Directors' interests in shares (continued)*

v   *Options (continued)*

	At 1 April 1994	Granted during the year	Exercised during the year	At 31 March 1995	Option Price (pence)	Exercise Price (pence)	Option Period
R W C Colvill							
Exercisable	195,504			**208,023**	227.0*		May 93–May 01
Not yet exercisable	50,393			**8,268**	257.0		Jan 00–Jun 00
Not exercisable							
(exceed MOV)	239,007			**235,310**	331.0*		May 94–May 04
		46,697			404.0		May 97–May 04
			80,000		206.0	418.5	
D K Hayes							
Exercisable	38			**535**	254.0		May 94–May 01
Not yet exercisable	10,339			**9,166**	231.0*		Jan 96–Jun 02
Not exercisable							
(exceed MOV)	194,507			**184,376**	330.0*		May 94–May 04
		55,919			404.0		May 97–May 04
		1,211**			322.0		Jan 02–Jun 02
			31,000		206.0	395.5	
			18,553		206.0	372.5	
			16,000		254.0	372.5	
			2,384**		151.0	391.5	
C Littmoden							
Exercisable	563			**27,359**	206.0		May 93–May 00
Not yet exercisable	12,996			**15,418**	206.0*		Jan 96–Jun 02
Not exercisable							
(exceed MOV)	257,245			**295,240**	311.0*		May 93–May 04
		64,791			404.0		May 97–May 04
		2,422**			322.0		Jan 02–Jun 02
B S Morris							
Exercisable	Nil			**Nil**			
Not yet exercisable	82,069			**53,620**	321.0*		May 95–May 02
Not exercisable							
(exceed MOV)	140,273			**145,788**	360.0*		May 95–May 04
		55,630			404.0		May 97–May 04
			62,090		254.0	410.5	
			14,090		254.0	420.0	
			2,384**		151.0	381.5	
J T Rowe							
Exercisable	80,252			**101,317**	213.0*		May 93–May 01
Not yet exercisable	9,356			**8,043**	229.0*		Jan 96–Jun 00
Not exercisable							
(exceed MOV)	204,743			**233,350**	335.0*		May 94–May 04
		49,672			404.0		May 97–May 04
		1,071**			322.0		Jan 00–Jun 00
			2,384**		151.0	388.5	

b   *Directors' interests in shares (continued)*

v   *Options (continued)*

	At 1 April 1994	Granted during the year	Exercised during the year	At 31 March 1995	Option Price (pence)	Exercise Price (pence)	Option Period
S J Sacher							
Exercisable	46,601			**905**	254.0		May 94–May 01
Not yet exercisable	14,633			**11,089**	227.0*		Jan 97–Jun 00
Not exercisable							
(exceed MOV)	293,354			**330,529**	310.0*		May 94–May 04
		73,019			404.0		May 97–May 04
		1,071**			322.0		Jan 00–Jun 00
			73,540		206.0	417.5	
			8,000		254.0	417.5	
			4,615**		182.0	381.0	
The Hon David Sieff							
Exercisable	766			**39,370**	206.0		May 93–May 00
Not yet exercisable	9,395			**10,606**	237.0*		Jan 97–Jun 02
Not exercisable							
(exceed MOV)	251,689			**312,693**	341.0*		May 93–May 04
		99,608			404.0		May 97–May 04
		1,211**			322.0		Jan 02–Jun 02
P P D Smith							
Exercisable	22,346			**1,213**	206.0		May 93–May 00
Not yet exercisable	9,825			**9,825**	229.0		Jan 99–Jun 99
Not exercisable							
(exceed MOV)	294,130			**287,814**	299.0*		May 93–May 04
		19,800			404.0		May 97–May 04
			14,628		175.0	411.5	
			32,621		206.0	411.5	
D G Trangmar							
Exercisable	127,897			**163,902**	191.0*		May 92–May 00
Not yet exercisable	7,152			**Nil**			
Not exercisable							
(exceed MOV)	323,641			**303,476**	277.0*		May 93–May 04
		15,840			404.0		May 97–May 04
			7,152**		151.0	376.5	
D G Lanigan							
Not yet exercisable	9,456			**Nil**			

Mr D G Lanigan has relinquished his rights to exercise the SAYE options he held.

*Weighted average price.

**SAYE grant or exercise.

12   Tangible fixed assets

a   Tangible assets

| | The Group | | | | The Company | | | |
	Land & buildings £m	Fixtures, fittings & equipment £m	Assets in the course of construction £m	Total £m	Land & buildings £m	Fixtures, fittings & equipment £m	Assets in the course of construction £m	Total £m
Cost of evaluation								
At 1 April 1994	2,700.0	931.5	21.4	**3,652.9**	2,384.6	730.1	14.5	**3,129.2**
Additions	64.8	194.6	107.5	**366.9**	38.8	157.6	77.5	**273.9**
Transfers	80.3	9.9	(90.2)	—	68.6	—	(68.6)	—
Disposals	(25.7)	(89.7)	—	**(115.4)**	(8.2)	(77.7)	—	**(85.9)**
Differences on exchange	2.5	2.6	0.1	**5.2**	—	—	—	—
At 31 March 1995	**2,821.9**	**1,048.9**	**38.8**	**3,909.6**	**2,483.8**	**810.0**	**23.4**	**3,317.2**
Accumulated depreciation								
At 1 April 1994	81.1	476.4	—	**557.5**	32.4	377.3	—	**409.7**
Depreciation for the year	14.8	135.9	—	**150.7**	5.3	112.9	—	**118.2**
Disposals	(6.8)	(85.1)	—	**(91.9)**	(0.5)	(75.6)	—	**(76.1)**
Differences on exchange	(3.6)	(0.1)	—	**(3.7)**	—	—	—	—
At 31 March 1995	**85.5**	**527.1**	—	**612.6**	**37.2**	**414.6**	—	**451.8**
Net book value								
At 31 March 1995	**2,736.4**	**521.8**	**38.8**	**3,297.0**	**2,446.6**	**395.4**	**23.4**	**2,865.4**
At 31 March 1994	2,618.9	455.1	21.4	3,095.4	2,352.2	352.8	14.5	2,719.5

Analysis of land & buildings at 31 March 1995

| | The Group | | | | The Company | | | |
	Freehold £m	Long, Leasehold £m	Short Leasehold £m	Total £m	Freehold £m	Long Leasehold £m	Short Leasehold £m	Total £m
At valuation	834.0	457.3	16.1	**1,307.4**	834.0	457.3	16.1	**1,307.4**
At cost	845.8	405.3	263.4	**1,514.5**	665.0	402.0	109.4	**1,176.4**
	1,679.8	862.6	279.5	**2,821.9**	1,499.0	859.3	125.5	**2,483.8**
Accumulated depreciation	8.1	1.6	75.8	**85.5**	2.7	1.5	33.0	**37.2**
Net book value								
At 31 March 1995	**1,671.7**	**861.0**	**203.7**	**2,736.4**	**1,496.3**	**857.8**	**92.5**	**2,446.6**
At 31 March 1994	1,566.0	857.4	195.5	2,618.9	1,400.1	854.3	97.8	2,352.2

b   Gerald Eve, Chartered Surveyors, valued the Company's freehold and leasehold properties in the United Kingdom and the Isle of Man as at 31 March 1982. This valuation was on the basis of open market value for existing use. At 31 March 1988, the directors, after consultation with Gerald Eve, revalued those of the Company's properties which had been valued as at 31 March 1982 (excluding subsequent additions and adjusted for disposals). The direscors' valuation was incorporated into the financial statements at 31 March 1988.

If the Company's land and buildings had not been valued at 31 March 1982 and 31 March 1988 their net book value would have been:

	1995 £m	1994 £m
At valuation at 31 March 1975	344.3	344.5
At cost	1,412.4	1,312.7
At 31 March	1,756.7	1,657.2
Accumulated depreciation	79.5	74.9
Net book value at 31 March	1,677.2	1,582.3

The company also valued its land and buildings in 1955 and in 1964. In the opinion of the directors unreasonable expense would be incurred in obtaining the original costs of the assets valued in those years and in 1975.

c The company does not maintain detailed records of cost and depreciation for fixtures, fittings and equipment. The accumulated cost figures represent reaonable estimates of the sums involved.

13 Fixed asset investments

a Investments

	The Group			The Company			
	Joint ventures £m	Other investments £m	Total £m	Shares in subsidiaries £m	Loans to subsidiaries £m	Joint venture £m	Total £m
Cost							
At 1 April 1994	6.3	9.2	**15.5**	685.8	49.9	6.3	**742.0**
Additions	9.8	27.4	**37.2**	39.6	15.0	—	**54.6**
Disposals (including share of losses)	(0.2)	(9.2)	**(9.4)**	(2.3)	—	(0.2)	**(2.5)**
Repayment of loan	—	—	—	—	(19.6)	—	**(19.6)**
At 31 March 1995	**15.9**	**27.4**	**43.3**	**723.1**	**45.3**	**6.1**	**774.5**

The investment in joint ventures represents the Company's 50% interest in Hedge End Park Ltd, a property development company, and a subsidiary's 50% interest in Braehead Park Joint Venture, an unincorporated venture. The partner in both joint ventures is J. Sainsbury plc.

Other investments comprise securities held by a subsidiary.

The book and market values of listed investments which form part of other investments are:

	Book value £m	Market value £m
Listed in the United Kingdom	14.4	14.4
Listed overseas	6.5	6.5
At 31 March 1995	20.9	20.9

b The Company's principal subsidiaries are set out below. A schedule of interests in all subsidiaries is filed with the Annual Return.

	Principal activity	Country of incorporation and operation	Proportion of shares held by:	
			The Company	A subsidiary
Marks and Spencer International Holdings Limited	Holding Company	Great Britain	100%	—
Marks and Spencer (Nederland) BV	Holding Company	The Netherlands	—	100%
Marks and Spencer US Holdings Inc	Holding Company	United States	100%	—
Marks and Spencer (France) SA	Retailing	France	—	100%
SA Marks and Spencer (Belgium) NV	Retailing	Belgium	—	100%
Marks and Spencer (España) SA	Retailing	Spain	—	80%
Marks and Spencer Stores BV	Retailing	The Netherlands	—	100%
Marks and Spencer (Ireland) Limited	Retailing	Republic of Ireland	—	100%

13 Fixed asset investments *(continued)*

	Principal activity	Country of incorporation and operation	Proportion of shares held by: The Company	A subsidiary
Marks & Spencer Canada Inc	Retailing	Canada	—	100%
D'Allaird's Stores Inc	Retailing	Canada	—	100%
Brooks Brothers Inc	Retailing	United States	—	100%
Brooks Brothers (Japan) Limited	Retailing	Japan	—	51%
Kings Super Markets Inc	Retailing	United States	—	100%
Marks and Spencer (Hong Kong) Limited	Retailing	Hong Kong	—	100%
Marks and Spencer Retail Financial Services Holdings Limited	Holding Company	Great Britain	100%	—
Marks and Spencer Financial Services Limited	Financial Activities	Great Britain	—	100%
Marks and Spencer Unit Trust Management Limited	Financial Activities	Great Britain	—	100%
Marks and Spencer Savings and Investments Limited	Financial Activities	Great Britain	—	100%
St Michael Finance Limited	Financial Activities	Great Britiain	100%	—
MS Insurance Limited	Financial Activities	Guernsey	—	100%
Marks and Spencer Finance (Nederland) BV	Finance	The Netherlands	—	100%
Marks and Spencer Finance Inc	Finance	United States	—	100%
Marks and Spencer Finance p.l.c.	Finance	Great Britain	100%	

All the companies incorporated in Great Britain are registered in England and Wales.

14 Debtors

	The Group 1995 £m	1994 £m	The Company 1995 £m	1994 £m
Amounts receivable within one year:				
Trade debtors	**32.9**	30.5	**17.5**	14.9
Customer balances	**370.6**	298.9	—	—
Amounts owed by Group companies	—	—	**1,046.0**	832.0
Other debtors	**48.2**	34.1	**29.4**	21.7
Prepayments and accrued income	**125.9**	116.5	**101.2**	95.0
	577.6	480.0	**1,194.1**	963.6
Amounts receivable after more than one year:				
Advance Corporation Tax recoverable on the proposed final dividend	**52.5**	46.6	**52.5**	46.6
Less amount offset against deferred taxation provision (see note 20)	**(16.1)**	(17.3)	**(13.9)**	(15.0)
	36.4	29.3	**38.6**	31.6
Customer balances	**423.8**	351.0	—	—
Other debtors	**22.1**	24.1	**15.0**	15.7
	482.3	404.4	**53.6**	47.3

Other debtors includes loans to employees, the majority of which are connected with house purchases. Last year, other debtors included an interest-free loan to an officer of the Company of £1,000. Transactions with directors are shown in note 11B(iv).

Prepayments and accrued income include £66.9m in respect of the UK pension scheme for 1995/96 (last year £64.7m in respect of 1994/95).

15   Current asset investments

	The Group		The Company	
	1995 **£m**	1994 £m	**1995** **£m**	1994 £m
Investments listed on a recognised stock exchange:				
Government securities	**13.4**	32.9	—	—
Listed in the United Kingdom	**19.6**	25.7	—	—
Listed overseas	**104.0**	78.0	—	—
Certificates of tax deposit	—	3.3	—	3.3
Unlisted:				
Securities	**56.1**	123.2	—	—
Other	**0.1**	0.8	—	—
	193.2	263.9	—	3.3

16   Cash in bank and in hand

Cash at bank includes commercial paper and short-term deposits with banks and other financial institutions.

17   Creditors: amounts falling due within one year

	The Group		The Company	
	1995 **£m**	1994 **£m**	**1995** £m	1994 £m
Bank loans, overdrafts and commercial paper	**273.9**	160.2	**45.2**	11.3
Trade creditors	**174.9**	162.8	**155.6**	144.4
Amounts owed to Group companies	—	—	**4.4**	5.7
Taxation	**317.9**	284.7	**294.4**	261.9
Social security and other taxes	**63.2**	63.1	**55.0**	53.3
Other creditors	**135.0**	146.6	**86.3**	86.6
Accruals and deferred income	**189.0**	177.4	**131.4**	125.2
Proposed final dividend	**209.9**	186.2	**209.9**	186.2
	1,363.8	1,181.0	**982.2**	874.6

18   Creditors: amounts falling due after more than one year

	The Group		The Company	
	1995 **£m**	1994 £m	**1995** **£m**	1994 £m
Repayable between one and two years:				
8¼% Guaranteed bonds 1996	**100.0**	—	—	—
Amounts owed to Group companies	—	—	**100.0**	—
Repayable between two and five years:				
8¼% Guaranteed bonds 1996	—	100.0	—	—
7⅜% Guaranteed notes 1998	**150.0**	150.0	—	—
US$ Promissory note 1998	**276.3**	303.1	—	—
Amount owed to Group companies	—	—	**150.0**	250.0
Other creditors	**32.7**	19.8	—	—
Repayable in five years or more:				
7¾% secured Debenture loan—1995/2000	—	15.0	—	15.0
Other creditors	**9.7**	11.4	—	—
	568.7	599.3	**250.0**	265.0

Creditors due after more than one year are analysed as:

	£m	£m	**£m**	£m
Long-term borrowings (see note 27)	**526.3**	568.1	**250.0**	265.0
Other long-term creditors	**42.4**	31.2	—	—
	568.7	599.3	**250.0**	265.0

18   Creditors: amounts falling due after more than one year *(continued)*

a   8¼% guaranteed bonds 1996
US$150m was raised in 1986 by the issue of a Eurobond at an annual interest rate of 8¼% maturing in 1996. Currency and interest swaps were arranged to provide £100m at floating interest rates below LIBOR.

b   7⅜% guaranteed notes 1998
£150m was raised in July 1993 by the issue of a Eurobond at an annual interest rate of 7⅜% maturing in 1998. Interest swaps were arranged to provide £150m at floating interest rates below LIBOR.

c   US$ promissory note 1998
A US$450m ten year Promissory note, bearing interest at US$ LIBOR maturing in 1998, was issued by a subsidiary of Marks and Spencer p.l.c. as part of the finance for the acquisition of Brooks Brothers Inc.

d   7¾% debenture—1995/2000
The debenture was a first mortgage debenture secured on certain freehold and leashold properties of the Company. On 31 January 1995, the Company redeemed this debenture at par. The debenture was subsequently cancelled.

The interest charges on the Eurobonds shown in note 5 represent floating rates.

19   Provisions for liabilities and charges

	The Group £m	The Company £m
At 1 April 1994	**40.9**	**35.1**
Utilised during the year	**(2.5)**	**(0.1)**
Differences on exchange	**(0.5)**	**—**
As at 31 March 1995	**37.9**	**35.0**

The provision utilised during the year mainly represents expenditure related to discontinued Canadian operations.

The provisions at 31 March 1995 include £35.0m for post-retirement health benefits and £2.9m for discontinued Canadian operations.

20   Deferred taxation

	The Group		The Company	
	1995 £m	1994 £m	**1995 £m**	1994 £m
Deferred tax provision arising on short-term timing differences	**27.6**	28.8	**25.4**	26.5
Deferred tax asset arising on post-retirement health benefits	**(11.5)**	(11.5)	**(11.5)**	(11.5)
	16.1	17.3	**13.9**	15.0
ACT recoverable offset against deferred tax provision (see note 14)	**(16.1)**	(17.3)	**(13.9)**	(15.0)
The movement in deferred tax comprises:				
At 1 April	**17.3**	12.2	**15.0**	9.6
(Credited)/charged to the profit and loss account (see note 6)	**(1.2)**	(5.1)	**(1.1)**	5.4
At 31 March	**16.1**	17.3	**13.9**	15.0

Deferred tax is not provided in respect of liabilities which might arise on the distribution of unappropriated profits of overseas subsidiaries.

21   Called up share capital

	The Company	
	1995	1994
	£m	£m
Authorised:		
3,200,000,000 ordinary shares of 25p each	**800.0**	800.0
Nil 7.0% cumulative preference shares of £1 each (last year 350,000)	—	0.4
Nil 4.9% cumulative preference shares of £1 each (last year 1,000,000)	—	1.0
	800.0	801.4
Allotted, called up and fully paid:		
2,795,906,297 ordinary shares of 25p each (last year 2,779,107,526	**699.0**	694.8
Nil 7.0% cumulative preference shares of £1 each (last year 350,000)	—	0.4
Nil 4.9% cumulative preference shares of £1 each (last year 1,000,000)	—	1.0
	699.0	696.2

12,771,763 ordinary shares having a nominal value of £3.2m were allotted during the year under the terms of the Company's share schemes which are described in note 10. The aggregate consideration received was £32.0m. Contingent rights to the allotment of shares are also described in note 10. In addition, 4,027,008 shares with a nominal value of £1.0m were allotted to shareholders making an election for scrip dividends. The nominal value of £1.0m in respect of scrip dividends was funded out of the share premium account.

On 21 October 1994, the Company redeemed both classes of cumulative preference share. A total premium of £0.1m was paid on redemption of the 1,000,000 4.9% cumulative preference shares and has been included in the preference dividend charge of £0.2m for the year (see note 8). The 350,000 7.0% cumulative preference shares were redeemed at par. Both classes of share have subsequently been cancelled.

22 Shareholders' funds

	The Group		The Company	
	1995 £m	1994 £m	1995 £m	1994 £m
Called up share capital (see note 21)	**699.0**	696.2	**699.0**	696.2
Share premium account:				
At 1 April	**162.3**	129.7	**162.3**	129.7
Shares issued relating to scrip dividends	**(1.0)**	(1.2)	**(1.0)**	(1.2)
Movement during the year	**28.8**	33.8	**28.8**	33.8
At 31 March	**190.1**	162.3	**190.1**	162.3
Revaluation reserve:				
At 1 April	**457.0**	448.9	**465.6**	464.1
Realised during the year	**(1.6)**	1.5	**(1.6)**	1.5
Transfer to profit and loss account reserve (see note below)	—	6.6	—	—
At 31 March	**455.4**	457.0	**464.0**	465.6
Capital reserve (see note below):				
At 1 April	—	—	—	—
Transfer from the profit and loss account reserve	**1.4**	—	**1.4**	—
Transfer to the profit and loss account reserve	**(1.4)**	—	**(1.4)**	—
At 31 March	—	—	—	—
Profit and loss account reserve:				
At 1 April	**2,008.5**	1,680.7	**2,279.4**	1,996.6
Realised revaluation reserve	**(1.6)**	(1.5)	**(1.6)**	1.5
Transfer from revaluation reserve (see note below)	—	(6.6)	—	—
Transfer to the capital reserve	**(1.4)**	—	**(1.4)**	—
Transfer from the capital reserve	**1.4**	—	**1.4**	—
Goodwill written off	—	(0.4)	—	—
Amounts added back in respect of scrip dividends (see note 8)	**16.4**	17.6	**16.4**	17.6
Undistributed surplus for the year	**335.6**	322.7	**282.3**	266.7
Exchange differences on foreign currency translation	**8.3**	(4.0)	—	—
At 31 March	**2,370.4**	2,008.5	**2,579.7**	2,279.4
Shareholders' funds	**3,714.9**	3,324.0	**3,932.8**	3,603.5

The transfer last year of £6.6m from the revaluation reserve to the profit and loss account reserve reflects an adjustment for the cumulative effect of exchange movements on the translation of the pre-acquisition net assets of overseas subsidiaries. These exchange movements are now dealt with through the profit and loss account reserve.

Following the redemption of both classes of cumulative preference share, and in accordance with the provisions of a capital reduction scheme approved by the court on 10 October 1994, a special capital reserve was set up equal to the nominal value of cumulative preference shares redeemed (£1.4m). This reserve was funded out of the profit and loss account reserve. Since the redemption of the cumulative preference shares, sufficient ordinary shares have been issued, so that, under the terms of the capital reduction scheme, this reserve is no longer necessary and accordingly the balance has been transferred back to the profit and loss account reserve.

Cumulative goodwill of £463.3m (last year £463.3m) arising on the acquisition of US, Canadian and Spanish subsidiaries has been written off against the profit and loss account reserve in the years of acquisition.

23   Reconciliation of movements in shareholders' funds

	The Group 1995 £m	The Group 1994 £m	The Company 1995 £m	The Company 1994 £m
Profit for the financial year	**623.8**	578.2	**570.5**	522.2
Dividends	**(288.2)**	(255.5)	**(288.2)**	(255.5)
	335.6	322.7	**282.3**	266.7
Other recognised gains and losses relating to the year	**8.3**	(4.0)	—	—
New share capital subscribed	**32.0**	38.2	**32.0**	38.2
Cumulative preference share capital redeemed	**(1.4)**	—	**(1.4)**	—
Goodwill written off	—	(0.4)	—	—
Amounts added back to profit and loss accout reserve in respect of scrip dividends (see note 8)	**16.4**	17.6	**16.4**	17.6
Net additions to shareholders' funds	**390.9**	374.1	**329.3**	322.5
Shareholders' funds at 1 April	**3,324.0**	2,949.9	**3,603.5**	3,281.0
Shareholders' funds at 31 March	**3,714.9**	3,324.0	**3,932.8**	3,603.5

24   Reconciliation of operating profit to net cash inflow from operating activities

	The Group 1995 £m	The Group 1994 £m
Operating profit	**896.5**	854.5
Depreciation	**150.7**	136.3
Increase in stocks	**(22.4)**	(10.0)
Increase in customer balances	**(144.5)**	(157.5)
Increase in other debtors	**(22.7)**	(1.5)
Increase in creditors	**51.2**	63.4
Net cash inflow from operating activities	**908.8**	885.2

25   Analysis of cash and non-cash equivalents included in net current assets

	1995 Cash and cash equivalents £m	1995 Non-cash equivalents £m	1995 Total £m	1994 Cash and cash equivalents £m	1994 Non-cash equivalents £m	1994 Total £m
Current asset investments	3.9	189.3	**193.2**	49.4	214.5	263.9
Cash at bank and in hand	455.7	280.0	**735.7**	428.6	122.2	550.8
Amounts due on purchase of investments included in other creditors	—	—	—	—	(8.0)	(8.0)
	459.6	469.3	**928.9**	478.0	328.7	806.7
Bank loans, overdrafts and commercial paper	(207.9)	(66.0)	**(273.9)**	(111.0)	(49.2)	(160.2)
	251.7	**403.3**	**655.0**	367.0	279.5	646.5

Cash and cash equivalent investments and deposits are assets with maturities of 90 days or less when acquired. Cash and cash equivalent bank loans, overdrafts and commercial paper are borrowings which are repayable in 90 days or less from the date of advance. All other investments and borrowings included above are classified as non-cash equivalents and are shown in the analysis of financing and treasury activities (see note 27).

26 Analysis of the movement in cash and cash equivalents

	The Group 1995 £m	1994 £m
At 1 April (see note 25)	367.0	88.7
Amounts included in cash flow statement	(88.5)	270.6
Foreign exchange movements on cash and cash equivalents	(26.8)	7.7
At 31 March (see note 25)	251.7	367.0

27 Analysis of financing and treasury activities

	Share capital and share premium £m	Long-term borrowings £m	Bank loans and overdrafts £m	Non-cash equivalent deposits £m	**Total** **£m**
At 1 April 1994	858.5	568.1	49.2	(328.7)	**1,147.1**
Amounts included in cash flow statement	30.6	(15.0)	16.8	(140.6)	**(108.2)**
Effect of foreign exchange rates	—	(26.8)	—	—	**(26.8)**
At 31 March 1995	**889.1**	**526.3**	**66.0**	**(469.3)**	**1,012.1**

28 Analysis of net group funds

	The Group 1995 £m	1994 £m
Analysis of net group funds:		
Fixed asset investments	27.4	9.2
Current asset investments	193.2	263.9
Cash at bank and in hand	735.7	550.8
Bank loans, overdrafts and commercial paper	(273.9)	(160.2)
Long-term borrowings	(526.3)	(568.1)
Amounts included in other long-term creditors due after more than one year	(27.4)	(15.5)
	128.7	80.1
Movement in net group funds:		
At 1 April	80.1	(125.4)
Amounts included in cash flow statement	48.6	205.5
At 31 March	**128.7**	80.1

29 Sundry cash flow information

Dividends paid include £0.8m (last year £0.7m) paid to minority shareholders in subsidiaries and a £0.1m premium paid on the redemption of the cumulative preference shares (see note 21).

The cash inflow from the sale of a subsidiary last year of £2.6m related to deferred consideration received on the disposal of Peoples Department Stores Inc to Wise Stores Inc.

30   Commitments and contingent liabilities

	The Group 1995 £m	The Group 1994 £m	The Company 1995 £m	The Company 1994 £m
a Commitments in respect of properties in the course of development	186.8	98.6	182.2	86.1
b Capital expenditure authorised by the directors but not yet contracted	279.3	191.3	218.0	169.7
c Deferred taxation not provided on the excess of capital allowances over depreciation on tangible assets	185.9	172.2	176.7	165.0
d Guarantees by the Company in respect of the Eurobonds and Promissory note issued by subsidiaries	—	—	526.3	553.1
e Guarantees by the Company of the commercial paper issued by St Michael Finance Limited	—	—	122.7	90.2
f Guarantees in relation to certain property lease disposals	—	7.2	—	7.2
g Guarantees by the Company of the liabilities of Marks and Spencer (Ireland) Limited	—	—	27.9	58.3

Marks and Spencer (Ireland) Limited has availed itself of the exemption provided for in s17 of the Companies (Amendment) Act 1986 (Ireland) in respect of the documents required to be annexed to its annual return.

h   In the opinion of the directors, the revalued properties will be retained for use in the business and the likelihood of any taxation liability arising is remote. Accordingly the potential deferred taxation in respect of these properties has not been quantified.

i   Other material contracts
In the event of a material change in the trading arrangements with certain warehouse operators, the Company has a commitment to purchase, at market value, fixed assets which are currently owned and operated by them on the Company's behalf.

j   Commitments under operating leases
At 31 March 1995 annual commitments under operating leases were as follows:

	The Group Land & buildings £m	The Group Other £m	The Company Land & buildings £m	The Company Other £m
Expiring within one year	5.6	1.1	—	0.3
Expiring in the second to fifth years inclusive	21.8	4.4	2.5	3.1
Expiring in five years or more	65.5	—	33.5	—
	92.9	5.5	36.0	3.4

31   Foreign exchange rates

The principal foreign exchange rates issued in the financial statements are as follows (local currency equivalent of £1):

	Sales Average rate 1995	Sales Average rate 1994	Profit average rate 1995	Profit average rate 1994	Balance sheet rate 1995	Balance sheet rate 1994
Republic of Ireland	1.01	1.04	1.01	1.04	1.00	1.03
France	8.32	8.62	8.31	8.60	7.81	8.46
Belgium	49.73	52.62	50.16	52.52	45.78	51.08
The Netherlands	2.71	2.83	2.71	2.84	2.49	2.79
Spain	204.48	202.43	203.63	203.02	205.23	202.08
United States	1.56	1.50	1.57	1.50	1.63	1.48
Canada	2.16	1.97	2.17	1.97	2.28	2.05
Hong Kong	12.10	11.59	12.12	11.59	12.59	11.47
Japan	153.84	162.02	154.89	162.80	140.73	152.54

GROUP FINANCIAL RECORD

For the years ended 31 March

	1995 £m 52 weeks	1994 £m 53 weeks	1993 £m 52 weeks	1992 £m 52 weeks	1991 £m 52 weeks
PROFIT AND LOSS ACCOUNT*					
Turnover:					
General	**3,889.0**	3,718.6	3,380.1	3,325.2	3,332.2
Foods	**2,682.0**	2,612.6	2,387.5	2,341.4	2,292.1
Financial Activities	**135.7**	122.8	109.9	98.2	91.5
Direct export sales outside the Group	**99.8**	87.2	73.3	62.7	59.0
Total turnover (excluding sales taxes)	**6,806.5**	6,541.2	5,950.8	5,827.5	5,774.8
Operating profit†:					
United Kingdom	**845.5**	790.2	665.0	622.5	591.8
Europe (excluding UK)	**20.7**	27.9	28.1	25.2	20.2
Rest of the World	**30.3**	36.4	28.7	15.3	10.9
Total operating profit	**896.5**	854.5	721.8	663.0	622.9
Retailing	**847.6**	813.1	689.0	640.2	602.9
Financial Activities	**48.9**	41.4	32.8	22.8	20.0
Loss on disposal of property and other fixed assests	**(5.4)**	(17.3)	(7.8)	(8.2)	(13.3)
Exceptional charges	**—**	—	—	(76.7)	(16.0)
Net interst income	**33.2**	14.3	22.5	10.8	13.3
Profit before taxation	**924.3**	851.5	736.5	588.9	606.9
Taxation on ordinary activities	**(299.5)**	(272.2)	(239.5)	(218.3)	(215.8)
Minority interests	**(1.0)**	(1.1)	(1.5)	(2.6)	(2.4)
Profit for the financial year	**623.8**	578.2	495.5	368.0	388.7
Dividends	**(288.2)**	(255.5)	(223.6)	(194.5)	(182.0)
Undistributed surplus	**335.6**	322.7	271.9	173.5	206.7
BALANCE SHEET‡					
Tangible fixed assets	**3,297.0**	3,095.4	2,908.6	2,776.7	2,612.6
Investments	**43.3**	15.5	19.4	4.7	—
Current assets	**2,365.8**	2,053.7	1,761.7	1,524.8	1,301.9
Total assets	**5,706.1**	5,164.6	4,689.7	4,306.2	3,914.5
Creditors due within one year	**(1,363.8)**	(1,181.0)	(1,230.7)	(1,168.8)	(896.7)
Total assets less current liabilities	**4,342.3**	3,983.6	3,459.0	3,137.4	3,017.8
Creditors due after more than one year	**(568.7)**	(599.3)	(446.4)	(401.5)	(549.6)
Provisions for liabilities and charges	**(37.9)**	(40.9)	(45.7)	(75.8)	(53.4)
Net assets	**3,735.7**	3,343.4	2,966.9	2,660.1	2,414.8
CASH FLOW					
Net cash inflow from operating activities#	**908.8**	885.2	763.1	688.2	677.6
Net cash outflow from returns on investments and servicing of finance	**(218.3)**	(197.6)	(170.7)	(160.5)	(152.5)
Tax paid	**(273.4)**	(231.8)	(215.5)	(216.2)	(231.9)
Net cash outflow from investing activities	**(397.4)**	(279.6)	(248.0)	(286.4)	(305.0)

*Restated for FRS 3 in 1992 and 1991. †Restated for 1994 and prior years to include profit share and to include results of the Republic of Ireland within Europe and MS Insurance within the Uunited Kingdom. ‡Restated for post-retirement health costs in 1992 and 1991. #Net of cash flows relating to exceptional previsions.

		1995 **52 weeks**	1994 53 weeks	1993 52 weeks	1992 52 weeks	1991 52 weeks
Net cash inflow/(outflow) before financing and treasury activities		**19.7**	176.2	128.9	25.1	(11.8)
Net cash (outflow)/inflow from financing and treasury activities		**(108.2)**	94.4	(143.8)	(68.6)	20.0
(Decrease)/increase in cash and cash equivalents		**(88.5)**	270.6	(14.9)	(43.5)	8.2
Increase in net funds		**48.6**	205.5	135.9	65.7	34.4
Gross margin*	Gross profit / Turnover	**35.1%**	35.1%	34.8%	33.8%	33.1%
Net margin*†	Operating profit / Turnover	**13.2%**	13.1%	12.2%	11.6%	10.8%
Profitability	Profit before tax / Turnover	**13.6%**	13.0%	12.4%	10.1%	10.5%
Earnings per share	Profit after tax, minority interests and preference dividends / Weighted average ordinary shares in issue	**22.4p**	20.9p	18.0p	13.5p	14.4p
Dividend per share		**10.3p**	9.2p	8.1p	7.1p	6.7p
Dividend cover	Earnings per share / Dividend per share	**2.2**	2.3	2.2	1.9	2.1
Return on equity	Profit after tax and minority interests / Average shareholders' funds	**17.7%**	18.4%	17.7%	14.6%	17.1%
Capital expenditure		**£366.9m**	£343.5m	£250.8m	£305.4m	£300.4m

•Based on operations reported as continuing operations
†Restated to include profit share

GROUP PRODUCTIVITY

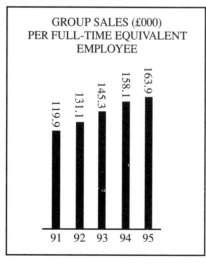

GROUP SALES (£000)
PER FULL-TIME EQUIVALENT
EMPLOYEE

119.9 131.1 145.3 158.1 163.9
91 92 93 94 95

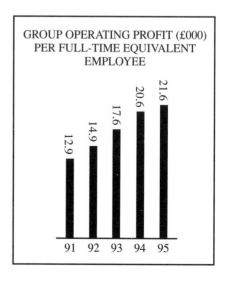

GROUP OPERATING PROFIT (£000)
PER FULL-TIME EQUIVALENT
EMPLOYEE

12.9 14.9 17.6 20.6 21.6
91 92 93 94 95

CHAPTER TWO

2.1.1

Balance sheet as at 30 September

	£		£
Current assets:		Capital	20,000
Bank	20,000		
	20,000		20,000

Comments The fact that Evans has increased the mortgage on his house does not appear in the balance sheet since this is a private transaction between Evans and the lender. The balance sheet tells us a little about the business but nothing at all about the owner. The business and its owner are entirely separate entities.

2.1.2

Balance sheet as at 4 October

	£		£
Current assets:		Capital	20,000
Stock	4,000		
Bank	16,000		
	20,000		20,000

Comments His mother is to work part-time in the shop and will receive £50 per week. This is to happen in the future and does not appear in this balance sheet. If he owed his mother her wages now they would appear as a current liability; £50 is not large enough to warrant a note at the foot of the balance sheet, but if Evans had entered into a contract for £50,000 it would be significant enough to be shown as a note. The same argument applies to the rent that does not become due until the end of the month.

2.1.3

Balance sheet as at 7 October

	£		£
Current assets:		Capital	20,000
Stock	13,700	Reserves:	
Bank	16,400	Profit	100
		Current liabilities:	
		Creditors	10,000
	———		———
	30,100		30,100
	═══		═══

Comments   He owes £10,000 for the cassettes that he has received and has made a profit of £100 which goes into reserves.

2.1.4

Balance sheet as at 8 October

	£		£
Current assets:		Capital	20,000
Stock	13,200	Reserves:	
Debtors	666	Profit	266
Bank	16,400	Current liabilities:	
		Creditors	10,000
	———		———
	30,266		30,266
	═══		═══

Comments: He is owed £666 for the cassettes and so debtors appear in the balance sheet and additional profit is added to the reserves.

2.1.5

Balance sheet as at 11 October

	£		£
Current assets:		Capital	20,000
Stock	13,200	Reserves:	
Debtors	666	Profit	216
Bank	16,350	Current liabilities:	
		Creditors	10,000
	———		———
	30,216		30,216
	═══		═══

Comments   The payment of the wages to his mother reduces the bank balance and the profit.

2.1.6   *Balance sheet as at 14 October*

	£	£		£
Fixed assets:			Capital	20,000
Premises		25,000	Reserves:	
Current assets:			Profit	216
Stock	13,200		Loan	15,000
Debtors	666		Current liabilities:	
Bank	6,350	20,216	Creditors	10,000
		45,216		45,216

Comments The bank loan is assumed to be for more than five years and so appears as a long-term liability between reserves and current liabilities. Evans has a fixed asset—premises—and his bank balance has been reduced by £10,000.

It would be good practice to redraw each of the balance sheets for Evans's business in the vertical form. That for 14 October would become:

Balance sheet as at 14 October

	£	£	£
Fixed assets:			
Premises			25,000
Current assets:			
Stock	13,200		
Debtors	666		
Bank	6,350	20,216	
Deduct Current liabilities:			
Creditors		10,000	
Working capital			10,216
Net capital employed			35,216
Less Loan			15,000
Net assets			20,216
Financed by:			
Capital			20,000
Reserves:			
Retained profit			216
Equity interest			20,216

2.2

	£	£		£	£
Fixed assets			Capital	200,000	
Land and buildings	160,000		Reserves	60,000	
Plant and machinery	50,000		Equity interest		260,000
Motor vehicles	10,000		Loan		70,000
		220,000			
Current assets:			Current liabilities:		
Stock	20,000		Creditors		40,000
Debtors	90,000				
Bank	40,000	150,000			
		370,000			370,000

2.3

Balance Sheet

	£	£	£
Goodwill			20,000
Fixed assets:			
Land and building		190,000	
Plant and machinery		110,000	
Furniture and fittings		80,000	380,000
Current assets:			
Stock	60,000		
Debtors	40,000		
Bank	10,000	110,000	
Deduct Current liabilities:			
Creditors	90,000		
Accruals	10,000	100,000	
Working capital			10,000
Net capital employed (total assets less current liabilities)			410,000
Less Long-term loan			50,000
Net assets			360,000
Financed by			
Share capital			290,000
Reserves			70,000
Equity interest			360,000

2.4	Fixed assets:	£	£		£	£
	Land and building	80,000		Capital		90,000
	Plant and machinery	60,000		Reserves		20,000
	Fixtures and fittings	20,000		Loan		70,000
	Motor vehicles	30,000	190,000			
	Current assets:			Current liabilities:		
	Stock	40,000		Creditors	90,000	
	Debtors	80,000		Accruals	50,000	140,000
	Bank	10,000	130,000			
			320,000			320,000

CHAPTER THREE

3.1.1

Income statement for the first four weeks

	£	£
Sales		4,230
Cost of goods sold:		
Opening stock	—	
Add Purchases	1,500	
	1,500	
Less Closing stock	50	1,450
Gross profit		2,780
Expenses:		
Rent	120	
Weekend help	60	
Fines	80	
Depreciation:		
Barrow	32	
Scales	4	296
NET PROFIT		2,484

Cash statement

	£	£
Opening balance		3,000
Add receipts		4,230
Cash available		7,230
Deduct Payments:		
Rent	90	
Weekend help	60	
Fines	80	
Fruit	1,500	
Barrow	832	
Scales	208	2,770
CASH IN HAND		4,460

Balance sheet as at end of first four weeks

	Cost	Depreciation	Net book value (NBV)		
	£	£	£		£
Fixed assets:				Capital	3,000
Scales	208	4	204	Reserves:	
Barrow	832	32	800	Profit	2,484
	1,040	36	1,004		
Current Assets:				Current liabilities:	
Stock		50		Rent due	30
Bank		4,460	4,510		
			5,514		5,514

The depreciation is calculated as follows:

1. The barrow cost £832 and is expected to last for two years. Tom Smith prepares his accounts every four weeks, and as there are 52 weeks in a year he has 52/4 = 13 accounting periods. In two years he will have 26 accounting periods. The barrow does not have any scrap value so the depreciation is 832/26 = £32.
2. Similarly the depreciation of the scales is over four years which is 4 × 13 = 52 periods. The calculation is 208/52 = £4.

Depreciation does not appear in the cash statement because it allocates the cost of the assets but does not cause any more money to leave Smith's business.

The sales figure is calculated by adding to the takings the expenses that have been paid out to them: £4,000 + £230 = £4,230.

The barrow and scales do not have a direct impact on the income statement because as far as Smith is concerned they are fixed assets.

The closing stock has been valued at the lower of cost or current market value.

3.1.2

Income statement for the second four weeks

	£	£
Sales		4,800
Cost of good sold:		
Opening stock	50	
Add Purchases	2,000	
	2,050	
Less Closing stock	100	1,950
Gross profit		2,850
Expenses:		
Rent	120	
Weekend help	60	
Fines	150	
Insurance	16	
Depreciation:		
Barrow	32	
Scales	4	382
NET PROFIT		2,468

Cash statement

	£	£
Opening balance		4,460
Add Receipts		4,800
Cash available		9,260
Deduct Payments:		
Insurance	208	
Wife	1,200	
Rent	90	
Fines	150	
Weekend help	60	
Fruit	2,000	3,708
CASH IN HAND		5,552

Balance sheet as at end of second four weeks

	Cost	Depreciation	Net book value (NBV)			
	£	£	£		£	£
Fixed assets:				Capital	3,000	
Scales	208	8	200	RESERVES		
Barrow	832	64	768	Profit b/fwd	2,484	
				Add This period	2,468	
	1,040	72	968			
					4,952	
				Less Drawings	1,200	3,752
Current assets:				Current liabilities:		
Stock		100		Rent due		60
Bank		5,552				
Insurance prepaid		192	5,844			
			6,812			6,812

The profit for the second period is £2,468. His cash balance at the end of the second period is £5,552. His financial position as reflected in the balance sheet is sound but he does seem to have rather too much money lying idle.

He has made a profit of £2,468 and has a great deal of cash, so he could afford to give his wife £1,800. It is good policy to retain some profit in the business to allow it to expand, so Smith should not give his wife much more than £1,800 as he would be approaching the total profit figure.

3.1.3

Income statement for the third four weeks

	£	£
Sales		4,100
Cost of goods sold:		
Opening stock	100	
Add Purchases	2,500	
	2,600	
Less Closing stock	200	2,400
Gross profit		1,700
Expenses:		
Rent	120	
Weekend help	60	
Fines	25	
Insurance	16	
Depreciation:		
Barrow	32	
Scales	4	257
Operating profit		1,443
Loss on sale of barrow		236
NET PROFIT		1,207

Cash statement

	£	£
Opening balance		5,552
Add Receipts		4,600
Cash available		10,152
Deduct Payments:		
Wife	1,450	
Rent	150	
Weekend help	60	
Fruit	2,500	
Van	3,003	7,163
CASH IN HAND		2,989

Balance sheet as at end of third four weeks

	Cost	Depreciation	Net book value (NBV)				
	£	£	£				£
Fixed assets:				Capital			3,000
Scales	208	12	196	RESERVES			
Van	3,003	—	3,003	Profit b/fwd	3,752		
				Add This period	1,207		
	3,211	12	3,199			4,959	
				Less Drawings	1,450		3,509
Current assets:				Current liabilities:			
Stock		200		Rent due		30	
Bank		2,989		Fine pending		25	55
Insurance prepaid		176	3,365				
			6,564				6,564

The loss on the sale of the barrow is calculated as follows:

	£
Cost of barrow	832
Less Depreciation (£32 × 3)	96
Book value at time of sale	736
Deduct Proceeds of sale	500
Loss on sale	236

The operating profit of £1,443 is the profit from normal business activities. The net profit of £1,207 is arrived at only after extraordinary items, such as the sale of the barrow, have been taken into account.

The accounting convention of anticipating losses has been taken into account in providing £25 for the anticipated fine.

The barrow has a full period's depreciation as it was sold on the last day of the period. The van is not depreciated at all as it was obtained on the last day of the period.

Smith has made a loss on the sale of his barrow of £236; his operating profit for the period is £1,443 and his financial position at the end of the period as revealed by the balance sheet is sound. It is interesting to note that his cash balance has fallen, mainly due to the purchase of the van.

3.1.4

Income statement for the fourth four weeks

	£	£
Sales		4,600
Cost of goods sold:		
Opening stock	200	
Add Purchases	4,000	
	4,200	
Less Closing stock	1,500	2,700
Gross profit		1,900
Over-provision for fine		
recovered		5
		1,905
Expenses:		
Vehicle running	200	
Rent	120	
Weekend help	60	
Insurance	16	
Vehicle licence	20	
Depreciation:		
Scales	4	
Van	85	505
NET PROFIT		1,400

Cash statement

	£	£
Opening balance		2,989
Add Receipts		4,500
Cash available		7,489
Deduct Payments:		
Wife	4,000	
Rent	120	
Weekend help	60	
Fruit	3,500	
Fine	20	
Vehicle running	200	
Licence	260	8,160
BANK OVERDRAWN		(671)

Balance sheet as at end of fourth four weeks

	Cost	Depreciation	Net book value (NBV)			
	£	£	£		£	£
Fixed assets:				Capital		3,000
Scales	208	16	192	RESERVES		
Van	3,003	85	2,918	Profit b/fwd	3,509	
				Add This period	1,400	
	3,211	101	3,110		4,909	
				Less Drawings	4,000	909
Current assets:				Current liabilities:		
Stock		1,500		Creditor	500	
Debtor		100		Rent due	30	
Insurance prepaid		160		Bank overdraft	671	1,201
Licence prepaid		240	2,000			
			5,110			5,110

The depreciation of the van is calculated as follows:

$$\text{Depreciation} \quad \frac{\text{Cost} - \text{Scrap value}}{\text{Life}} = \frac{3,003 - 793}{26} = \frac{2,210}{26} = £85$$

The over-provision for the fine of £5 is treated as an additional receipt. This is because the last period's profit was reduced by £5, and to compensate for that this period's profit is increased by £5.

The vehicle licence is treated as apportioned expenditure. Only one-thirteenth of it is used up in this period and shown in the income statement as an expense. The balance is shown on the balance sheet as an asset.

Despite being profitable, Smith has a bank overdraft of £671, and it is essential for him to convince his wife that she can manage on £1,000 per month, or less, if he is to survive in the short term.

In the longer term it may be that his business will pick up and his situation improve as he begins to gain a better understanding of his new situation.

Smith's net profit for the period is £1,400. Smith's financial position at the end of the period is somewhat precarious as previously stated. If he can learn from his experience and obtain his wife's cooperation, he should overcome this problem, with the aid of the bank. It might be prudent for him to obtain overdraft facilities of £2,000 and prepare a cash flow forecast.

His balance sheet does not accurately represent the worth of his business as assets are valued on the basis of historical costs, less depreciation, and no account has been taken of goodwill, which would be whatever he could persuade a purchaser to give him for his business as a going concern.

3.2

1.   *Balance sheet as at 31 August 1997*

	Cost	Depreciation	Net book value (NBV)
	£'000s	£'000s	£'000s
Fixed assets:			
Land and buildings	280	100	180
Plant and machinery	76	61	15
Vehicles	20	16	4
	376	177	199
Current assets:			
Stock	18		
Debtor	14		
Bank	1	33	
Less Current liabilities:			
Creditors	30		
Accruals	10	40	
Net current liabilities/working capital			(7)
NET CAPITAL EMPLOYED			192
Less Loan			60
Net assets			132
Owner's equity:			
Capital			80
Reserves			
Retained profit			52
			132

2. More than one year because the retained profit of £52,000 is greater than this year's profit of £24,000.
3. The creditors of £30,000 greatly exceed the debtors of £14,000 and bank balance of £1,000 so Brown may experience difficulty in paying his way.

CHAPTER FOUR

4.1

		1997	1998

1. Net profit as a percentage of net capital employed

$$\frac{110 \times 100}{630} = \quad 17.46 \text{ per cent}$$

$$\frac{100 \times 100}{645} = \qquad\qquad\qquad 15.5 \text{ per cent}$$

In 1998 if the extraordinary items are excluded there is a loss of £150,000, viz.

Gain on sale of investment	60,000
Gain on change in accounting basis	190,000
	250,000

This indicates the extent of the collapse in operating viability on a consistent basis with the 1997 accounts.

2. Debtors' ratio (£'000s) $\quad = \quad \dfrac{\text{Debtors}}{\text{Credit sales}} \times 365$

$$\frac{230 \times 365}{1,700} = \quad 49.4 \text{ days}$$

$$\frac{370 \times 365}{1,300} = \qquad\qquad\qquad 103.9 \text{ days}$$

This shows that debt collection has slipped dramatically and is in keeping with the reported problems in the accounting department.

3. *Current ratio*
    Current assets : Current liabilities
    720 : 490   1.47 : 1
    775 : 440   1.76 : 1

4. *Quick ratio*
    Quick assets : Current liabilities
    530 : 490   1.08:1
    620 : 440   1.41:1

5.   *Creditors' ratio*   1997   1998

$$\frac{\text{Creditors}}{\text{Credit purchases}} \times \quad 365$$

$$\frac{300 \times 365}{870} \quad = \qquad\qquad 125.9 \text{ days}$$

$$\frac{240 \times 365}{790} \quad = \qquad\qquad\qquad\qquad 110.9 \text{ days}$$

4.2

	1998	1997	1996	1995	1994

1. *Return on equity*

$$\frac{\text{Profit before tax and exceptional items} \times 100}{\text{Shareholders' funds}}$$

	1998	1997	1996	1995	1994
$\dfrac{219.5 \times 100^*}{617.8}$	35.5%	31.3%	28.6%	29.5%	26.9%

2. *Return on capital employed*

$$\frac{\text{Profit before tax and exceptional items} \times 100}{\text{Net capital employed (Total assets} - \text{Current liabilities)}}$$

	1998	1997	1996	1995	1994
$\dfrac{219.5 \times 100}{1279.4}$	17.2%	14.6%	12.5%	14%	16.4%

3. *Interest cover*

$$\frac{\text{Profit before interest charges}}{\text{Interest charges}}$$

	1998	1997	1996	1995	1994
$\dfrac{249.7}{30.2}$	8.3 times	5.8 times	4.9 times	4.1 times	8.7 times

4. *Fixed asset turnover*

$\dfrac{\text{Sales}}{\text{Fixed assets}}$	$\dfrac{2934.4}{921.6}$	3.2 times	2.9 times	2.7 times	2.8 times	2.1 times

5. *Percentage growth in sales year on year*

$$\frac{(\text{Sales for 1998} - \text{Sales for 1997}) \times 100}{\text{Sales for 1997}}$$

	1998	1997	1996	1995	1994
$\dfrac{(2934.4 - 2757.8) \times 100}{2757.8}$	6.4%	14.5%	1.4%	36.3%	—

6. *Percentage growth in profit year on year*

$$\frac{(\text{Profit for 1998} - \text{Profit for 1997}) \times 100}{\text{Profit for 1997}}$$

$$\frac{(219.5 - 181.7) \times 100}{181.7} \qquad 20.8\% \qquad 15.8\% \qquad 7\% \qquad -1.4\% \qquad —$$

*The worked examples are figures for 1998 taken from the five-year summary in question 4.2. Other results have been obtained by using figures for the relevant years as given in question 4.2.

Interpretation

The ROCE is at a reasonable level when compared with the return that could be earned by investing the money safely in the Post Office, bank or building society.

Interest cover shows that profits are adequate to support the current borrowing. The fixed assets are being employed effectively.

The percentage growth in sales year on year fluctuates rather worryingly, but profits present a period of steady growth after 1995.

Summary

The income statements indicate that this organization is in the oil business, so it would be helpful to have average figures for this sector to facilitate comparison. The business appears to be going through an unsettled period as demonstrated by the ROCE, but profits are growing well.

4.3	1994	1995	1996	1997	1998
A *Profitability Ratios*					

1. Return on capital employed

$$\frac{\text{Profit before tax} \times 100}{\text{Net capital employed}} = \frac{294.7 \times 100^*}{1306.3} \qquad 22.6\% \quad 18.7\% \quad 12.8\% \quad 13.1\% \quad 16.3\%$$

2. Profitability of sales

$$\frac{\text{Profit before tax} \times 100}{\text{Sales}} = \frac{294.7 \times 100}{2910} \qquad 10.1\% \quad 7.8\% \quad 5.8\% \quad 5.8\% \quad 6.9\%$$

3. Return on equity

$$\frac{\text{Profit before tax} \times 100}{\text{Shareholders' equity}} = \frac{294.7 \times 100}{961.8} \qquad 30.6\% \quad 25.9\% \quad 18.1\% \quad 17.7\% \quad 28.3\%$$

B *Liquidity ratios*	1994	1995	1996	1997	1998

1. Current ratio

Current assets : Current liabilities

690.3 : 600.6

	1.1 : 1	1.6 : 1	2 : 1	1.9 : 1	1.7 : 1

2. Quick ratio

Quick assets : Current liabilities

(690.3–463.9)

226.4 : 600.6

	0.4 : 1	0.5 : 1	0.9 : 1	0.8 : 1	0.8 : 1

3. Gearing ratio

$$\frac{\text{Long/medium/short-term debt} \times 100}{\text{Shareholders' equity}}$$

$$\frac{(301.3 + 54.8) \times 100}{961.8}$$

	37%	40%	42%	37%	68%

4. Times interest earned (interest cover)

$$\frac{\text{Profit before interest charges}}{\text{Interest charges}}$$

$$\frac{342.2}{47.5}$$

	7.2 times	6.3 times	5.8 times	6.6 times	6.4 times

C *Efficiency ratios*

1. Age of debtors

$$\frac{\text{Sales}}{\text{Debtors}} = \text{times turned over} : \frac{365}{\text{times}}$$

$$= \text{collection days}$$

$$\frac{2910}{124.2} = 23.4$$

$$\frac{365}{23.4}$$

	15.6 days	13.8 days	16.7 days	14.3 days	20.4 days

2. Age of stock (rate of stock turnover)

$$\frac{\text{Cost of sales}}{\text{Stock}} = \text{times, then} \frac{365}{\text{times}}$$

$$= \text{days to sell stock}$$

$$\frac{2910-283.3}{463.9} = 5.7 \text{ times, then} \frac{365}{5.7}$$

	64 days	79.3 days	73 days	67.6 days	66.4 days

3. Fixed asset turnover

	1994	1995	1996	1997	1998

$$\frac{\text{Sales}}{\text{Fixed assets}} = \text{number of times}$$

$$\frac{2910}{(841.8+372)}$$

2.4 times   3.3 times   3.7 times   3.6 times   3.6 times

4. Sales per employee

$$\frac{\text{Sales}}{\text{Employees}} = \frac{2,910,000,000}{58,769}$$

£49,493.2   £52,610.7   £54,710.1   £56,496.1   £62,182.8

*Worked examples for 1994; other results obtained similarly by using five-year summary in question 4.3.

Interpretation

Profitability as measured by the ROCE is fluctuating as is the profitability of sales. This could indicate an organization that is going through a period of reorganization and the final year indicates that it is beginning to benefit from its hard work. The return on equity follows a similar pattern.

The current and quick ratios are low and have a slight tendency to fluctuate, although overall they appear to be under control. They indicate an organization in the retail sector rather than manufacturing, which would need more working capital.

The gearing ratio shows a large increase in the final year, with additional borrowing used to buy additional fixed assets, possibly to support the reorganization, but the interest cover remains at over six times. This demonstrates that profits can easily support the increased gearing.

Debtors pay in less than three weeks, which is extremely fast for most businesses, and indicates that the sales are largely for cash, showing an organization in the retail sector, but not food.

The stock is turned over in about ten weeks, which again supports the view that the orgainization is in the retail sector.

The fixed assets are being effectively employed, and sales per employee are increasing well.

Summary

This organization appears to be in the retail sector and to have gone through a period of reorganization as shown by the ROCE and profitability of sales. The benefits of this reorganization are now being felt, but it is dangerous to assume this on the evidence of 1998 alone. It would be interesting to see the next few years' figures and the average for the sector for reasons of comparison. It appears that management has perceived a problem and taken action it feels necessary to correct the situation.

4.4

	1994	1995	1996	1997	1998

A *Profitability ratios*

1. Return on capital employed

$$\frac{\text{Profit before tax} \times 100}{\text{Net capital employed}} = \frac{175.9 \times 100*}{825.1}$$

| | 21.3% | 18.4% | 19.6% | 21.5% | 16.2% |

2. Profitability of sales

$$\frac{\text{Profit before tax} \times 100}{\text{Sales}} = \frac{175.9 \times 100}{3593}$$

| | 4.9% | 5.5% | 5.9% | 6.7% | 6.9% |

3. Return on equity

$$\frac{\text{Profit before tax} \times 100}{\text{Shareholders' equity}} = \frac{175.9 \times 100}{690.1}$$

| | 25.5% | 26% | 26.8% | 28.8% | 20.2% |

B *Liquidity ratios*
1. Current ratio

Current assets : Current liabilities
      256.6 : 431.6

| | 0.6 : 1 | 0.6 : 1 | 0.5 : 1 | 0.4 : 1 | 0.8 : 1 |

2. Quick ratio

Quick assets : Current liabilities
(256.6−182.5) : 431.6

| | 0.2 : 1 | 0.2 : 1 | 0.2 : 1 | 0.1 : 1 | 0.6 : 1 |

3. Gearing ratio

$$\frac{\text{Long/medium/short-term debt} \times 100}{\text{Shareholders' equity}}$$

$$\frac{(120.4 + 8.8) \times 100}{690.1}$$

| | 18.7% | 34.9% | 29.3% | 33.2% | 24.3% |

4. Times interest earned (interest cover)

$$\frac{\text{Profit before interest charges}}{\text{Interest charges}}$$

$$\frac{185.5}{9.6}$$

| | 19.3 times | 11.8 times | 8.1 times | 8.8 times | 9.2 times |

C *Efficiency ratios*
1. Age of debtors

$$\frac{\text{Sales}}{\text{Debtors}} = \text{times turned over, then}$$

$$\frac{365}{\text{times}} = \text{collection days}$$

$$\frac{3593}{13.6} = 264.2 \text{ times}$$

	1994	1995	1996	1997	1998

$$\frac{365}{264.2}$$

1.4 days 3.5 days 2.1 days 1.3 days 2.9 days

2. Age of stock (rate of stock turnover)

$$\frac{\text{Cost of sales}}{\text{Stock}} = \text{times, then} \quad \frac{365}{\text{times}}$$

$$= \text{days to sell stock}$$

$$\frac{3593 - 154.5}{182.5} = 18.8 \text{ times, then} \quad \frac{365}{18.8} \quad 19.4 \text{ days} \quad 21.8 \text{ days} \quad 23.1 \text{ days} \quad 23.7 \text{ days} \quad 25.6 \text{ days}$$

3. Fixed asset turnover

$$\frac{\text{Sales}}{\text{Fixed assets}} = \text{number of times}$$

$$\frac{3593}{(598.9 + 401)} \quad 3.6 \text{ times} \quad 2.9 \text{ times} \quad 2.7 \text{ times} \quad 2.5 \text{ times} \quad 2.2 \text{ times}$$

4. Sales per employee

$$\frac{\text{Sales}}{\text{Employees}} = \frac{3,593,000,000}{62,652} \quad £57,348.5 \quad £57,802.2 \quad £62,355.6 \quad £64,908.0 \quad £72,371.0$$

*Worked examples for 1994; other results obtained similarly by using five-year summary in question 4.4.

Interpretation

Profitability, as measured by ROCE, is fluctuating rather than increasing, but this is affected by increases in the net capital employed. Profitability of sales is showing a steady increase.

Return on equity is increasing until 1998, when there is a drop caused by a large increase in shareholders' equity.

Liquidity, as measured by both the current and quick ratios, appears low, but the business is able to survive on them. An organization that sells for cash and receives credit from its suppliers is indicated—probably a food retailer.

Gearing ratio is at a reasonable level and the interest cover is good.

Debtors are paying extremely quickly, supporting the view that this is largely a cash business.

Stock is being sold in about three weeks, which for most businesses would be very fast, but for retail food is not exceptional.

Fixed assets are apparently being employed less effectively in later years, but on further inspection this is being affected by increases in the investment in fixed assets.

Sales per employee are improving.

Summary

This appears to be a well-managed organization that has gone through a period of expansion, as demonstrated by the additional investment from which it is yet to benefit fully in terms of the ROCE. It is probably in the retail food sector, enabling it to turn stock over quickly, keep debtors to a minimum and have negative working capital. Average figures for the sector would be helpful for purposes of comparison.

CHAPTER FIVE

5.1   Reconciliation of operating profit to net cash flow from operations.

	£'000s	£'000s
Operating profit		68
Add Increase in creditors		80
		148
Less Increase in stocks	40	
Increase in debtors	100	140
		8

Cash flow statement for year ending 31 December 1997

	£'000s
Net cash inflow from operating activities	8
Less Purchase of fixed assets	(200)
Net cash outflow before financing	(192)
Financing:	
Issue of ordinary shares	200
Increase in cash	8

5.2   Reconciliation of net profit to cash flow from operations.

	£'000s	£'000s
Operating profit (£460 − £152 − £70)		238
ADD Depreciation	70	
Loss on sale of plant and machinery	22	
(sale price £24,000, cost £50,000, Depn £4,000)		
Increase in provisions	2	
Decrease in stock	20	114
		352
Deduct Increase in debtors	40	
Decrease in creditors	14	
		54
Net cash flow		298

Davies Ltd
Cash flow statement for year ending 31 March 1997

	£'000s	£'000s
Net cash inflow from operating activities		298
Less Corporation tax	104	
Plant and machinery purchased	150	
Dividends paid	40	294
Net cash flow		4
Increase in cash		4

CHAPTER SEVEN

7.1

Overhead apportionment

	Casting £	Finishing £	Packing £	Total £
Company admin.	600	1,200	1,200	3,000
Clerical and indirect wages	450	900	900	2,250
Maintenance of equipment	562	169	169	900
Management salaries	400	800	800	2,000
Depreciation of equipment	1,125	337	338	1,800
Rent and rates	120	120	240	480
Expense supplies	75	150	150	375
	3,332	3,676	3,797	10,805
Labour hours	400	800	800	
Labour hour rate	8.33	4.59	4.75	

Direct labour hours are calculated by dividing the direct labour cost by 5 (hourly rate).

Cost of one de luxe model

	£	£
Direct materials		1,980
Direct wages		4,400
Prime/direct cost		6,380
Overhead cost		
Casting 160 × £8.33 = 1,332.8		
Finishing 400 × £4.59 = 1,836		
Packing 320 × £4.75 = 1,520		4,688.8
Total cost of one de luxe model		11,068.8 ÷ 5,000 = £2.21

Cost of one standard model

	£	£
Direct materials		2,720
Direct wages		5,600
		———
Prime/direct cost		8,320
Overhead cost		
Casting 240 × £8.33 = 1,999.2		
Finishing 400 × £4.59 = 1,836		
Packing 480 × £4.75 = 2,280		6,115.2
		———
Total cost of one standard model		14,435.2 ÷ 10,000 = £1.44

In apportioning the overhead costs among the three departments the following steps were taken:

1. *Company administration*
   Apportioned on the basis of the direct labour hours. The total overhead was £3,000 and the total direct labour hours 2,000.

$$\frac{400}{2,000} \times £3,000 = £600 \text{ to casting}$$

$$\frac{800}{2,000} \times £3,000 = £1,200 \text{ to finishing}$$

$$\frac{800}{2,000} \times £3,000 = £1,200 \text{ to packing}$$

2. *Clerical and indirect wages*
   Apportioned on the basis of the direct wages. The total overhead was £2,250 and the total direct wages £10,000.

$$\frac{2,000}{10,000} \times £2,250 = £450 \text{ to casting}$$

$$\frac{4,000}{10,000} \times £2,250 = £900 \text{ to finishing}$$

$$\frac{4,000}{10,000} \times £2,250 = £900 \text{ to packing}$$

3. *Maintenance of equipment*
    Apportioned on the basis of the book value of the equipment and rounded off to the nearest £1. The total overhead was £900 and the total value of equipment £80,000.

    $$\frac{50,000}{80,000} \times £900 = £562.5 = £562 \text{ to casting}$$

    $$\frac{15,000}{80,000} \times £900 = £168.75 = £169 \text{ to finishing}$$

    $$\frac{15,000}{80,000} \times £900 = £168.75 = £169 \text{ to packing}$$

4. *Management salaries*
    Apportioned on the basis of the direct labour hours. The total overhead was £2,000 and the total direct labour hours 2,000.

    $$\frac{400}{2,000} \times £2,000 = £400 \text{ to casting}$$

    $$\frac{800}{2,000} \times £2,000 = £800 \text{ to finishing}$$

    $$\frac{800}{2,000} \times £2,000 = £800 \text{ to packing}$$

5. *Depreciation of equipment*
    Apportioned on the basis of the book value of the equipment. The total overhead was £1,800 and the total value of equipment £80,000.

    $$\frac{50,000}{80,000} \times £1,800 = £1,125 \text{ to casting}$$

    $$\frac{15,000}{80,000} \times £1,800 = £337.50 = £337 \text{ to finishing}$$

    $$\frac{15,000}{80,000} \times £1,800 = £337.50 = £338 \text{ to packing}$$

Note The £337.50 has been rounded up on one case and down in the other in order to ensure that the total is correct.

6. *Rent and rates*
    Apportioned on the basis of floor area. The total overhead was £480 and the total floor area 8,000 sq. ft.

$$\frac{2,000}{8,000} \times £480 = £120 \text{ to casting}$$

$$\frac{2,000}{8,000} \times £480 = £120 \text{ to finishing}$$

$$\frac{4,000}{8,000} \times £480 = £240 \text{ to packing}$$

7.2   Hit Limited

Overhead apportionment January 1998

	Production department		Service department
	X	Y	
	£'000s	£'000s	£'000s
Allocated expenses	65	35	50
Apportionment of service department's expenses in the ratio 70 : 30	35	15	(50)
Overhead to be charged	100	50	—

7.3   Scope Limited
Assembly department—overhead absorption methods:
1. *Specific units*

$$\frac{\text{Overhead}}{\text{Number of units}} = \frac{25,000}{5,000} = \underline{\underline{£5 \text{ per unit}}}$$

2. *Direct materials*

$$\frac{\text{Overhead}}{\text{Direct materials}} \times 100 = \frac{£25,000}{50,000} \times 100 = 50\%$$

3. *Direct labour*

$$\frac{\text{Overhead}}{\text{Direct labour}} \times 100 = \frac{£25,000}{100,000} \times 100 = 25\%$$

4. *Prime cost*

$$\frac{\text{Overhead}}{\text{Prime cost}} \times 100 = \frac{£25,000}{153,000} \times 100 = 16.3\%$$

5. *Direct labour hours*

$$\frac{\text{Overhead}}{\text{Direct labour hours}} = \frac{£25,000}{10,000} = £2.50 \text{ per direct labour hours}$$

6. *Machine hours*

$$\frac{\text{Overhead}}{\text{Machine hours}} = \frac{£25,000}{2,500} = £10 \text{ per machine hour}$$

7.4   Davies Limited

1.   (a) *Direct labour hours*

$$\frac{\text{Overhead}}{\text{Direct labour hours}} = \frac{70,000}{15,000} = 4.67 \text{ DLH}$$

Therefore for job number 22 : £4.67 × 10 = £46.7

(b) *Machine hours*

$$\frac{\text{Overhead}}{\text{Machine hours}} = \frac{70,000}{5,000} = 14 \text{ per MH}$$

Therefore for job number 22 : £14 × 4   =   £56

Selling price of job number 22	*Direct labour hours* £	*Machine hours* £
Direct materials	25	25
Direct wages	30	30
Prime costs	55	55
Overhead	46.7	56
Total cost	101.7	111
Profit 25%	25.4	27.75
Selling price	127.1	138.75

2.   As the department appears more labour intensive than machine intensive, use the direct labour hour method.

CHAPTER EIGHT

8.1

Standard cost of 20 miles £410 × 20	=	£	8,200	
Actual cost of 20 miles	=	£	8,654	
Total variance		£	454	adverse
Material				
Standard cost of materials 20 × £200	=	£	4,000	
Actual cost of materials	=	£	4,347	
Total material variance	=	£	347	adverse
Material usage variance £20 × 10	=	£	200	adverse
Material price variance 0.7 × 210	=	£	147	adverse
		£	347	adverse
Labour				
Standard cost of labour 20 × £210	=	£	4,200	
Actual cost of labour	=	£	4,307	
Total labour variance	=	£	107	adverse
Labour efficiency variance 10 × £7	=	£	70	favourable
Labour rate variance 590 × £0.3	=	£	177	adverse
	=	£	107	adverse
TOTAL VARIANCE £107 A × £347 A	=	£	454	adverse

8.2

Standard cost of 80,000 sq. ft insulation £430 × 80	=	£	34,400	
Actual cost of 80,000 sq. ft insulation	=	£	33,952	
Total variance	=	£	448	favourable
Material				
Standard cost of materials 800 × £18	=	£	14,400	
Actual cost of materials 840 × £18.3	=	£	15,372	
Total material variance	=	£	972	adverse
Material usage variance 40 × £18	=	£	720	adverse
Material price variance 840 × £0.3	=	£	252	adverse
	=	£	972	adverse
Labour				
Standard cost of labour 150 × 80	=	£	12,000	
Actual cost of labour £7.2 × 1400	=	£	10,080	
	=	£	1,920	favourable
Labour efficiency variance 200 × £7.5	=	£	1,500	favourable
Labour rate variance 1,400 × £0.3	=	£	420	favourable
	=	£	1,920	favourable
Overhead variance	=	£	500	adverse
TOTAL VARIANCE £927A, £1920F, £500A	=	£	448	favourable

8.3

Standard cost of 8,000 miles £88 × 80	=	£	7,040	
Actual cost of 8,000 miles (820 × £1.85 + 750 × £7.2)	=	£	6,917	
Total variance	=	£	123	favourable

Material

Standard cost of materals £1.8 × 800	=	£	1,440
Actual cost of materials £1.85 × 820	=	£	1,517
Total material variance	=	£	77 adverse
Material usage variance 20 × £1.8	=	£	36 adverse
Material price variance 820 × £0.05	=	£	41 adverse
	=	£	77 adverse

Labour

Standard cost of labour 80 × £70	=	£	5,600
Actual cost of labour 750 × £7.20	=	£	5,400
	=	£	200 favourable
Labour efficiency variance 50 × £7	=	£	350 favourable
Labour rate variance 750 × £0.2	=	£	150 adverse
		£	200 favourable

CHAPTER NINE

9.1

	Jul £	Aug £	Sept £	Oct £	Nov £	Dec £
Opening balance	1,500	1,270	1,790	(3,140)	(1,700)	440
Sales receipts	2,400	2,800	3,200	3,600	3,800	2,600
Legacy	—	—	—	—	—	3,000
TOTAL CASH AVAILABLE	3,900	4,070	4,990	460	2,100	6,040
Payments:						
Labour	1,000	650	550	500	450	350
Materials	900	1,020	1,080	1,200	780	660
Variable expenses	180	200	130	110	100	90
	400	260	220	200	180	140
Fixed expenses	150	150	150	150	150	150
Capital expenditure	—	—	6,000	—	—	—
TOTAL PAYMENTS	2,630	2,280	8,130	2,160	1,660	1,390
TOTAL CASH −TOTAL PAYMENTS						
Balance carried forward	1,270	1,790	(3,140)	(1,700)	440	4,650

You can see that there is a cash crisis in September and October. If the owner of the business had been monitoring his forecast he would have been aware of this up to 12 months before it occurred. This would have given him the opportunity to obtain bank overdraft facilities in good time or perhaps to have rescheduled his capital outlay. If he could delay this for three months the amount of overdraft that he requires would be nil.

9.2

Mary's delicatessen

	Nov £	Dec £	Jan £	Feb £	Mar £	Apr £
Receipts:						
Opening balance	(1,050)	(2,100)	(500)	(1,575)	6,575	350
Cash receipts	5,400	9,000	6,300	20,700	3,600	7,200
Received from debtors	800	600	1,000	700	2,300	400
Total cash	5,150	7,500	6,800	19,825	12,475	7,950
Payments:						
Cash	2,250	3,750	2,625	8,625	1,500	3,000
Previous credit purchases	3,000	2,250	3,750	2,625	8,625	1,500
Wages	2,000	2,000	2,000	2,000	2,000	2,000
	7,250	8,000	8,375	13,250	12,125	6,500
BALANCE CARRIED FORWARD	(2,100)	(500)	(1,575)	6,575	350	1,450

CHAPTER TEN

10.1

Units	Unit selling price	Variable cost	Contribution per unit	Total contribution
10,000	£10	£8	£2	£20,000
15,000	£9.50	£8	£1.50	£22,500
20,000	£9	£8	£1	£20,000
25,000	£8.50	£8	£0.50	£12,500

It seems that the greatest constibution is at 15,000 units, giving £22,500 and a profit of (£22,500 −10,000), i.e. £12,500 provided customers are not upset by receiving smaller quantities than before, good use can be made of the capacity that is released; 15,000 units should be produced and sold giving £2,500 more profit than at present.

10.2

1. Contribution per hour (SP −VC) £65 −£35   =   £30

$$\text{Break-even point} \ = \ \frac{\text{Total fixed costs}}{\text{Contribution per hr}} \ = \ \frac{£15,000}{30} \ = 500 \text{ hours}$$

2. To make a profit of £9,000 need to sell 500 hours $+ \ \dfrac{9,000}{30}$

$$= 500 + 300 = 800 \text{ hours}$$

3. If the hours sold fell to 300, loss would be (500 −300) × £30

$$= £6,000$$

4. Sales 900 × £65   =   £58,500
    Variable cost 900 × £35   =   £31,500
    Fixed costs   =   £15,000
                                   ‾‾‾‾‾‾‾
    Total cost   =   £46,500
                                   ‾‾‾‾‾‾‾

                                   £15,000
    Break-even point   =   ───────   = 500 hours
                                     30

10.3

Product	A	B	C
Selling price per unit	£2.0	£3.5	£3.0
Variable cost per unit	£1.5	£2.5	£1.7
Contribution per unit	£0.5	£1.0	£1.3

Option

1. (A) 20,000 × £0.5 = £10,000; (B) 10,000 × £1.0 = £10,000; (C) 15,000 × £1.3 = £19,500
    Total contribution £39,500

2. (A) ———; (B) 20,000 × £1.0 = £20,000; (C) 21,000 × £1.3 = £27,300
    Total contribution £47,300

3. (A) 30,000 × £0.5 = £15,000; (B) ———; (C) 24,000 × £1.3 = £31,200
    Total contribution £46,200

4. (A) 30,000 × £0.5 = £15,000; (B) 20,000 × £1 = £20,000; (C) ———
    Total contribution £35,000

Alternative 2 maximizes the contribution and provided it would have no serious marketing consequences should be the chosen option. There is however a risk in ignoring the demand for product A.

CHAPTER ELEVEN

11.1   In answering this question we have to decide which costs will be altered by stopping production and buying the product from outside suppliers. If this were done the savings would be prime cost £60,000, which is the cost of production in terms of materials and labour, and the variable overhead of £30,000 which would largely be made up of power costs. It is assumed that the product manager would not be made redundant. The working capital would be released so that the interest of £1,800 would be saved.

The cost of buying from outside would be £9 plus the fixed costs of the department which would still have to be met. These are:

	£
Product manager's salary	20,000
Depreciation of department machinery	6,000
Overhead allocated from other departments	24,000
	50,000

which is £4.17 per unit. This makes the cost of buying £13.17 per unit (£9 + £4.17) which is more than the production cost of £11.67 + interest on the working capital of 15p per unit (£11.82). In this case it is better for the organization to continue to manufacture itself.

If we assume that the plant manager is made redundant at no additional cost then the cost of buying in becomes:

	£
Depreciation of department machinery	6,000
Allocated overheads	24,000
	30,000

which is £2.50 per unit making the cost of buying £11.50. This is much closer to the production cost of £11.67 and changes the decision in that it is now apparently better to buy in the product than make it.

11.2

	X £	£	Y £	£
Sales 14,000 @ £10		140,000		140,000
Fixed costs	24,000		72,000	
Variable costs				
14,000 @ £7	98,000			
14,000 @ £4			56,000	
		122,000		128,000
Surplus		18,000		12,000

Method X is favoured here but what would be the decision if sales reach 32,000 units?

CHAPTER TWELVE

12.1   Savings discounted at 10 per cent p.a.

			£		FACTOR		£
Year 0	—		8,000	×	1	—	8,000
1	+		1,000	×	.909	+	909
2	+		2,000	×	.826	+	1,652
3	+		4,000	×	.750	+	3,000
4	+		2,000	×	.683	+	1,366
5	+		1,000	×	.621	+	621

PRESENT VALUE	7,548
NET PRESENT VALUE (XPV)	−452

Purchase does not yield the target 10 per cent.

12.2   Present value of £5,500 p.a. for 10 years discounted at 12 per cent = £28,250. Project does earn the target 12 per cent. NPV @ 12 per cent = +£3,250.

12.3   £5,000 p.a. for five years is earned by £20,000 now. £1 p.a. for five years is earned by £4 now. From the five-year line in the DCF table at the end of the book this is seen to be 8 per cent. A surplus of 1 per cent (gross) is hardly worth the investment.

12.4

	Year	£	Factor	£
Cost of insulation	0	24,000 × 1	24,000
Savings			
	1	5,000 × 0.9174	4,587
	2	5,000 × 0.8417	4,209
	3	5,000 × 0.7722	3,861
	4	5,000 × 0.7084	3,542
	5	5,000 × 0.6499	3,250
	6	5,000 × 0.5963	2,982
	7	5,000 × 0.5470	2,735

PRESENT VALUE	25,166
NET PRESENT VALUE (NPV)	+1,166

The discounted savings exceed the cost of insulation so it is worth going ahead and insulating the building.

An alternative approach that can be employed when the same sum of money is involved over a number of years is to use the cumulative table under column 4 (see DCF Tables, pages 231–237) if the savings occur at the year end, or column 5, 'Present value of £1 received continuously', if the savings or cash inflow are continuous throughout the period. In this example the calculation will then become:

	£
Cost of insulation	24,000
Savings using column 4 and year 7 of present value tables	
£5,000 × 5.0330 PRESENT VALUE	25,165
NET PRESENT VALUE	+1,165

Using column 5 and year 7 we have

Cost of insulation	24,000
Savings £5,000 × 5.2562 PRESENT VALUE	26,281
NET PRESENT VALUE	+2,281

In this example we have greater NPV because the savings are achieved right throughout each year rather than waiting until the year end.

To use IRR approach we start from the position of a positive NPV of £1,166 when 9 per cent is applied as the cost of capital as calculated above. To obtain a negative NPV a greater cost of capital must be used.

Try 12%

	Year	*Factor*	*Present value*
		£	£
Cost	0	24,000 × 1	24,000
Savings	1	5,000 × 0.8929	4,465
	2	5,000 × 0.7979	3,990
	3	5,000 × 0.7118	3,559
	4	5,000 × 0.6355	3,178
	5	5,000 × 0.5674	2,837
	6	5,000 × 0.5066	2,533
	7	5,000 × 0.4523	2,262
	PRESENT VALUE		22,824
	NET PRESENT VALUE (NPV)		−1,176

Using interpolation to find the IRR we have

$$9\% + 3 \left(\frac{1,165}{2,341} \right) = 9\% + (3 \times 0.50) = 9\% + 1.50 = 10\%$$

This gives an IRR of approximately 10 per cent which is greater than the required 9 per cent so the insulation would be carried out.

12.5

		£
Year 0 additional cost of the advanced machine (£30,000 − £15,000)		15,000

Savings obtained:
Raw material costs reduced from £10,000 to
£6,000 a year for five years

		£
£4,000 × 3.4331		13,732
Additional scrap year 5, £2,000 × 0.5194		1,039
PRESENT VALUE		14,771
NET PRESENT VALUE		−229

The discounted savings engendered by the expensive machine are less than its additional cost so it is better to buy the cheaper machine. However, it is a marginal decision as the difference is only £229.

If the continuous table is used we have:

	£
£4,000 × 3.6682	14,673
£2,000 × 0.5194	1,039
PRESENT VALUE	15,712
NET PRESENT VALUE	+ 712

This gives a positive NPV and reverses the decision, which highlights the fact that the basis on which the estimates are being made must be clearly understood. In this case the decision will probably be based on personal preference.

The solution to the question using the IRR approach becomes:

Advanced model using 13 per cent

Year		Factor £	Present value £	Present value £
0	Additional outlay	15,000 × 1		15,000
1–5	Savings	4,000 × 3.5172	14,069	
5	Additional scrap	2,000 × 0.5428	1,086	
	PRESENT VALUE			15,155
	NET PRESENT VALUE			+155

There is a negative NPV when 14 per cent is employed as calculated previously so we can see at a glance that the IRR is going to be around 14 per cent. Using interpolation we have

$$13\% + 1 \left(\frac{155}{384} \right) = 13\% + (1 \times 0.4) = 13\% + 0.4 = 13.4\%$$

This gives an IRR of approximately 13 per cent which our previous calculations indicated it would be. It becomes a marginal decision whether to buy the advanced or standard machine and it will be made on grounds of personal preference.

CHAPTER FOURTEEN

14.1

1.
$$\text{Return} = \frac{50}{2.50} = 20 \text{ per cent}$$

Present value of business = 500,000 × £2.5 = £1,250,000

If loan £500,000 raised capital employed = £1,750,000

$$\text{Weighted average cost capital} = \frac{1,250,000}{1,750,000} \times 25 \text{ per cent} + \frac{500,000}{1,750,000} \times 18 \text{ per cent}$$
$$= 23 \text{ per cent}$$

$$\text{Return on project} \quad \frac{200,000}{500,000} = 40\% > 23 \text{ per cent}$$

If project lasts 10 years discounting at 23 per cent

$$\text{NPV} = 200,000 \times 3.92 - 500,000 = £284,000$$

2. Gearing increases from nil to 500,000 : 1,250,000 = 1 : 2.5
   Greater financial risk to shareholders, but compensated for by increased return from 20 per cent to 25 per cent.

14.2

The traditional view is that the cost of capital can indeed be reduced by increasing the proportion of debt to equity but that there is a limit to this process. Eventually the increased financial risk will increase the cost of both equity and debt prohibitively. Thus, if we increase our gearing ratio to 1, i.e. equal parts of debt and equity, our cost of capital should fall as shown below:

	Market value	Cost
Equity	£10 million	18 per cent
Debt	£10 million	10 per cent
	Weighted average 14 per cent	

If, however, we increase the gearing ratio to 5, massively loading the financing in favour of debt, the effect of financial risk is clearly seen.

	Market value	*Cost*
Equity	£10 million	25 per cent*
Debt	£50 million	20 per cent*
	Weighted average 20.83 per cent	

*These figures are illustrative and were not taken from data given in the question.

The position can be illustrated graphically (Figure A14.1).

The view of the adherents to the Modigliani/Miller theory, however, is that the cost of capital is unaffected by the capital structure. As gearing increases the cost of equity increases such as precisely to offset the reducing effect of the increased debt. Thus:

With gearing ratio of 1

	Market value	*Cost*
Equity	£10 million	24.54 per cent
Debt	£10 million	10 per cent
	Weighted average at 17.27 per cent	

With gearing ratio of 5

	Market value	*Cost*
Equity	£10 million	53.62 per cent*
Debt	£50 million	10 per cent
	Weighted average unchanged at 17.27 per cent	

*Adjusts itself through the mechanism of a fall in the share price caused by the market operation of arbitrage.

Again this may be represented graphically (Figure A14.2).

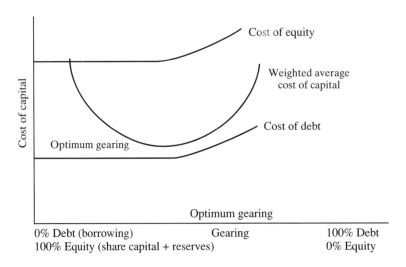

Figure A14.1   Cost of capital graph

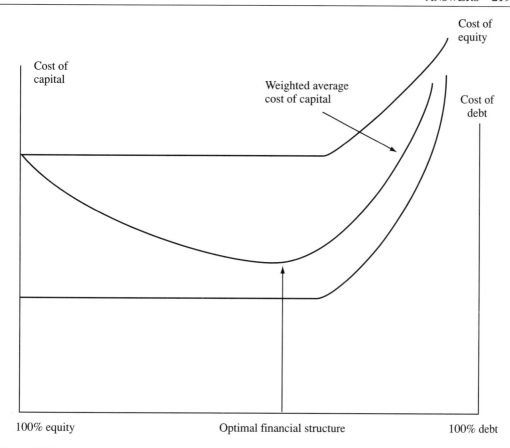

Figure A14.2

CHAPTER FIFTEEN

15.1

(i) Raw materials turnover	$=$	$\dfrac{\text{Raw material stock}}{\text{Daily purchase of raw materials}}$	$=$	$\dfrac{9,000}{6,400 \times 0.05} = 28.1$ days +
(ii) *Add* finished goods turnover	$=$	$\dfrac{\text{Finished goods stock}}{\text{Daily cost of goods sold}}$	$=$	$\dfrac{42,000}{6,400 \times 0.2} = 32.8$ days +
(iii) *Add* Age of debtor	$=$	$\dfrac{\text{Debtors}}{\text{Daily sales}}$	$=$	$\dfrac{36,000}{6,400 \times 0.25} = 22.5$ days
				83.4 days −
(iv) *Less* Age of creditors	$=$	$\dfrac{\text{Creditors}}{\text{Daily purchases}}$	$=$	$\dfrac{6,000}{6,400 \times 0.05} = 18.8$ days

Total working capital cycle   64.6 days

CHAPTER SEVENTEEN

17.1   The cost per unit is given by:

$$\text{Unit variable cost} \ + \ \frac{\text{Total fixed costs}}{\text{Unit sales}} \ = \ \text{£30} \ + \ \frac{\text{£600,000}}{\text{60,000}} \ = \ \text{£40}$$

In order to calculate the 25 per cent mark-up we have:

$$\text{Mark-up} \ = \ \frac{\text{Unit cost}}{(1- \text{Return on sales})} \ = \ \frac{\text{£40}}{(1-0.25)} \ = \ \frac{\text{£40}}{0.75} \ = \ \text{£53.33}$$

The firm would charge £53.33 for each and make a profit of £13.33 on every unit sold.

17.2

$$\text{Break even} \ = \ \frac{\text{Fixed cost}}{\text{Contribution}} \ = \ \frac{\text{Fixed cost}}{\text{Selling price} - \text{Variable cost}}$$

$$= \ \frac{\text{£600,000}}{\text{£53.33} - \text{£30}} \ = \ \frac{\text{£600,000}}{\text{£23.33}} \ = \ \text{25,717.959 units}$$

$$= \ \text{25,718 units}$$

The firm must sell 25,718 units in order to break even.

If it wished to break even at 60,000 units sold then the contribution per unit would have to be £10, i.e. £600,000 fixed costs ÷ 60,000 units and the selling price would be £30 + £10 = £40 and applying the formula we have

$$\frac{\text{Fixed costs}}{\text{SP} - \text{VC}} \ = \ \frac{\text{£600,000}}{\text{£40} - \text{£30}} \ = \ \frac{\text{£600,000}}{10} \ = \ \text{60,000 units}$$

and the break-even price would be £40 per unit.

17.3   In a normal competitive market the main factor which influences the price an organization can charge for its goods or services is the price of competing goods or services. The firm can then consider whether it can charge more or less than its competitors and devise a marketing strategy.

CHAPTER EIGHTEEN

18.1

		Electronic Appliances Ltd			
Profitability ratios		1995	1996	1997	
Return on capital employed %		14.5	8.1	9.2	
Profit margin %		15.3	11.9	10.6	
					(Prime costs—under control)
Overheads:					
Production %		26.2	30.4	32.8	
Technical dept %		7.2	8.6	9.2	
Sales dept %		6.2	7.0	7.7	
Capital turnover	Times	0.94	0.68	0.87	valued at direct cost
Work in progress	Months	6.9	8.8	10.2	valued at production cost
Work in progress	Months	4.0	4.6	5.0	compared with actual cost
Stocks	Months	7.4	8.6	11.1	
Debtors	Months	2.5	2.7	2.9	
Fixed capital	Months	7.5	12.0	9.4	
Liquidity ratios					
Current ratio	Times	4.5	4.2	2.1	
Acid test ratio	Times	1.7	1.5	0.72	

Analysis

The return on capital employed shows a large decline between 1995 and 1996, 14.5 per cent down to 8 per cent, and then a slight recovery to 9.2 per cent in 1997.

The profit margin reflects a similar decline from 15.3 per cent to 10.6 per cent over the three years, although the decline is much greater between 1995 and 1996.

The prime costs are under control and increase in the proportions expected to support the increased sales.

The overheads for the production, technical and sales departments are all increasing steadily and will need to be controlled in future.

The rates of capital turnover are slowing, most noticeably in the case of work in progress and stocks.

The liquidity ratios are declining and the business is obviously failing to generate sufficient funds for its needs. It gives every impression of being an organization run by an enthusiast to meet his needs. He will take on any work that he sees to be a challenge, which maintains his interest and enthusiasm but this is bad for the business.

He needs to decide what his business is about and endeavour to achieve longer runs. This will reduce his overhead costs per unit produced and increase the overall efficiency of the organization.

The calculations for 1995 have been made on the basis below:

Return on capital employed $\dfrac{76,660}{530,544} \times 100 = 14.5$ per cent

Profit margin (sales) $\dfrac{76,660}{500,607} \times 100 = 15.3$ per cent

Overheads (sales):

Production $\dfrac{130,870}{500,607} \times 100 = 26.2$ per cent

Technical $\dfrac{36,104}{500,607} \times 100 = 7.2$ per cent

Sales $\dfrac{31,082}{500,607} \times 100 = 6.2$ per cent

Capital turnover $\dfrac{500,607}{530,544} = 0.94$ times

Work in progress (at direct cost) $\dfrac{185,974}{106,203} = 1.75$ times; $\dfrac{12}{1.75} = 6.9$ months

Work in progress (at production cost) $\dfrac{(185,974 + 130,780)}{106,203} = 2.98$ times; $\dfrac{12}{2.98} = 4$ months

Stocks (at actual cost of finished goods) $\dfrac{115,321}{71,019} = 1.62$ times; $\dfrac{12}{1.62} = 7.4$ months

Debtors $\dfrac{500,607}{105,001} = 4.77$ times; $\dfrac{12}{4.77} = 2.5$ months

Fixed capital (fixed assets) $\dfrac{500,607}{310,481} = 1.61$ times; $\dfrac{12}{1.61} = 7.5$ months

The other ratios have all been fully investigated earlier.

18.2

Ratio analyses of Marks and Spencer Plc (based on the financial statements on pages 154–182)

		1994	1995
1.	Gross profit to net capital employed $\dfrac{\text{Gross profit} \times 100}{\text{Net capital employed}}$ (see note 3)	$\dfrac{2{,}294.2 \times 100}{3{,}983.6} = 57.6\%$	$\dfrac{2{,}389.4 \times 100}{4{,}342.3} = 55.0\%$
2.	Net profit to net capital employed $\dfrac{\text{Net profit} \times 100}{\text{Net capital employed}}$	$\dfrac{851.5 \times 100}{3{,}983.6} = 21.4\%$	$\dfrac{942.3 \times 100}{4{,}342.3} = 21.7\%$
3.	Gross profit on sales (gross margin) $\dfrac{\text{Gross profit} \times 100}{\text{Sales}}$	$\dfrac{2{,}294.2 \times 100}{6{,}541.2} = 35.1\%$	$\dfrac{2{,}389.4 \times 100}{6{,}806.5} = 35.1\%$
4.	Net profit on sales (net margin) $\dfrac{\text{Net profit} \times 100}{\text{Sales}}$	$\dfrac{851.5 \times 100}{6{,}541.2} = 13.0\%$	$\dfrac{942.3 \times 100}{6{,}806.5} = 13.8\%$
5.	Current ratio Current assets : current liabilities	$2{,}053.7 : 1{,}181.0 = 1.7 : 1$	$2{,}365.8 : 1{,}363.8 = 1.7 : 1$
6.	Quick ratio (acid test) Quick assets : current liabilities	$1{,}294.7 : 1{,}181.0 = 1.1 : 1$	$1{,}506.5 : 1{,}363.8 = 1.1 : 1$
7.	Capital gearing ratio $\dfrac{\text{Fixed interest borrowing} \times 100}{\text{Equity interest}}$ (see note 18)	$\dfrac{568.1 \times 100}{3{,}324} = 17.1\%$	$\dfrac{526.3 \times 100}{3{,}714.9} = 14.2\%$

Continued on next page

18.2 *continued*

8. *Times interest earned*

$$\frac{\text{Profit before fixed interest charges}}{\text{Fixed interest charges (note 5)}}$$

N/A as interest received exceeds interest paid

9. *Debtors' ratio*

$$\frac{\text{Credit sales} \div \text{into 365}}{\text{Customer and trade debtors}} \quad \text{(note 14)}$$

$$\frac{6,541.2}{329.4} = \frac{365}{19.8} = 18 \text{ days} \qquad \frac{6,806.5}{403.5} = \frac{365}{16.8} = 22 \text{ days}$$

10. *Creditors' ratio*

$$\frac{\text{Purchases (note 3)} \div \text{into 365}}{\text{Trade Creditors}} \quad \text{(note 17)}$$

$$\frac{4,247}{162.8} = \frac{365}{26.1} = 14 \text{ days} \qquad \frac{4,417.1}{174.9} = \frac{365}{25.2} = 14.5 \text{ days}$$

(There is no information on purchases so we compromise with the 'cost of sales' figure.) Is this a useful ratio with the available information?

11. *Stock turnover*

$$\frac{\text{Cost of sales} \div \text{into 365}}{\text{Closing stock}}$$

$$\frac{4,247}{354.6} = \frac{365}{12} = 30 \text{ days} \qquad \frac{4,417.1}{377} = \frac{365}{11.7} = 31 \text{ days}$$

12. *Fixed assets*

$$\frac{\text{Sales}}{\text{Tangible fixed assets}}$$

$$\frac{6,541.2}{3,095.4} = 2.1 \text{ times} \qquad \frac{6,806.5}{3,297} = 2.1 \text{ times}$$

13. *Sales per employee*

$$\frac{\text{Sales}}{\text{Number of employees}} \quad \text{(note 10)}$$

$$\frac{6,541,200,000}{41,386} = £158,053 \qquad \frac{6,806,500,000}{41,535} = £163,874$$

Marks and Spencer is a highly successful company. Do you feel that this has been reflected in the ratios calculated? Would the figures differ significantly in other organizations?

GLOSSARY

Absorption costing   A costing system that absorbs all the overhead costs.

Accounting period   Normally 12 months as far as the financial accounts are concerned, to coincide with the tax year. So far as the management accounts are concerned it can be any period ranging from one week to one year. It is generally thought necessary to provide management information at least once every four weeks.

Accounting rate of return (ARR)   The average annual return on a capital investment.

Acid test (Quick ratio)   Test of the ability of an organization to pay its way in the short term, given by the ratio of quick assets to current liabilities.

Activity based costing   A costing system that is based on the use of cost drivers. Allocation of costs on the basis of the use a product makes of a service.

Articles of association   Internal rules that state the rights and duties of directors and shareholders of a company.

Assets   Items belonging to the organization that have either a long-term or short-term value. Those having a long-term value are items like machinery and plant. They are called fixed assets.

Authorized capital   The total amount of money that the organization is authorized to raise by the issue of share capital. The authorized capital is subject to stamp duty and so organizations do not state high authorized capital figures when they are first formed. The authorized share capital is not set for all time and can be varied if necessary.

Bad debts   Debt that has not been possible to collect.

Balance sheet   Statement of the financial position of an organization.

Book value   The value at which an asset is shown in the balance sheet.

Break even   The level of activity at which neither a profit nor a loss is made.

Budget   A budget is a forecast or estimate of the events over a stated future interval of time, e.g. one year, five years or five months.

Budgetary control   Methods of monitoring the performance.

Capital budgeting   Budgeting for the purchase of fixed assets.

Capital employed   The total of the assets owned. The net capital employed is more usually used in calculating ratios and is the total assets less the current liabilities.

Capital expenditure   Expenditure that results in the acquisition of fixed assets.

Capital items   Items that last for several years. Examples are machinery used in manufacture, motor vehicles, land and buildings.

Cash flow statement   Statement showing cash movements. May be on a daily, weekly, monthly, quarterly or annual basis.

Cash operating cycle   The time a business takes to generate cash from its activities.

Credit terms   Providing or receiving goods or services for which payment will be made at a later date.

Creditors   People to whom the business owes money for goods or services received.

Creditors' ratio   Time taken to pay suppliers.

Current assets   Assets that are normally used up in one financial period and change from day to day.

Current liabilities   Liabilities that must be settled within a short time: they fluctuate from day to day.

Current ratio   Measure of the organization's ability to pay its way in the period between about three and nine months in the future. Given by the ratio of current assets to current liabilities.

Debenture   A certificate issued by a company acknowledging a debt.

Debtors   People who owe money to the organization.

Debtors' ratio   Time taken to collect money that is owing from customers.

Depreciation   Method of allocating the cost of a fixed asset over its useful life.

Differential costs   Costs that are altered by the suggested action.

Discounted cash flow (DCF)   Future cash flows discounted to give their present value.

Dividend   Distribution of profits to the shareholders. Usually expressed as a dividend of *x*p in the £ on the nominal value of their shares.

Dividend cover   The number of times the earnings cover the declared dividend.

Earnings   Moneys received or due for goods or services provided by the organization.

Earnings per share   The profits available to be distributed, divided by the number of shares.

Equity   The equity of the business is the part that belongs to the owners. What remains after all outside interests have received their money.

Equity capital   *As* for *equity.*

Expenses   Moneys paid or due to be paid by the organization for revenue goods or services it has received.

Extraordinary items   Items that do not result from normal trading activities, e.g. sale of fixed assets.

Fixed assets   Assets held for many years to earn profits. Examples are land and buildings and plant and machinery.

Fixed cost   Cost that is incurred as a result of management policy and does not vary with the activity level. Examples are salaries, rates, depreciation.

Fixed overheads   Expenses that do not vary with the level of activity.

Gearing   Relationship between the share capital and loan capital of a business.

Gearing ratio   Loan capital as a percentage of the owner's equity.

Goodwill   The excess over the book value of a business that is received when sold.

Gross margin   Gross profit.

Gross profit   Sales minus cost of goods sold.

Historical cost   The cost at which the assets were obtained.

Hyde approach   A method of reducing the impact of inflation on profits.

Income statement   Used to calculate the profit or loss of an organization in an accounting period. Made up of
1. *Manufacturing account* showing the costs of goods made.
2. *Trading account* showing the gross profit or loss; the difference between the cost price and selling price of the goods.
3. *Profit and loss account* showing the net profit or loss.

Insolvency   Failure to meet financial obligations.

International rate of return (IRR)   The return on a capital scheme when time value of money is taken into account.

Inventory   Stock.

Issued capital   The shares that have been issued (sold) by the organization in order to raise money.

Job cost   Cost of a single job or operation.

Just in time   Method of stock control under which the supplier acts as the stock holder and delivers supplies so that they can go straight to the production line.

Labour hour rate   The amount to be charged for each labour hour in order to recover overheads.

Liabilities   Moneys that the organization owes.

Limiting factor   The item which is in short supply and so limits the activity of an organization. It might be sales, cash, materials or skilled staff.

Liquidity   Ability to pay bills as they fall due.

Loan capital   Borrowed money.

Long-term liabilities   Long-term debts.

Machine hour rate   The role to be charged for each machine hour in order to recover overheads.

Margin   Gross profit as a percentage of sales.

Margin of safety   The excess of sales over the break-even point.

Marginal cost   The cost of one more.

Market penetration   Setting a low price to capture a high market share.

Market skimming   Setting a high price to profit by skimming the luxury end of the market.

Mark-up   The percentage added to the cost price of goods to arrive at the selling price.

Market value of share   Price that the share would realize if sold.

Memorandum of association   Constitution of the company.

Net assets   Total assets less current liabilities.

Net capital employed   The resources that are employed in the business for more than one year; enables the return on the long-term investment to be found. The net capital employed is calculated by deducting the current liabilities from the total assets.

Net present value (NPV)   The present value of the future cash flows arising from a capital investment compared with the present value of the cost of that investment.

Net profit   Profit before tax after all expenses have been deducted.

Nominal value   Face value of a share.

Off balance sheet finance   Finance that is not fully recorded on the balance sheet, but often hidden as investment in subsidiary companies.

Ordinary shares   Share capital that is not entitled to a fixed rate of dividend.

Overtrading   Expanding the business faster than cash resources will allow.

Payback   Period or time taken to recover the initial outlay.

Percentage methods   Approach to the recovery of overheads by adding a percentage to the wages, materials or prime cost.

Preference shares   Share capital that has a fixed rate of dividend and receives its dividends before the rest of the share capital.

Pricing   Methods of arriving at the price to charge for a service or product.

Pricing strategies   Approaches to pricing in the market.

Primary ratio   Net profit as a percentage of the net capital employed.

Prime costs   Direct materials, direct labour and direct expenses added together.

Profit   Surplus of earnings over expenses.

Profitability   Return on sales or return on investment.

Public limited company (plc)   Limited company that conforms to Common Market regulations.

Quick assets   Those that are quickly and easily realizable—normally debtors and cash.

Quick ratio   Acid test.

Reconciliation   Reconciling two different numbers, eg bank and cash balances and profits in funds generated.

Relevant costs   Costs that affect the decision maker.

Reserves   Profits that are retained in the business—rarely cash.

Retained profits   Reserves.

Revenue expenditure   Expenditure that is completely used up or discharged in one year.

Revenue items   Items that are completely used up or discharged in one year. Examples are salaries, wages, heating, raw materials.

Revenue reserves   Distributable to shareholders.

Share capital   The amount received from the shareholders of the business.

Share premium   A capital reserve (one which cannot be distributed to the shareholders) created when the company sells its shares at a price in excess of the nominal value.

Spreadsheet   A piece of software which appears as a matrix of interrelated cells and which is capable of performing mathematical computations.

Standard cost   Predetermined or expected cost.

Stock   Finished goods, work in progress and raw materials.

Stock turnover   Number of times the stock is turned over in a financial period, given by the ratio of cost of goods sold to cost of stock.

Times interest earned   Profit before interest charges divided by the interest charges.

Turnover   Total sales value.

Variable costs   Costs that alter with the level of activity, eg raw materials.

Variable overheads   Indirect expenses that vary with activity level.

Variances   Differences between standard and actual performance.

Work in progress (WIP)   Partly finished items.

Working capital   Capital needed to keep the business operating until more money is obtained from operations. It is current assets minus current liabilities.

Working capital cycle   Time taken to turn stock into cash.

BIBLIOGRAPHY

Andrews, V. L., and P. Hunt, *Financial Management Cases and Readings,* Irwin, Homewood, Illinois, 1976. Revised edition.

Anthony, R. N., and J. Dierdon, *Management Control Systems,* Irwin, Homewood, Illinois, 1980. 4th edition.

Bierman, H., and S. Smidt, *The Capital Budgeting Decision,* Macmillan, New York: Collier, Macmillan, London, 1980. 5th edition.

Bredy, R. A., S. C. Myers, and A. J. Marcus, *Fundamentals of Corporate Finance,* McGraw-Hall, New York, 1995. Industrial edition.

Bromwich, M., *The Economics of Capital Budgeting,* Penguin, Harmondsworth, Middlesex, 1978. 2nd reprint.

Bull, R. J., *Accounting in Business,* Butterworths, London, 1980. 4th edition.

Carsberg, B. V., and A. Hope, *Business Investment Decisions Under Inflation,* Institute of Chartered Accountants, London, 1976.

Clarkson, C. P. E., and B. J. Elliott, *Managing Money and Finance,* Gower, Aldershot, 1983.

Emmanuel, C. R., T. Oltey, and K. A. Merchant, *Accounting for Management Control,* Chapman & Hall, London, 1990. 2nd edition.

Glautier, M. W. E., and B. Underdown, *Accounting Theory and Practice,* Pitman, London, 1982. 2nd edition.

Goch, D., *Finance and Accounts for Managers,* Pan, London, 1980. Revised edition.

Hartley, W. C. F., *Introduction to Business Accounting for Managers,* Pergamon, Oxford, 1980. 3rd edition.

Hindmarch, A., M. Atchison, and R. Marke, *Accounting: An Introduction,* Macmillan, London and Basingstoke, 1977. 1st edition.

Horngren, C. T., *Cost Accounting—A Managerial Emphasis,* Prentice-Hall, London, 1982. 5th edition.

Hunt, P., C. N. Williams, and G. Donaldson, *Basic Business Finance Text,* Irwin, Homewood, Illinois, 1961. Revised edition.

Hyde, W., *Interim Guidelines on Inflation Accounting,* Accounting Standards Committee, 1977.

Lauderback, J. G., and M. L. Hirsch, *Cost Accounting,* Kent, Boston, Mass., 1982.

Merrett, A. J., and A. Sykes, *The Finance and Analysis of Capital Projects,* Longman, London, 1973. 2nd edition.

Miller, M. H., and F. Modigliani, *Dividend Policy, Growth and the Valuation of Shares*, in *Journal of Business*, Vol. 34, 1961, pages 411-433.

Newbould, G. D., *Business Finance*, Harrap, London, 1970.

Pile, R. and R. Dobbins, *Investment Decisions and Financial Strategy*, Philip Allan, Hemel Hempstead, 1986.

Puxty, A. G. and C. J. Dodds, *Financial Management and Meaning*, Chapman & Hall, London, 1991. 2nd edition.

Samuels, J. M., F. M. Wilkes and R. E. Brayshaw, *Management of Company Finance*, Chapman & Hall, London, 1990. 5th edition.

Siegel, G. and H. Ramanaushas-Marconi, *Behavioral Accounting*, Chapman & Hall, London, 1989.

Sizer, J., *An Insight into Management Accounting*, Pitman, London, 1979. 2nd edition.

Taylor, A. H., and R. E. Palmer, *Financial Planning for Managers*, Pan, London, 1980. Revised edition.

Van Horne, J. C., *Financial Management and Policy*, Prentice-Hall, London, 1983. 6th edition.

Van Horne, J. C., *Fundamentals of Financial Management*, Prentice-Hall International, London, 1986.

Watts, M., *Elements of Finance for Managers*, Macdonald & Evans, Plymouth, 1976.

Wert, J. E., and C. L. Prather, *Financing Business Firms*, Irwin, Homewood, Illinois, 1975. 5th edition.

Weston, J. F., and E. F. Brigham, *Managerial Finance*, Holt, Rinehart & Winston, London, 1978. 6th edition.

Wilson, R. M. S., *Financial Control—A Systems Approach*, McGraw-Hill, London, 1974.

Wright, M. G., *Discounted Cash Flow*, McGraw-Hill, London, 1973. 2nd edition.

Wright, M. G., *Financial Management*, McGraw-Hill, Maidenhead, 1970.

DCF TABLES

	Year	Amount to which £1 will accumulate	Present value of £1	Present value of £1 received at end of period	Present value of £1 received continuously	Amount received at end of year which will recover initial investment of £1	Amount received at end of year which will recover initial investment of £1	Year	
	1	1.0100	0.9901	0.9901	0.9950	1.0100	1.0050	1	
	2	1.0201	0.9803	1.9704	1.9802	0.5075	0.5050	2	
	3	1.0303	0.9706	2.9410	2.9557	0.3400	0.3383	3	
	4	1.0406	0.9610	3.9020	3.9214	0.2563	0.2550	4	
	5	1.0510	0.9515	4.8534	4.8777	0.2060	0.2050	5	
	6	1.0615	0.9420	5.7955	5.8244	0.1725	0.1717	6	
	7	1.0721	0.9327	6.7282	6.7618	0.1486	0.1479	7	
	8	1.0829	0.9235	7.6517	7.6899	0.1307	0.1300	8	
	9	1.0937	0.9143	8.5660	8.6088	0.1167	0.1162	9	
	10	1.1046	0.9053	9.4713	9.5186	0.1056	0.1051	10	
	11	1.1157	0.8963	10.3676	10.4194	0.0965	0.0960	11	
1.0%	12	1.1268	0.8874	11.2551	11.3113	0.0888	0.0884	12	1.0%
	13	1.1381	0.8787	12.1337	12.1943	0.0824	0.0820	13	
	14	1.1495	0.8700	13.0037	13.0686	0.0769	0.0765	14	
	15	1.1610	0.8613	13.8651	13.9343	0.0721	0.0718	15	
	16	1.1726	0.8528	14.7179	14.7913	0.0679	0.0676	16	
	17	1.1843	0.8444	15.5623	15.6399	0.0643	0.0639	17	
	18	1.1961	0.8360	16.3983	16.4801	0.0610	0.0607	18	
	19	1.2081	0.8277	17.2260	17.3120	0.0581	0.0578	19	
	20	1.2202	0.8195	18.0456	18.1356	0.0554	0.0551	20	
	21	1.2324	0.8114	18.8570	18.9511	0.0530	0.0528	21	
	22	1.2447	0.8034	19.6604	19.7585	0.0509	0.0506	22	
	23	1.2572	0.7954	20.4558	20.5579	0.0489	0.0486	23	
	24	1.2697	0.7876	21.2434	21.3494	0.0471	0.0468	24	
	25	1.2824	0.7798	22.0232	22.1331	0.0454	0.0452	25	
	1	1.0200	0.9804	0.9804	0.9902	1.0200	1.0099	1	
	2	1.0404	0.9612	1.9416	1.9609	0.5150	0.5100	2	
	3	1.0612	0.9423	2.8839	2.9126	0.3468	0.3433	3	
	4	1.0824	0.9238	3.8077	3.8457	0.2626	0.2600	4	
	5	1.1041	0.9057	4.7135	4.7604	0.2122	0.2101	5	
	6	1.1262	0.8880	5.6014	5.6573	0.1785	0.1768	6	
	7	1.1487	0.8706	6.4720	6.5365	0.1545	0.1530	7	
	8	1.1717	0.8535	7.3255	7.3985	0.1365	0.1352	8	
	9	1.1951	0.8368	8.1622	8.2436	0.1225	0.1213	9	
	10	1.2190	0.8203	8.9826	9.0721	0.1113	0.1102	10	
	11	1.2434	0.8043	9.7868	9.8844	0.1022	0.1012	11	
2.0%	12	1.2682	0.7885	10.5753	10.6807	0.0946	0.0936	12	2.0%
	13	1.2936	0.7730	11.3484	11.4615	0.0881	0.0872	13	
	14	1.3195	0.7579	12.1062	12.2269	0.0826	0.0818	14	
	15	1.3459	0.7430	12.8493	12.9773	0.0778	0.0771	15	
	16	1.3728	0.7284	13.5777	13.7130	0.0737	0.0729	16	
	17	1.4002	0.7142	14.2919	14.4343	0.0700	0.0693	17	
	18	1.4282	0.7002	14.9920	15.1415	0.0667	0.0660	18	
	19	1.4568	0.6864	15.6785	15.8347	0.0638	0.0632	19	
	20	1.4859	0.6730	16.3514	16.5144	0.0612	0.0606	20	
	21	1.5157	0.6598	17.0112	17.1808	0.0588	0.0582	21	
	22	1.5460	0.6468	17.6580	17.8340	0.0566	0.0561	22	
	23	1.5769	0.6342	18.2922	18.4745	0.0547	0.0541	23	
	24	1.6084	0.6217	18.9139	19.1024	0.0529	0.0523	24	
	25	1.6406	0.6095	19.5235	19.7180	0.0512	0.0507	25	

	Year	Amount to which £1 will accumulate	Present value of £1	Present value of £1 received at end of period	Present value of £1 received continuously	Amount received at end of year which will recover initial investment of £1	Amount received at end of year which will recover initial investment of £1	Year	
	1	1.0300	0.9709	0.9709	0.9854	1.0300	1.0149	1	
	2	1.0609	0.9426	1.9135	1.9420	0.5226	0.5149	2	
	3	1.0927	0.9151	2.8286	2.8708	0.3535	0.3483	3	
	4	1.1255	0.8885	3.7171	3.7726	0.2690	0.2651	4	
	5	1.1593	0.8626	4.5797	4.6481	0.2184	0.2151	5	
	6	1.1941	0.8375	5.4172	5.4980	0.1846	0.1819	6	
	7	1.2299	0.8131	6.2303	6.3233	0.1605	0.1581	7	
	8	1.2668	0.7894	7.0197	7.1245	0.1425	0.1404	8	
	9	1.3048	0.7664	7.7861	7.9023	0.1284	0.1265	9	
	10	1.3439	0.7441	8.5302	8.6575	0.1172	0.1155	10	
	11	1.3842	0.7224	9.2526	9.3907	0.1081	0.1065	11	
3.0%	12	1.4258	0.7014	9.9540	10.1026	0.1005	0.0990	12	3.0%
	13	1.4685	0.6810	10.6350	10.7937	0.0940	0.0926	13	
	14	1.5126	0.6611	11.2961	11.4647	0.0855	0.0872	14	
	15	1.5580	0.6419	11.9379	12.1161	0.0838	0.0825	15	
	16	1.6047	0.6232	12.5611	12.7486	0.0796	0.0784	16	
	17	1.6528	0.6050	13.1661	13.3626	0.0760	0.0748	17	
	18	1.7024	0.5874	13.7535	13.9588	0.0727	0.0716	18	
	19	1.7535	0.5703	14.3238	14.5376	0.0698	0.0688	19	
	20	1.8061	0.5537	14.8775	15.0995	0.0672	0.0662	20	
	21	1.8063	0.5375	15.4150	15.6451	0.0649	0.0639	21	
	22	1.9161	0.5219	15.9369	16.1748	0.0627	0.0618	22	
	23	1.9736	0.5067	16.4436	16.6890	0.0608	0.0599	23	
	24	2.0328	0.4919	16.9355	17.1883	0.0590	0.0582	24	
	25	2.0938	0.4776	17.4131	17.6731	0.0574	0.0566	25	
	1	1.0400	0.9615	0.9615	0.9806	1.0400	1.0197	1	
	2	1.0816	0.9246	1.8861	1.9236	0.5302	0.5199	2	
	3	1.1249	0.8890	2.7751	2.8302	0.3603	0.3533	3	
	4	1.1699	0.8548	3.6299	3.7020	0.2755	0.2701	4	
	5	1.2167	0.8219	4.4518	4.5403	0.2246	0.2203	5	
	6	1.2653	0.7903	5.2421	5.3463	0.1908	0.1870	6	
	7	1.3169	0.7599	6.0021	6.1213	0.1666	0.1634	7	
	8	1.3686	0.7307	6.7327	6.8665	0.1485	0.1456	8	
	9	1.4233	0.7026	7.4353	7.5831	0.1345	0.1319	9	
	10	1.4802	0.6756	8.1109	8.2721	0.1233	0.1209	10	
	11	1.5395	0.6496	8.7605	8.9345	0.1141	0.1119	11	
4.0%	12	1.6010	0.6246	9.3851	9.5715	0.1066	0.1045	12	4.0%
	13	1.6651	0.6006	9.9856	10.1841	0.1001	0.0982	13	
	14	1.7317	0.5775	10.5631	10.7730	0.0947	0.0928	14	
	15	1.8009	0.5553	11.1184	11.3393	0.0899	0.0882	15	
	16	1.8730	0.5339	11.6523	11.8838	0.0858	0.0841	16	
	17	1.9479	0.5134	12.1657	12.4074	0.0822	0.0806	17	
	18	2.0258	0.4936	12.6593	12.9108	0.0790	0.0775	18	
	19	2.1068	0.4746	13.1339	13.3949	0.0761	0.0747	19	
	20	2.1911	0.4564	13.5903	13.8604	0.0736	0.0721	20	
	21	2.2788	0.4388	14.0292	14.3079	0.0713	0.0699	21	
	22	2.3699	0.4220	14.4511	14.7382	0.0692	0.0679	22	
	23	2.4647	0.4057	14.8568	15.1520	0.0673	0.0660	23	
	24	2.5633	0.3901	15.2470	15.5499	0.0656	0.0643	24	
	25	2.6658	0.3751	15.6221	15.9325	0.0640	0.0628	25	

	Year	Amount to which £1 will accumulate	Present value of £1	Present value of £1 received at end of period	Present value of £1 received continuously	Amount received at end of year which will recover initial investment of £1	Amount received at end of year which will recover initial investment of £1	Year	
	1	1.0500	0.9524	0.9524	0.9760	1.0500	1.0246	1	
	2	1.1025	0.9070	1.8594	1.9055	0.5378	0.5248	2	
	3	1.1576	0.8638	2.7232	2.7908	0.3672	0.3583	3	
	4	1.2155	0.8227	3.5460	3.6399	0.2820	0.2752	4	
	5	1.2763	0.7835	4.3295	4.4368	0.2310	0.2254	5	
	6	1.3401	0.7462	5.0757	5.2016	0.1970	0.1923	6	
	7	1.4071	0.7107	5.7864	5.9299	0.1728	0.1686	7	
	8	1.4775	0.6768	6.4632	6.6235	0.1547	0.1510	8	
	9	1.5513	0.6446	7.1078	7.2841	0.1407	0.1373	9	
	10	1.6289	0.6139	7.7217	7.9132	0.1295	0.1264	10	
	11	1.7103	0.5847	8.3064	8.5124	0.1204	0.1175	11	
5.0%	12	1.7959	0.5568	8.8633	9.0830	0.1128	0.1101	12	5.0%
	13	1.8856	0.5303	9.3936	9.6263	0.1065	0.1039	13	
	14	1.9799	0.5051	9.8986	10.1441	0.1010	0.0986	14	
	15	2.0789	0.4810	10.3797	10.6370	0.0963	0.0940	15	
	16	2.1829	0.4581	10.8378	11.1065	0.0923	0.0900	16	
	17	2.2920	0.4363	11.2741	11.5536	0.887	0.0866	17	
	18	2.4066	0.4155	11.6896	11.9795	0.0855	0.0835	18	
	19	2.5270	0.3957	12.0853	12.3850	0.0827	0.0807	19	
	20	2.6533	0.3769	12.4622	12.7712	0.0802	0.0783	20	
	21	2.7860	0.3589	12.8212	13.1391	0.0780	0.0761	21	
	22	2.9253	0.3418	13.1630	13.4894	0.0760	0.0741	22	
	23	3.0715	0.3256	13.4886	13.8230	0.0741	0.0723	23	
	24	3.2251	0.3101	13.7986	14.1408	0.0725	0.0707	24	
	25	3.3864	0.2953	14.0939	14.4434	0.0710	0.0692	25	
	1	1.0600	0.9434	0.9434	0.9714	1.0600	1.0294	1	
	2	1.1236	0.8900	1.8334	1.8879	0.5454	0.5297	2	
	3	1.1910	0.8396	2.6730	2.7524	0.3741	0.3633	3	
	4	1.2626	0.7921	3.4651	3.5680	0.2886	0.2803	4	
	5	1.3382	0.7473	4.2124	4.3375	0.2374	0.2305	5	
	6	1.4185	0.7050	4.9173	5.0634	0.2034	0.1975	6	
	7	1.5036	0.6651	5.5824	5.7482	0.1791	1.1740	7	
	8	1.5938	0.6274	6.2098	6.3943	0.160	0.1564	8	
	9	1.6895	0.5919	6.8017	7.0038	0.1470	0.1428	9	
	10	1.7908	0.5584	7.3601	7.5787	0.1359	0.1319	10	
	11	1.8983	0.5268	7.8869	8.1212	0.1268	0.1231	11	
6.0%	12	2.0122	0.4970	8.3838	8.6329	0.1193	0.1158	12	6.0%
	13	2.1329	0.4688	8.8527	9.1157	0.1130	0.1097	13	
	14	2.2609	0.4423	9.2950	9.5711	0.1076	0.1045	14	
	15	2.3966	0.4173	9.7122	10.0008	0.1030	0.1000	15	
	16	2.5404	0.3936	10.1059	10.4061	0.0990	0.0961	16	
	17	2.6928	0.3714	10.4773	10.7885	0.0954	0.0927	17	
	18	2.8543	0.3503	10.8276	11.1493	0.0924	0.0897	18	
	19	3.0256	0.3305	11.1581	11.4896	0.0896	0.0870	19	
	20	3.2071	0.3118	11.4699	11.8107	0.0872	0.0847	20	
	21	3.3996	0.2942	11.7641	12.1136	0.0850	0.0826	21	
	22	3.6035	0.2775	12.0416	12.3993	0.0830	0.0806	22	
	23	3.8197	0.2618	12.3034	12.6689	0.0813	0.0789	23	
	24	4.0489	0.2470	12.5504	12.9232	0.0797	0.0774	24	
	25	4.2919	0.2330	12.7834	13.1631	0.0782	0.0760	25	

Year	Amount to which £1 will accumulate	Present value of £1	Present value of £1 received at end of period	Present value of £1 received continuously	Amount received at end of year which will recover initial investment of £1	Amount received at end of year which will recover initial investment of £1	Year
	1	1.0700	0.9346	0.9346	0.9669	1.0700	1.0342	1
	2	1.1449	0.8734	1.8080	1.8706	0.5531	0.5346	2
	3	1.2250	0.8163	2.6243	2.7151	0.3811	0.3683	3
	4	1.3108	0.7629	3.3872	3.5044	0.2952	0.2854	4
	5	1.4026	0.7130	4.1002	4.2421	0.2439	0.2357	5
	6	1.5007	0.6663	4.7665	4.9316	0.2098	0.2028	6
	7	1.6058	0.6227	5.3893	5.5758	0.1856	0.1793	7
	8	1.7182	0.5820	5.9713	6.1779	0.1675	0.1619	8
	9	1.8385	0.5439	6.5152	6.7407	0.1535	0.1484	9
	10	1.9672	0.5083	7.0236	7.2666	0.1424	0.1376	10
	11	2.1049	0.4751	7.4987	7.7582	0.1334	0.1289	11
7.0%	12	2.2522	0.4440	7.9427	8.2175	0.1259	0.1217	12	7.0%
	13	2.4098	0.4150	8.3577	8.6469	0.1197	0.1156	13
	14	2.5785	0.3878	8.7455	9.0481	0.1143	0.1105	14
	15	2.7590	0.3624	9.1079	9.4231	0.1098	0.1061	15
	16	2.9522	0.3387	9.4466	9.7736	0.1059	0.1023	16
	17	3.1588	0.3166	9.7632	10.1011	0.1024	0.0990	17
	18	3.3799	0.2959	10.0591	10.4072	0.0994	0.0961	18
	19	3.6165	0.2765	10.3356	10.6933	0.0968	0.0935	19
	20	3.8697	0.2584	10.5940	10.9606	0.0944	0.0912	20
	21	4.1406	0.2415	10.8355	11.2105	0.0923	0.0892	21
	22	4.4304	0.2257	11.0612	11.4440	0.0904	0.0874	22
	23	4.7405	0.2109	11.2722	11.6623	0.0887	0.0857	23
	24	5.0724	0.1971	11.4693	11.8662	0.0872	0.0843	24
	25	5.4274	0.1842	11.6536	12.0569	0.0858	0.0829	25
	1	1.0800	0.9259	0.9259	0.9625	1.0800	1.0390	1
	2	1.1664	0.8573	1.7833	1.8537	0.5608	0.5395	2
	3	1.2597	0.7938	2.5771	2.6789	0.3880	0.3733	3
	4	1.3605	0.7350	3.3121	3.4429	0.3019	0.2905	4
	5	1.4693	0.6806	3.9927	4.1504	0.2505	0.2409	5
	6	1.5869	0.6302	4.6229	4.8054	0.2163	0.2081	6
	7	1.7138	0.5835	5.2064	5.4120	0.1921	0.1848	7
	8	1.8509	0.5403	5.7466	5.9736	0.1740	0.1674	8
	9	1.9990	0.5002	6.2469	6.4936	0.1601	0.1540	9
	10	2.1589	0.4632	6.7101	6.9750	0.1490	0.1434	10
	11	2.3316	0.4289	7.1390	7.4209	0.1401	0.1348	11
8.0%	12	2.5182	0.3971	7.5361	7.8337	0.1327	0.1277	12	8.0%
	13	2.7196	0.3677	7.9038	8.2159	0.1265	0.1217	13
	14	2.9372	0.3405	8.2442	8.5698	0.1213	0.1167	14
	15	3.1722	0.3152	8.5595	8.8975	0.1168	0.1124	15
	16	3.4259	0.2919	8.8514	9.2009	0.1130	0.1087	16
	17	3.7000	0.2703	9.1216	9.4818	0.1096	0.1055	17
	18	3.9960	0.2502	9.3719	9.7420	0.1067	0.1026	18
	19	4.3157	0.2317	9.6036	9.9828	0.1041	0.1002	19
	20	4.6610	0.2145	9.8181	10.2058	0.1019	0.0980	20
	21	5.0338	0.1987	10.0168	10.4123	0.0998	0.0960	21
	22	5.4365	0.1839	10.2007	10.6035	0.0980	0.0943	22
	23	5.8715	0.1703	10.3711	10.7806	0.0964	0.0928	23
	24	6.3412	0.1577	10.5288	10.9445	0.0950	0.0914	24
	25	6.8485	0.1460	10.6748	11.0963	0.0937	0.0901	25

	Year	Amount to which £1 will accumulate	Present value of £1	Present value of £1 received at end of period	Present value of £1 received continuously	Amount received at end of year which will recover initial investment of £1	Amount received at end of year which will recover initial investment of £1	Year	
	1	1.0900	0.9174	0.9174	0.9581	1.0900	1.0437	1	
	2	1.1881	0.8417	1.7591	1.8371	0.5685	0.5443	2	
	3	1.2950	0.7722	2.5313	2.6436	0.3951	0.3783	3	
	4	1.4116	0.7084	3.2397	3.3834	0.3087	0.2956	4	
	5	1.5386	0.6499	3.8897	4.0622	0.2571	0.2462	5	
	6	1.6771	0.5963	4.4859	4.6849	0.2229	0.2135	6	
	7	1.8280	0.5470	5.0330	5.2562	0.1987	0.1903	7	
	8	1.9926	0.5019	5.5348	5.7803	0.1807	0.1730	8	
	9	2.1719	0.4604	5.9952	6.2612	0.1668	0.1597	9	
	10	2.3674	0.4224	6.4177	6.7023	0.1558	0.1492	10	
	11	2.5804	0.3875	6.8052	7.1070	0.1469	0.1407	11	
9.0%	12	2.8127	0.3555	7.1607	7.4783	0.1397	0.1337	12	9.0%
	13	3.0658	0.3262	7.4869	7.8190	0.1336	0.1279	13	
	14	3.3417	0.2992	7.7862	8.1315	0.1284	0.1230	14	
	15	3.6425	0.2745	8.0607	8.4182	0.1241	0.1188	15	
	16	3.9703	0.2519	8.3126	8.6813	0.1203	0.1152	16	
	17	4.3276	0.2311	8.5436	8.9226	0.1170	0.1121	17	
	18	4.7171	0.2120	8.7556	9.1440	0.1142	0.1094	18	
	19	5.1417	0.1945	8.9501	9.3471	0.1117	0.1070	19	
	20	5.6044	0.1784	9.1285	9.5334	0.1095	0.1049	20	
	21	6.1088	0.1637	9.2922	9.7044	0.1076	0.1030	21	
	22	6.6586	0.1502	9.4424	9.8612	0.1059	0.1014	22	
	23	7.2579	0.1378	9.5802	10.0051	0.1044	0.0999	23	
	24	7.9111	0.1264	9.7066	10.1371	0.1030	0.0986	24	
	25	8.6231	0.1160	9.8226	10.2582	0.1018	0.0975	25	
	1	1.1000	0.9091	0.9091	0.9538	1.1000	1.0484	1	
	2	1.2100	0.8264	1.7355	1.8209	0.5762	0.5492	2	
	3	1.3310	0.7513	2.4869	2.6092	0.4021	0.3833	3	
	4	1.4641	0.6830	3.1699	3.3258	0.3155	0.3007	4	
	5	1.6105	0.6209	3.7908	3.9773	0.2638	0.2514	5	
	6	1.7716	0.5645	4.3553	4.5696	0.2296	0.2188	6	
	7	1.9487	0.5132	4.8684	5.1080	0.2054	0.1958	7	
	8	2.1436	0.4665	5.3349	5.5974	0.1874	0.1787	8	
	9	2.3579	0.4241	5.7590	6.0424	0.1736	0.1655	9	
	10	2.5937	0.3855	6.1446	6.4469	0.1627	0.1551	10	
	11	2.8531	0.3505	6.4951	6.8147	0.1540	0.1467	11	
10.0%	12	3.1384	0.3186	6.8137	7.1490	0.1468	0.1399	12	10.0%
	13	3.4523	0.2897	7.1034	7.4529	0.1408	0.1342	13	
	14	3.7975	0.2633	7.3667	7.7292	0.1357	0.1294	14	
	15	4.1772	0.2394	7.6061	7.9803	0.1315	0.1253	15	
	16	4.5950	0.2176	7.8237	8.2087	0.1278	0.1218	16	
	17	5.0545	0.1978	8.0216	8.4163	0.1247	0.1188	17	
	18	5.5599	0.1799	8.2014	8.6050	0.1219	0.1162	18	
	19	6.1159	0.1635	8.3649	8.7765	0.1195	0.1139	19	
	20	6.7275	0.1486	8.5136	8.9325	0.1175	0.1120	20	
	21	7.4002	0.1351	8.6487	9.0743	0.1156	0.1102	21	
	22	8.1403	0.1228	8.7715	9.2032	0.1140	0.1087	22	
	23	8.9543	0.1117	8.8832	9.3203	0.1126	0.1073	23	
	24	9.8497	0.1015	8.9847	9.4268	0.1113	0.1061	24	
	25	10.8347	0.0923	9.0770	9.5237	0.1102	0.1050	25	

	Year	Amount to which £1 will accumulate	Present value of £1	Present value of £1 received at end of period	Present value of £1 received continuously	Amount received at end of year which will recover initial investment of £1	Amount received at end of year which will recover initial investment of £1	Year	
	1	1.1300	0.8850	0.8850	0.9413	1.1300	1.0624	1	
	2	1.2769	0.7831	1.6681	1.7743	0.5995	0.5636	2	
	3	1.4429	0.6931	2.3612	2.5115	0.4236	0.3982	3	
	4	1.6305	0.6133	2.9745	3.1639	0.3362	0.3161	4	
	5	1.8424	0.5428	3.5172	3.7412	0.2843	0.2673	5	
	6	2.0820	0.4803	3.9975	4.2521	0.2602	0.2352	6	
	7	2.3526	0.4251	4.4226	4.7042	0.2261	0.2126	7	
	8	2.6584	0.3762	4.7988	5.1043	0.2084	0.1959	8	
	9	3.0040	0.3329	5.1317	5.4584	0.1949	0.1832	9	
	10	3.3946	0.2946	5.4262	5.7718	0.1843	0.1733	10	
	11	3.8359	0.2607	5.6869	6.0491	0.1758	0.1653	11	
13.0%	12	4.3345	0.2307	5.9176	6.2945	0.1690	0.1589	12	13.0%
	13	4.8980	0.2042	6.1218	6.5116	0.1634	0.1526	13	
	14	5.5348	0.1807	6.3025	6.7038	0.1587	0.1492	14	
	15	6.2543	0.1599	6.4624	6.8739	0.1547	0.1455	15	
	16	7.0673	0.1415	6.6039	7.0244	0.1514	0.1424	16	
	17	7.9861	0.1252	6.7291	7.1576	0.1486	0.1397	17	
	18	9.0243	0.1108	6.8399	7.2754	0.1462	0.1374	18	
	19	10.1974	0.0981	6.9380	7.3798	0.1441	0.1355	19	
	20	11.5231	0.0868	7.0248	7.4721	0.1424	0.1338	20	
	21	13.0211	0.0768	7.1016	7.5538	0.1408	0.1324	21	
	22	14.7138	0.0680	7.1695	7.6260	0.1395	0.1311	22	
	23	16.6266	0.0601	7.2297	7.6900	0.1383	0.1300	23	
	24	18.7881	0.0532	7.2829	7.7466	0.1373	0.1291	24	
	25	21.2305	0.0471	7.3300	7.7967	0.1364	0.1283	25	
	1	1.1400	0.8772	0.8772	0.9373	1.1400	1.0669	1	
	2	1.2996	0.7695	1.6467	1.7594	0.6073	0.5684	2	
	3	1.4815	0.6750	2.3216	2.4806	0.4307	0.4031	3	
	4	1.6890	0.6921	2.9137	3.1132	0.3432	0.3212	4	
	5	1.9254	0.5194	3.4331	3.6682	0.2913	0.2726	5	
	6	2.1950	0.4556	3.8887	4.1549	0.2572	0.2407	6	
	7	2.5023	0.3996	4.2883	4.5819	0.2332	0.2182	7	
	8	2.8526	0.3506	4.6389	4.9565	0.2156	0.2018	8	
	9	3.2519	0.3075	4.9464	5.2851	0.2022	0.1892	9	
	10	3.7072	0.2697	5.2161	5.5733	0.1917	0.1794	10	
	11	4.2262	0.2366	5.4527	5.8261	0.1834	0.1716	11	
14.0%	12	4.8179	0.2076	5.6603	6.0479	0.1767	0.1653	12	14.0%
	13	5.4924	0.1821	5.8424	6.2424	0.1713	0.1602	13	
	14	6.2613	0.1597	6.0021	6.4130	0.1666	0.1559	14	
	15	7.1379	0.1401	6.1422	6.5627	0.1628	0.1524	15	
	16	8.1372	0.1229	6.2651	6.6940	0.1596	0.1494	16	
	17	9.2765	0.1078	6.3729	6.8092	0.1569	0.1469	17	
	18	10.5752	0.0946	6.4674	6.9103	0.1546	0.1447	18	
	19	12,0557	0.0829	6.5504	6.9989	0.1527	0.1429	19	
	20	13.7435	0.0728	6.6231	7.0766	0.1510	0.1413	20	
	21	15.6676	0.0638	6.6870	7.1448	0.1496	0.1400	21	
	22	17.8610	0.0560	6.7429	7.2046	0.1483	0.1388	22	
	23	20.3616	0.0491	6.7921	7.2571	0.1472	0.1378	23	
	24	23.2122	0.0431	6.8351	7.3032	0.1463	0.1369	24	
	25	26.4619	0.0378	6.8729	7.3435	0.1455	0.1362	25	

	Year	Amount to which £1 will accumulate	Present value of £1	Present value of £1 received at end of period	Present value of £1 received continuously	Amount received at end of year which will recover initial investment of £1	Amount received at end of year which will recover initial investment of £1	Year	
	1	1.1500	0.8696	0.8696	0.9333	1.1500	1.0715	1	
	2	1.3225	0.7561	1.6257	1.7448	0.6151	0.5731	2	
	3	1.5209	0.6575	2.2832	2.4505	0.4380	0.4081	3	
	4	1.7490	0.5718	2.8550	3.0641	0.3503	0.3264	4	
	5	2.0114	0.4972	3.3522	3.5977	0.2983	0.2780	5	
	6	2.3131	0.4323	3.7845	4.0617	0.2642	0.2462	6	
	7	2.6600	0.3759	4.1604	4.4652	0.2404	0.2240	7	
	8	3.0590	0.3269	4.4873	4.8160	0.2229	0.2076	8	
	9	3.5179	0.2843	4.7716	5.1211	0.2096	0.1953	9	
	10	4.0456	0.2472	5.0188	5.3864	0.1993	0.1857	10	
	11	4.6524	0.2149	5.2337	5.6171	0.1911	0.1780	11	
15.0%	12	5.3503	0.1869	5.4206	5.8177	0.1845	0.1719	12	15.0%
	13	6.1528	0.1625	5.5831	5.9921	0.1791	0.1669	13	
	14	7.0757	0.1413	5.7245	6.1438	0.1747	0.1628	14	
	15	8.1371	0.1229	5.8474	6.2757	0.1710	0.1593	15	
	16	9.3576	0.1069	5.9542	6.3904	0.1679	0.1565	16	
	17	10.7613	0.0929	6.0472	6.4901	0.1654	0.1541	17	
	18	12.3755	0.0808	6.1280	6.5769	0.1632	0.1520	18	
	19	14.2318	0.0703	6.1982	6.6523	0.1613	0.1503	19	
	20	16.3665	0.0611	6.2593	6.7178	0.1598	0.1489	20	
	21	18.8215	0.0531	6.3126	6.7749	0.1584	0.1476	21	
	22	21.6447	0.0462	6.3587	6.8245	0.1573	0.1465	22	
	23	24.8915	0.0402	6.3988	6.8676	0.1563	0.1456	23	
	24	28.6252	0.0349	6.4338	6.9051	0.1554	0.1448	24	
	25	32.9190	0.0304	6.4641	6.9377	0.1547	0.1441	25	
	1	1.1600	0.8621	0.8621	0.9293	1.1600	1.0760	1	
	2	1.3456	0.7432	1.6052	1.7305	0.6230	0.5779	2	
	3	1.5609	0.6407	2.2459	2.4211	0.4453	0.4130	3	
	4	1.8106	0.5523	2.7982	3.0165	0.3574	0.3315	4	
	5	2.1003	0.4761	3.2743	3.5298	0.3054	0.2833	5	
	6	2.4364	0.4104	3.6847	3.9722	0.2714	0.2517	6	
	7	2.8262	0.3538	4.0386	4.3537	0.2476	0.2297	7	
	8	3.2784	0.3050	4.3436	4.6825	0.2302	0.2136	8	
	9	3.8030	0.2630	4.6065	4.9660	0.2171	0.2014	9	
	10	4.4114	0.2267	4.8332	5.2103	0.2089	0.1919	10	
	11	5.1173	0.1954	5.0286	5.4210	0.1989	0.1845	11	
16.0%	12	5.9360	0.1685	5.1971	5.6026	0.1924	0.1785	12	16.0%
	13	6.8858	0.1452	5.3423	5.7592	0.1872	0.1736	13	
	14	7.9875	0.1252	5.4675	5.8941	0.1829	0.1697	14	
	15	9.2655	0.1070	5.5755	6.0105	0.1794	0.1664	15	
	16	10.7480	0.0930	5.6685	6.1108	0.1764	0.1636	16	
	17	12.4677	0.0802	5.7487	6.1972	0.1740	0.1614	17	
	18	14.4625	0.0691	5.8178	6.2718	0.1719	0.1594	18	
	19	16.7765	0.0596	5.8775	6.3360	0.1701	0.1578	19	
	20	19.4608	0.0514	5.9288	6.3914	0.1687	0.1565	20	
	21	22.5745	0.0443	5.9731	6.4392	0.1674	0.1553	21	
	22	26.1864	0.0382	6.0113	6.4803	0.1664	0.1543	22	
	23	30.3762	0.0329	6.0442	6.5158	0.1654	0.1535	23	
	24	35.2364	0.0284	6.0726	6.5464	0.1647	0.1528	24	
	25	40.8742	0.0245	6.0971	6.5728	0.1640	0.1521	25	

INDEX